Tzeruf Basics
a Kabbalah Meditation:

Tzeruf Basics
a Kabbalah Meditation

BY

DANIEL A. ELIAS

TZERUF CO

Author: *Daniel A. Elias, J.D.*

Publisher: Tzeruf Co. - (tzeruf.com)
P.O. Box 391
Hemet, CA 92546-0391
USA

SAN Number   853-0203

Copyright © 2012 by Tzeruf Co.
Printed in the U.S.A.

All rights reserved.

No part of this publication may be reproduced or transmitted in any form or by any means, electronic or mechanical, including photocopying, recording, or by any information storage and retrieval system, without permission in writing from the Tzeruf Co.

First Edition Published 2012

Publisher's Cataloging-in-Publication data

Author: Elias, Daniel A.

Title: Tzeruf Basics, a Kabbalah Meditation.   Illustrated by Daniel Elias.

English Paperback   ISBN   978-0-9792826-0-7

LCCN   2012933696

I dedicate this book to

Rabbi Abraham Abulafia, ben Samuel,

who dedicated his life's work to spread this meditation technique to the world.

This meditation is more powerful than praying

-- Abulafia

Table of Contents

Calling in the Name of XII
I Will Bless You XIV
The Commandment XV
Preface XVII
About Tzeruf 1
The Hebrew Alphabet 12
The Mystical Letters 17
Alphabet in the Mouth 45
Hebrew Vowels Markings 48
The Sacred Hebrew Language 57
Letters linked to a Word's meaning 75
The Different Names of God 76
Learning Hebrew 85
The Torah 87
Concentrating the Torah Power 95
Your Neighbor 95
Intro to the Soul 98
Creating a Vessel in Yesod 102
Level 4 - Spiritual 119
Level 3 - Mental 129
Level 2 - Emotional 137
Level 1 - Physical Action 144
Soul Development 148
Intro to the Meditations 156
Preliminary Prayers 169
  Dedication 171

Rabbi Vital Prayer 172
Song of Sea End 175
Prophecy Prayer - Psalm 7 179
Midnight Psalm - Psalm 111 182
Shortest Psalm - Psalm 117 184
Shema 185

GALGAL SQUARE 189
Galgal Square 193
Galgal Reversed 195
Galgal Triangle 197

ALEF WITH IHVH 211
Alef 213

THE 72 NAMES 217
72 Names RAW 221
72 Names Seeded 223
72 Names Spaced 225
72 Names Pointed 227
Memorizing 228

THE 72 ANGELS 229
72 Angels 1 231
72 Angels 2 232
72 Angels 3 233
72 Angels 4 234
72 Angels 5 235
72 Angels 6 236
72 Angels 7 237
72 Angels 8 238
72 Angels 9 239

LATER KABBALISTS 241
Later Kabbalists - Table 1 245
Later Kabbalists - Table 2 247

ABOUT PSALM 119 249
Psalm 119 251

SUPPLICATION 273
ADVANCED MEDITATIONS 274
APPENDIX 277
ABOUT THE AUTHOR 281
INDEX 283

CALLING IN THE NAME OF ...

Genesis 4:26

וּלְשֵׁת גַּם־הוּא יֻלַּד־בֵּן
son – begot   he – also   and to Seth

וַיִּקְרָא אֶת־שְׁמוֹ אֱנוֹשׁ
Enosh   his name – that   he called

אָז הוּחַל לִקְרֹא בְּשֵׁם יְהוָה׃
ihvh   in name   to call   he began   then

26 And to Seth, to him also there was born a son; and he called his name Enos: then began men to **call upon the name of the LORD.**

Genesis 12:8

וַיַּעְתֵּק מִשָּׁם הָהָרָה מִקֶּדֶם לְבֵית־אֵל
El - to Beth   from east   the mount   from there   and he did same

וַיֵּט אָהֳלֹה בֵּית־אֵל מִיָּם וְהָעַי מִקֶּדֶם
from east   and Hai   from Sea   El - Beth   his tent   and he pitched

וַיִּבֶן־שָׁם מִזְבֵּחַ לַיהוָה וַיִּקְרָא בְּשֵׁם יְהוָה׃
ihvh   in name   and he called   to ihvh   altar   there - and he built

8 And he removed from thence unto a mountain on the east of Beth-el, and pitched his tent, having Beth-el on the west, and Hai on the east: and there he builded an altar unto the LORD, and **called upon the name of the LORD.**

Genesis 13:4

אֶל־מְקוֹם הַמִּזְבֵּחַ אֲשֶׁר־עָשָׂה שָׁם בָּרִאשֹׁנָה
in first   there   made – which   the altar   place - unto

וַיִּקְרָא שָׁם אַבְרָם בְּשֵׁם יְהוָה׃
ihvh   in name   Abram   there and he called

4 Unto the place of the altar, which he had made there at the first: and there Abram **called on the name of the LORD.**

Genesis 21:33

וַיִּטַּע אֵשֶׁל בִּבְאֵר שָׁבַע

     Sheba   in Beer   tamarisk tree   and he planted

וַיִּקְרָא־שָׁם בְּשֵׁם יְהוָה אֵל עוֹלָם׃

    forever   El   ihvh   in name   there - and he called

33 And Abraham planted a grove in Beer-sheba, and **called there on the name of the LORD,** the everlasting God.

Genesis 26:25

וַיִּבֶן שָׁם מִזְבֵּחַ

    altar   there   and he built

וַיִּקְרָא בְּשֵׁם יְהוָה וַיֶּט־שָׁם אָהֳלוֹ

  his tent   there - and he pitched   ihvh   in name   and he called

וַיִּכְרוּ־שָׁם עַבְדֵי־יִצְחָק בְּאֵר׃

    well   Isaac - servants   there - and they dug

25 And he builded an altar there, and **called upon the name of the LORD,** and pitched his tent there: and there Isaac's servants digged a well.

Exodus Ch 34:5

וַיֵּרֶד יְהוָה בֶּעָנָן וַיִּתְיַצֵּב עִמּוֹ שָׁם

  there   with him   and he stood   in cloud   ihvh   and descended

וַיִּקְרָא בְשֵׁם יְהוָה׃

    ihvh   in name   and he called

5 And the LORD descended in the cloud, and stood with him there, and **proclaimed the name of the LORD.**

I Will Bless You

Exodus Ch 20:24

בְּכָל־הַמָּקוֹם אֲשֶׁר אַזְכִּיר אֶת־שְׁמִי
the place - in all   which   I will mention   my name - that

אָבוֹא אֵלֶיךָ וּבֵרַכְתִּיךָ:
I will come   unto you   and I will bless you

24 ....in all places **where I record my name** I will come unto thee, and I will bless thee.

Exodus 33:12

וַיֹּאמֶר מֹשֶׁה אֶל־יְהוָֹה
and he said   Moses   ihvh - unto

רְאֵה אַתָּה אֹמֵר אֵלַי הַעַל אֶת־הָעָם הַזֶּה
see   you   say   unto me   the upon   the people - that   the this

וְאַתָּה לֹא הוֹדַעְתַּנִי אֵת אֲשֶׁר־תִּשְׁלַח עִמִּי
and you   not   let me know   that   which - you send   with me

וְאַתָּה אָמַרְתָּ יְדַעְתִּיךָ בְשֵׁם וְגַם־מָצָאתָ חֵן בְּעֵינָי:
and you   you said   I know you   in name   and also - you found   grace   in my eyes

12 And Moses said unto the LORD, See, thou sayest unto me, Bring up this people: and thou hast not let me know whom thou wilt send with me. Yet thou hast said, **I know thee by name,** and thou hast also found grace in my sight.

Psalms 91:14

כִּי בִי חָשַׁק וַאֲפַלְּטֵהוּ אֲשַׂגְּבֵהוּ כִּי־יָדַע שְׁמִי:
like   in me   desire   and I deliver him   I elevate him   like - he knows   my name

14 Because he hath set his love upon me, therefore will I deliver him: I will set him on high, because he hath **known my name.**

The Commandment

The ten commandments is a term applied to ten of the most significant laws in the *Bible*. These ten commandments appears in three places in the *Bible*. However, the labels the *Bible* puts on the ten commandments are different than what is popularly named. Only once is a label of commandment labeled, and then it's labeled as "the commandment".

What is "the" commandment? It is generally accepted that the commandment that is most significant to God is the prohibition of idol worship. Another commandment that is closely related to this is the prohibition is using the four letter name of God, the shem hamephorash or the tetragramaton יְהֹוָה , "in vain."

Commandments

In Exodus 20:1 the ten commandments are referred to as the **"speakings."**

וַיְדַבֵּר	אֱלֹהִים	אֵת	כָּל־הַדְּבָרִים	הָאֵלֶּה	לֵאמֹר׃
and he spoke	Elohim	that	the speakings – all	the these	to say

Exo 20:1 And God spake all these words, saying,

The Statutes and the Judgments

In Deuteronomy 5:1 the ten commandments are referred to as **"the statutes and the judgments"**.

וַיִּקְרָא	מֹשֶׁה	אֶל־כָּל־יִשְׂרָאֵל	וַיֹּאמֶר	אֲלֵהֶם
and he called	Moses	unto - all - Israel	and he said	unto them

שְׁמַע	יִשְׂרָאֵל	אֶת־הַחֻקִּים	וְאֶת־הַמִּשְׁפָּטִים
listen	Israel	that - the statutes	and that - the judgments

אֲשֶׁר	אָנֹכִי	דֹּבֵר	בְּאָזְנֵיכֶם	הַיּוֹם
which	I am	speaking	in your ears	the day

וְלִמַּדְתֶּם אֹתָם וּשְׁמַרְתֶּם לַעֲשֹׂתָם׃

    to do them   and heed them   to them   and learn them

Deut 5:1. And Moses called all Israel, and said to them, Hear, O Israel, the **statutes and judgments** which I speak in your ears this day, that you may learn them, and keep, and do them.

THE COMMANDMENT, THE STATUES AND THE JUDGMENTS

In Deuteronomy 6:1 the direct translation is "**the commandment (singular), the statutes and the judgments.**"

וְזֹאת הַמִּצְוָה   הַחֻקִּים וְהַמִּשְׁפָּטִים

and the judgments   the statutes   the commandment   and this

אֲשֶׁר צִוָּה יְהוָה אֱלֹהֵיכֶם לְלַמֵּד אֶתְכֶם לַעֲשׂוֹת בָּאָרֶץ

in land   to do   that you   to teach   your Elohim   ihvh   command   which

אֲשֶׁר אַתֶּם עֹבְרִים שָׁמָּה לְרִשְׁתָּהּ׃

to possess   there   passings over   that you   which

Deut 6:1. Now these are the commandments, the statutes, and the judgments, which the Lord your God commanded to teach you, that you might do them in the land to which you are going to possess;

THE COMMANDMENT....NOT "TO SHAV" (לַשָּׁוְא)

לֹא תִשָּׂא אֶת־שֵׁם־יְהוָה אֱלֹהֶיךָ לַשָּׁוְא

to vain   your Elohim   ihvh - name - that   you lift   not

כִּי לֹא יְנַקֶּה יְהוָה אֵת אֲשֶׁר־יִשָּׂא אֶת־שְׁמוֹ לַשָּׁוְא׃

to vain   his name – that   he lift – which   that   ihvh   he will hold innocent   not   like

Ex 20:7 You shall not take the name of the Lord your God **in vain**; for the Lord will not hold him guiltless who takes his name **in vain**.

לֹא תִשָּׂא אֶת־שֵׁם־יְהוָה אֱלֹהֶיךָ לַשָּׁוְא

to vain   your Elohim   ihvh – name – that   you lift   don't

כִּי לֹא יְנַקֶּה יְהוָה אֵת אֲשֶׁר־יִשָּׂא אֶת־שְׁמוֹ לַשָּׁוְא׃

to vain   his name – that   he lift - which   that   ihvh   he will hold innocent   not   like

Duet 5:11 Thou shalt not take the name of the LORD thy God **in vain:** for the LORD will not hold him guiltless that taketh his name **in vain**.

Preface

Book Objectives.

The first objective of the book is to provide the basic tables necessary to begin tzeruf vocal meditations.

The second objective is to give one the necessary basic understanding of the activities that are needed in addition to the vocalizations. In order to give an overview I could only touch on a small portion of the subjects involved. This overview is to alert the reader of various related Kabbalah concepts and to seek further in depth information on the subjects in which they are most interested in.

Knowledge of Kabbalah.

A person reading this book needs to have a prior basic knowledge of Kabbalah and the sefirot (the plural of the word of seferah). After a person has read several basic books on Kabbalah, this book will seem more understandable. Many of the topics quickly covered could fill a whole book. There are so many topics that are related to this meditation.

Translations

One Hebrew word of a verse contains so much subtle information. There is the root, the prefix, the affix, dropped weak letters, gutturals, dagesh lene, dagesh forte, it's sentence grammatical name, etc. There is only space for a one word translation. Much of the English grammar has been left out by necessity; ie. the translation "the" was put in only when there was a specific prefix letter Heh.

Every expression in the [ongoing] present tense can variably be expressed in the future tense as well as in the past tense. This is because anything that is ongoing is in the present and has already happened and will continue to happen.

I would have preferred to translate the tenses of the verbs as they actually appear instead of looking to the sentence meaning to infer the past, present or future. However in order to make the translations simple to understand for the majority of people who do not understand this concept I have inferred verb tenses to optimize understanding.

The vast majority of the Hebrew words in the *Bible* are very easy to translate. Generally everyone agrees on their meanings and these words are used in everyday life in Israel. But many the hard Hebrew words with uncertain roots are such that even experts question their meanings and translations.

The Eskimos have 20 words for snow. This same principle applies to the Hebrew words found in the *Torah*. There may be 20 Hebrew words that have been translated with the same English word, but each of these similar Hebrew words have an extensive detailed specific and differing explanation.

When I was translating verses I listed hard to translate words and made notes on what other translators have put for a meaning and what possible roots the word could be derived from. In the end on those words it's a best estimate as to their meanings.

JEWISH

There are people who are "below standard" proudly allegedly claiming they are Jewish by birth. However, by the substandard way they act, their statement doesn't mean they are special. Being Jewish means loving God and following his laws, the *Torah*. Anyone can do this. Anyone that doesn't cannot make any claim to fame.

Some people think that they are not Jewish and feel funny studying Hebrew and reading the *Torah* in Hebrew. If you need to be accepted socially then there is still a conversion process available. At sometime in the future conversions will cease to be accepted according to the *Talmud*.

On a final note, "A Gentile who studies the *Torah* is as great as the high priest" (B. K. 38a).

About Tzeruf

Tzeruf is the "calling in the name of the Lord," as it is translated in the *King James Bible*.

It consists of the combining verbally in an organized manner...

1) the Hebrew alphabet letters and saying their sounds out loud,

2) combining with different vowels sounds,

3) combining with the sacred name,

the shem hameforash ... AKA .... tetragrammaton ... AKA ... HaVaYaH, ... AKA ...

In the advanced methods there is an additional step where one writes by hand the various alphabet letters as well as vocalizing.

Where did it originate?

The first reference to this meditation is found at Genesis 4:26. There it states that Adam's son, Seth, had a son named Enosh, who began "calling in the name of the Lord." Other former patriarchs have also done this "calling." Abraham and Isaac, are described in biblical verses to also having done this "calling."

This meditation has been around for more than 5,800 years. "The" Adam from the book of Genesis (Gen 2:7) , wrote about these "callings" in a book. Traditionally the book is referred to simply as *The Book of Adam.*

The book of Adam has been handed down from Adam to each succeeding generation. From Seth it eventually trickled down to Abraham, to Isaac, to Joseph, to Moses, to Samuel, to David, to King Solomon, to numerous prophets, to Rabbi Akiva, to Rabbi Simeon, and after that it was disseminated to those well advanced in the knowledge of Kabbalah. This book was a most guarded secret. Many of the followers of the Baal Shem Tov said he had this book in his possession when he was alive. His students would look at this book and say they could not understand what it meant. It contains the most treasured of mystical secrets. Tzeruf meditation is among these mystical secrets.

ANCIENT KNOWLEDGE

One of Noah's sons, named Shem, had a grandson, named Eiver. Shem lived 600 years, and was still alive when Abraham was alive. Shem was even alive when Jacob and Esau were born.

Both Shem and Eiver established a *Torah* academy that taught mysticism to the Israelites for many years. This academy of Shem & Eiver went along with the Israelites to Egypt when they moved there during the time Joseph was is charge of Egypt. It is said that this academy was responsible for passing down this most advanced mystical esoteric knowledge to Moses who demonstrated it's power to the world.

EXODUS 24:12

> And the LORD said unto Moses, Come up to me into the mount, and be there: and I will give thee tables of stone, and a law, and commandments which I have written; that thou mayest teach them.

EXODUS 31:18

> And he gave unto Moses, when he had made an end of communing with him upon mount Sinai, two tables of testimony, tables of stone, written with the finger of God.

These "Tables of Testimony " given to Moses are said to be similar in content to the Sumerian writings, and the Sumerian table, the "Table of Destiny."

Much has been lost of man's history and knowledge of the past since the burning of; Egyptian library in the Temple of Ptah in Memphis; the great library in Alexandria and the Bruchion branches of that library; European libraries; and the Chinese wholesale book burning in 213 B.C. The only great ancient civilization libraries that escaped man's destruction are the large collections of texts in Tibet. [1]

Who Exposed Tzeruf Meditation?

At the end of the 13th century, a Rabbi named Abraham Abulafia, ben Samuel, decided to publish tzeruf meditation to the world. He made the teaching of these techniques the main focus of his life's work. Rabbi Abulafia, on the Isle of Crete, wrote the first known writings detailing these techniques. He founded a school which specialized in this meditation. These mystical writings and teachings were the main impetus behind it's spreading to other parts of the world. Abulafia called his system "the Kabbalah of letters," and has stated that this meditation is more powerful than praying.

Three students of Rabbi Abulafia helped further spread the techniques by publishing their own books. Rabbi Cordovero, a student of Rabbi Abulafia, wrote the classic *Pardes Rimonim*. Rabbi Gikatilla was another of Abulafia's students. He was the successor of Rabbi Abulafia's school. He is best known for writing the classic book *Gates of Light*.

The renown Rabbi Vital was another student of Abulafia. He is known for writing several books on tzeruf techniques. The most notable one is *Shaarey Kedusha*. Rabbi Vital is mainly known as the official note keeper for the Arizal, AKA the Ari. The Ari developed a different style of Kabbalah meditation that is a more refined meditation, yet more difficult, not as dangerous, yet takes more time and skill to manifest notable results.

How do you do it?

The basic method is simply seeing with your eyes the written Hebrew letters, and simultaneously vocalizing with the sounds of those letters with vowel sounds, all done in a specific sequence and mixing this with other letters and the shem hamephorash or other

---

[1] Before World War II, the Germans sent an official expedition to Tibet to find out more about what was said in some vedas, regarding a detailed description of the construction of a vamana, a flying saucer. It described the magnetizing of spinning mercury, a metal and a liquid. (The U-boat U-864, sunk on route to Japan at the end of WWII, contained "advanced airplane designs" and a cargo of 67 tons of liquid mercury). The Germans allegedly built this advanced flying machine in part from these vedas descriptions. The Germans have various names for them such as the Bell and Haunebu. Such is an example of man's lost knowledge and lost civilizations.

names of God. The Objective is to bring down the "influx" from the higher spiritual dimensions. This "influx" can be described as a spiritual food that makes the soul alive. This meditation should be done daily. The time needed to complete a session of this meditation is generally from a half hour to an hour of time, but an intense advanced session can last as much as 2 or 3 hours.

What are the Benefits?

Tzeruf meditation does not leave you with an "I feel good" feeling after you have finished a session. You may feel a slight light headed feeling after a meditation session but it will go away in a short time and is not significant. It usually takes several weeks of consistent meditation before one notices any results. A spiritual energy emerges from the spiritual dimension of your subconscious, and descends through your mental, emotional and physical levels. This energy feeds the soul just like food feeds your body. This spiritual energy is not like physical energy. It is an energy that activates the spiritual plane.

Events

The effect of this type of meditation manifests itself in events. These events present themselves as a mysterious or coincidental expression. You will be attracted to various situations or opportunities. These situations will have a special perception to them. It is hard to describe it, but you will know that the situation is different. If you stop the meditations for a while, you will notice that these coincidental events stop occurring.

These events appear as opportunities that are mystical in nature. They seem to defy statistics. They will appear to be more than just a coincidence. An example would be of a person learning some important fact right before a problem situation arises. Because of this learning of this important fact, one will save time and money, and will have prevented a situation that would have developed into a major problem. It is like an angel giving you a gift.

Perceptions

After daily doing vocal meditations for a long period of time, you will notice a difference in your perceptions. They will be more intense. You will perceive more of a persons spiritual character when you are around them. You will have strong feelings about situations, good or bad. Then typically after you have made a hard decision regarding a pressing situation, you become aware that you had the inner insight and are amazed with the outcome. Your life will become improved and more directed.

However, sometimes bad things will happen to you. And when they do, they will seem intense. These events occur to teach you how to be wise and to test your character.

Many people expect, after doing a significant amount of any type of meditation, that they will reach a fabulous "feel good" state of splendor. A teacher of Zen meditation will typically have a constant smile and act like he has reached a state of ecstasy (maybe even on the drug ecstasy) as he teaches others who desperately want to be in that ecstatic state. The effects from tzeruf meditation are in some respects the opposite.

You will develop an increased awareness of other people's vanity. People assign false values to many things and for their own justifications. You will have this extra sensitive awareness to the point that it will bother you.

You will be more sensitive and see real and potential threats from organizations of other people. You will apply more time thinking and learning how to protect yourself. Also, it is not uncommon for you to be more sensitive to bad people. You may also find jealousy developing in others for no apparent reasons. They somehow will sense your nourished soul or realize your increased perceptiveness.

MEMORIES

You will have many memories of things that you have done in the past, or things you have said, that shows to yourself how much of a beast you were. Unpleasant events that you were or were not responsible for and haven't thought of for years will just drop into your mind. You will also think about the opportunities you had and should have exploited but didn't. You will wish that you could go back and change things.

DREAMS

You will have vivid dreams. These dreams will foretell you of what will happen to you in the short term. You will have to interpret these dreams because they won't be clear as to what they mean. You will find out later what their meanings were after events have transpired. Because of the uncertainty of the interpretations of these dreams you will need to become more attentive in order to avoid misfortune. Eventually the interpretations of your dreams will become more certain.

Dreams are derived from your soul ascending to the upper spiritual worlds during sleep. This "ascending up" refers more to going to a higher spiritual dimension rather than up from the physical ground level.

As you are sleeping your soul experiences various things in these upper worlds, then returns to your body before awakening. Dreams are a small part of what you remembered from your experiences in the upper world while you slept.

As one advances spiritually, these advanced dream states take one to an mystical level of spirituality. Dreams are just the entrance and the tip of the iceberg in entering the spiritual supernal worlds. All the renown mystical Rabbi's talk about this advanced experience.

Higher States

Abulafia talks about a trembling that happens before one enters into a state of prophesy.

> "All your body will begin to tremble, and your limbs begin to shake, and you will fear a great fear .... the body will tremble, like a rider riding a racing horse, and the soul is happy and joyful, while the horse vibrates beneath him" "And you shall feel another spirit awakening within yourself and strengthening you and encompassing your entire body and you feeling pleasure" (*Otzar Eden Ganuz*)

After numerous of these experiences, Abulafia states that the meditator reaches his sought after destination; the vision of a human form...

Danger

In meditation, if a person is not pure, evil forces such as people and spirits will be attracted and surround a person and spirits can even in extreme cases enter one's body. These forces will wrongly influence, incite, and cause misery because this is how these forces derive their pleasure. It's not uncommon for a person to start up daily tzeruf meditation and experience numerous negative events. When this happens, one needs to consider what actions he or she is doing that is not in alignment with biblical principles. Most people do not even realize their actions are violations. For example, "Lashone Harah", translated as "the bad tongue," is one of the violations that is done by many people, and these people do it all day long not knowing the consequences. Know the no's and the go's.

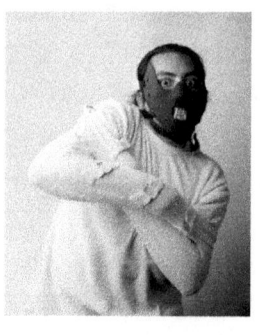

The sages of old have warned that the advanced tzeruf meditations can become extremely dangerous. They site well known cases of people going insane. The danger stems from a person not being spiritually pure as a large amount of influx from an intense meditation descends and enters into the person's soul. If the person has violated the commandments and ordinances detailed in the *Bible*, this influx will tend to bring about, severely, the "effect" as in cause and effect, of any his or her impure actions. By doing extensive and/or advanced meditations, these actions can light his soul on fire. His imagination will get the better of him to the point that he will not be able to distinguish reality from imagination.

The word crown in Hebrew is Keter. According to Rabbi Abulafia, when these letters are rearranged or permuted, it will spell out "karet." This means "cut off." Thus, a person can become "cut off" if he is not spiritually pure and attempts to meditate using these techniques and using God's sacred name at the highest spiritual level of Keter, the Crown.

Regarding being cut off Abulafia states,

> "Your mind will become confused, your thoughts confounded, and you will not find the way to escape the daydreams of your mind. The power of your imagination will overtake you, making you imagine many utterly worthless fantasies. Your imagination will grow strong, your intellectual reasoning will weaken, until your daydreams cast you into a great sea." He concludes, "You will not have the wisdom to ever escape from it, and you will drown in the sea of imagination."

When you use your imagination intensely it overpowers what your eyes are seeing. The state Abulafia describes is where you are permanently in a little bit of a conscious state and in a lot of a dreaming state. You attach wrong meanings to facts. It's like living a mirage.

The Commandment regarding using god's name.

This meditation technique uses God's only true supreme name; the shem hameforash AKA the tetragrammaton. The ten speakings, commonly known as the ten commandments, are the most significant laws in the *Bible*. One of these commandments is the prohibition on using God's name, the shem haMeforash, "in vain."

"Taking the name" when translated literally is "lifting the name." In the *Bible* the word "vain" is found in the following verses;

Exodus 20:7

You shall not take the name of the LORD your God **in vain**; for the Lord will not hold him guiltless who takes his name **in vain**.

Deut 5:11

Thou shalt not take the name of the LORD thy God **in vain**: for the LORD will not hold him guiltless that taketh his name **in vain**.

The translation "Lord" as used in the *Bible* is directly translated as the four letter shem haMeforash, יהוה, the sacred name of God.

"In Vain?" What does the translation "vain" mean? The translated English word "vain" in the original language of Hebrew is to shav; לְשָׁוְא.

Shav has been given numerous translations. Some of the typical translations one hears are; an exhaled breath, meaninglessness, casually without reverence, cursing, self gratification, and many others. Shav means falsehood. The word specifically relates to oath-taking, but is a multi dimensional word that makes it allegorically translatable to many definitions.

Using the shem hameforash in a false manner would be using it "vainly" for gratification of the ego or self adornment. Basically it's trying to be like a God.

Provoking God

It's best not to provoke God. People who do things that God perceives as abominable, are certain to suffer.

There was this Roman General who, after conquering Jerusalem, killed a pig in the holiest of holies room of the second temple. Afterwards, he totally destroyed the second temple and plowed it under so no stone was on top of another. His name was Titus. Titus Flavius Vespasianus—commonly known as Vespasian. No retribution happened to him while in the Temple's holy of holies room. The high priests would die if they were not pure when entering into the holy of holies room. Yet nothing happened to Titus.............right away............. but.......... shortly afterwards, he started to die a most excruciating death.

A mosquito flew up his nose and lodged near his brain. This bug lived there and fed itself from his brain for seven years. During this time Titus would hear loud knocking sounds in his brain and experience extreme and excruciating pain. In the end he died a horrific and prolonged and painful death. After he died they opened his skull and found that the insect had grown to the size of a sparrow. It had a beak like brass and claws like iron. He died at the age of 41.

ABOUT TZERUF

The Letters

The Hebrew Alphabet

In the beginning of language the first stage of writing there was just pictures.

Next came something like the Egyptian hieroglyphics that told a story. But thousands of pictures had to be learned. Sounds were also linked to the pictures. A good example of this is the Chinese writing.

Horizon

Changed to Assent

Descent

Dawn

Rain

King (one who is between heaven and earth)

Rumblings of Carriages

Then came the third stage of language that was more efficient. Pictures developed into symbols, the alphabet letters, that had attached to them sounds. When this was combined with other alphabet symbol letters and sounds, words developed, and then sentences.

BEGINNINGS OF THE ALPHABET

In ancient times the Hebrew people and the Phoneticians were located along the coastal regions of what is modern day Lebanon, Syria and Israel. Both cultures lived next to each other and shared common alphabet symbols.

The Phoenicians were ship traders and because of their extensive traveling and trading, they are known to have spread their common alphabet throughout the Mediterranean sea. The Phoenicians taught the other cultures whom they traded with how to read and write. They are known for spreading the alphabet to the Greeks and hence to the civilized world. One of the thriving Phoenician seaports in the city of Byblos (modern day Jubayl in Lebanon) had major exports of papyrus (like paper, used for writing) throughout the Mediterranean area. The name of this port city is where the root of the modern day word "bible" is derived from.

Tradition is that these shared sacred alphabet symbols were handed down from Adam to the Hebrew people from generation to generation. The ancient Hebrews had what they called a "sacred" alphabet of 22 symbols linked to mystical sounds. The Phoenicians also had a very similar alphabet of 22 symbols which they called "magic signs." They basically had the same alphabet. These alphabet symbols were adopted by the Greeks and other civilizations who then transformed the symbols to suite their own cultures. The old Hebrew letters in time also went under transformations, but kept the 22 alphabet concepts and their sounds. This transformation is what we see in today's world as alphabet symbols similar to old Aramaic. The final result of today's Hebrew letters came from Ezra the scribe by his converting the ancient Hebrew alphabet script into an Aramaic morphology (ketav meruba).

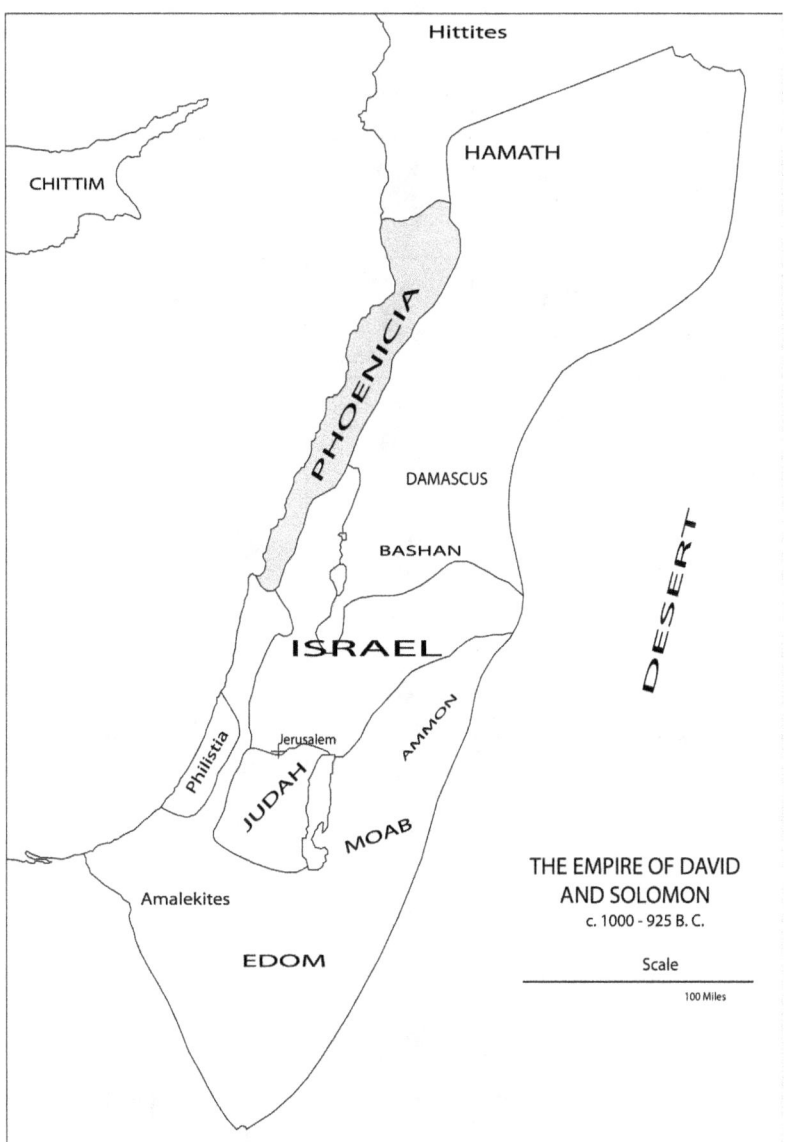

COMPARISON OF ALPHABET SYMBOLS

LETTER NAME	MODERN-HEBREW	ARAMAIC	PHOENICIAN	LITERAL MEANING
ALEF	א			Ox, Bull
BET	ב			Tent, House
GIMEL	ג			Camel
DALET	ד			Door
HEH	ה			Window, Fence
VAV	ו			Nail
ZAYIN	ז			Weapon
KHET	ח			Fence, Hedge, Chamber
TET	ט			to Twist, a Snake
YOD	י			Closed Hand
CAF	כ			Arm, Wing, Open Hand

THE HEBREW ALPHABET

Letter Name	Modern Hebrew	Aramaic	Phoenician	Literal Meaning
LAMED	ל	ל	∠	Cattle Goad, Staff
MEM	מ	מ	ᛘ	Water
NUN	נ	נ	ᏉI	Fish
SAMEC	ס	ס	‡	a Prop
AYIN	ע	ע	O	Eye
PEI	פ	פ	⊃	Mouth
TZADI	צ	צ	ᛣ	Fish-Hook
KUF	ק	ק	Φ	Back of the Head
RESH	ר	ר	⊲	Head
SHIN	ש	ש	W	Teeth
TAV	ת	ת	X	Sign, Cross

THE HEBREW ALPHABET

16

The Mystical Letters

Each Hebrew alphabet letter symbol has a concept of creation linked to it. The "sacred" or "magical" link to the alphabet letters is such that the subconscious automatically knows which concept of creation is represented by the written Hebrew letter symbol. Further, each concept of creation represented by a letter has associated with it a specific sound that is linked to that concept or Hebrew letter.

Each Hebrew letter actually represents an early pictographic symbol. For example the letter Bet ב (as used in the word Bethlehem, meaning 'house of bread') represents an image of a house. It shows a roof, wall, foundation, and entrance.

All letters are a composite of other letters except the Yod. All letters have a composite form and a fundamental form.

The Composite form is the font style that we see from the ink on the paper. This is where two or more letters are combined to make a new letter. In the case of an Alef, it has a diagonal line, a Vav, and two yods above and below the line.

The Fundamental form is where a letter must contain certain

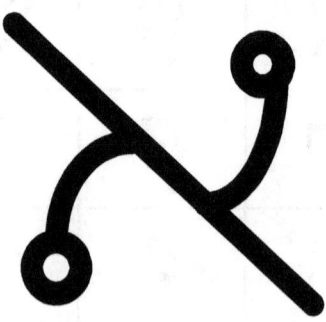

Fundamental Form of Alef

elements to be considered a valid letter. With an Alef the letters must have a diagonal line, high on the left and low on the right, and two points above and below the diagonal line. Further, these two points need to be connected to the diagonal line.

The font composite form or font style of a letter may vary significantly. Such as the diagonal line on the Alef may be thin or very wide. The same is true of the two points above and below the line, but fundamentally there must be no more or no less than two. The two points can connect to the line many ways, but fundamentally they must be connected to the line.

The Hebrew language is referred to as the "Lashon Ha-Kodesh", the holy language. It is said to be the only language spoken in heaven. It earns this designation based on it's letters.

What follows is an explanation of the meanings of each Hebrew alphabet letter which only resembles the tip of an iceberg. These following letters are four dimensional and the short explanations are impossible to depict them in their true lights.

ALEF - Ox

Alef is the first letter of the alphabet and has a numerical value of one. It looks like a line with two points on each side. It is composed of a slanted Vav with two Yods on both sides.

The Alef symbolizes the uniting of opposites, the duality in life, a coming together; God/mankind, man/woman, day/night, Heaven/Earth, ying/yang, etc. This is where God takes on a definition since he separated himself from creation. It is symbolic of the sefirah Keter. It is symbolic of the power of the one and only Omnipotent God. It represents sovereignty, infiniteness, and eternalness.

Construction

The Aleph is a consonant yet in the Hebrew language, it is a silent consonant and is only a place holder for a vocal sound. There are three Hebrew letters that are put together to make the form of the Aleph; the upper Yod (value 10), the slanted Vav (value 6), and the lower Yod (value 10). Adding the gematria values of these three letters equals 26, which is the same numerical value as God's true supreme name the Shem Hamephorish. Alef is worthy of being a name of HaShem. More names of God start with this letter than any other letters. It is the first letter of the substantial name EHIEH. The name for man, Adam, also begins with an Alef. The upper Yod represents God, the lower Yod represents man. The diagonal between represents the separation from God, and the *Torah* which bridges that separation. It is the only letter that faces to the right, all Hebrew letters face to the left. It is related to the word aloof, meaning emperor.

Numbers

Alef enabled the reality of all numbers. It's the prime factor in all the combinations of letters. It's numerical value of one represents the everything, the indivisible God. In a certain aspect Alef is not a number. If Alef ceased to exist, consequently then all other numbers would cease to exist. If all numbers failed to exist, that would not negate the existence of the Alef. This shows that if all of creation failed to exist, the creator would remain. Therefore this shows that all of creation is dependant on the creator. The reality is the other numbers are based on the Alef just as the creation is based on the creator. Alef does not change from it's unity to multiplicity but other numbers are derived from it. Every one of the creations will be found in relation to the unity, the creator. Thus we are likened to the numbers. Aleph is the beginning of the four degrees of numbers; units, tens, hundreds, and thousands (thousands headed by Alef again in Hebrew numerical writing). Alef is one and also one thousand with demonstrates that the beginning is also the end. It represents the singular and the many that are all connected.

BET - HOUSE

Bet is the second letter of the alphabet and has a numerical value of two. This is a double letter. This letter symbolizes a shelter. It has a roof, a wall, a foundation, and an entrance.

The left upper corner points upward to signify the acknowledgment of the Creator. The open side of the enclosure teaches that we should be open to guests. Bet means house and symbolizes that man makes himself a mini sanctuary. We spend most of our time in "houses", also meaning structures or buildings. One's body is the house of the soul. All of creation is a house in relation to God. As a preposition it means "in." It symbolizes that everything must have a line of separation and thus an enclosure. Each person separates from another. Everywhere in God's creation there is diversity.

GIMEL - CAMEL

Gimel is the third letter of the alphabet and has a numerical value of three. This is a double letter. It looks like a mother with a small child hanging on to her hand. It symbolizes the mother, father producing a child. This concept is to nourish until completely ripe, as in a mother nurturing a child to maturity with the child as a benefactor. It is the union of two creating a third. It symbolizes two opposing factors blended and forming a third that is better. It represents reproduction. It is the unifying and harmony of opposites.

Gimel also represents foot walking meaning progress. The camel in olden days represented this movement. The letter depicts a camel's long neck. It also means to deal, to recompense for a benefit, also reward & punishment. It signifies that every word and action is stored and one has to account for them.

DALET - ENTRANCE, EXIT

Dalet is the fourth letter of the alphabet and has a numerical value of four. This is a double letter. This letter is a depiction of a top view of an open door or a gate. It is a doorway to what we ultimately seek, inner knowledge and wisdom. It is the cycle of the old fading away and the new coming forth. It is destruction and regeneration. It represents a beneficiary. It represents humbleness of a poor person (dal).

It means the four directions of a plane. God created the universe with four spiritual levels. These four worlds or levels are emanation, creation, formation, and action. Many aspects of life are in four levels; mineral, plant, animal, man; earth water fire air, etc.

HEH - Window

Heh is the fifth letter of the alphabet. It's numerical value is five. It is composed of a Dalet and a small Vav. The Heh has a small opening to one side. It symbolizes being inside and looking out a widow. It means to "breathe" allowing in air and light in. The letter's sound is the sound of an exhalation of the breath. It actually has no tonal sound. God created the upper and lower worlds with an effortless exhalation. The small window in the top of the Heh also represents repentance.

It indicates femininity. At the end of a word it is used to form the feminine gender of a noun. As a prefix to a word, it indicates a specific member of the class. As a prefix it is used as a definite particle to give emphasis. It denotes creation. Freedom of choice.

In the shem hamephash this letter appears twice. The letter value of five has an allusion to the five books of *Torah* revealing it's mysteries. This letter relates to time; past, present and unity, or completeness. It is expression and revelation. It is common in all languages as a sound used to get attention (hey!) and laughing (haha). It represents mans thought, speech, action, and dimensions of malkut revealing man's soul.

VAV - NAIL OR HOOK

Vav is the sixth letter of the alphabet. It's value is six. It is formed as a letter Yod, then progresses on a path downwards.

It denotes physical completion. God created the world in six days. An object contains six dimensions; above and below, right and left, before and behind. Space has 6 directions. In the Hebrew language, when the Vav is attached to the beginning of a word it denotes a conjunction. It unites concepts. A joining together. It looks like a man standing, connecting heaven and earth, with his head in heaven. In the first sentence of the *Torah* when the Vav appears first it talks of a uniting of heaven and earth. The Aleph appears six times in first sentence of the *Torah*. Alef is equal to a thousand and thus represents six thousand years of struggle before the Messiah comes.

A Vav before a verb reverses the past and future tense and is read as meaning the opposite of what it would be if the Vav were not there. This shows a connection between future and past. It is called the Vav that reverses time.

The shem hamephorash has a Vav between two Hehs. This connects the upper Heh with lower Heh, represents light coming straight to below.

ZAYIN - Sword

Zayin is the seventh letter of the alphabet with a numerical value of 7. It is composed of a Vav with a Yod on top as a crown. It represents returning light up the Vav, spreading out to a crown. The Vav is masculine. Zayin is actually is feminine, as alluded "a woman of valor is a crown to her husband" (Proverbs). The seventh day shabbat is called a bride.

It looks like a weapon. It means the controlling of an opposite force by will. Seven denotes a perfection. Creation was not finished until the seventh day. It was a day of rest from the mundane, into a day involved with the spiritual world. Sabbath is rest from the struggle. Seven represents six directions plus one; the individual focal point. It signifies both fight for sustenance and armament, a sword. It means this in the sense of survival of fittest. It means a scepter gained through effort. As it says at the end of the story of creation, the seventh day is a "made to do" day. This means it is left for man to do.

Talmud says all 7's are precious. It is the day of rest encoded in all cycles of creation. It is seven weeks after Peasach when the *Torah* was received. All holidays are in first 7 months of year. Smita rest for the land is on the 7th year. Seven times seven is the jubilee year. 6000 years plus 1000 years of the messiah reign equals mans time of existence. Passover lasts 7 days. One eats matza for seven days. The festival of Succot lasts seven days. The bride & groom celebrate for seven days. There are seven lower sefirot on every level of creation.

KHET - WALL, HEDGE

Khet. This is the eighth letter of the alphabet with a numerical value of 8. It is constructed with one side a Vav other a Zayin with a connector to bridge between both. Vav masculine, Zayin feminine, and the connector between them is the third partner (God).

It is going beyond seven, to transcend the physical limitations by going to eight. It's the plane above nature. Anything transcending nature is always depicted with the value of eight. When referring to messianic times anything dealing with miracles is always symbolized as eight. Circumcision is performed on the 8th day. A brit or circumcision is a covenant, more specifically an eternal contract. There is the eighth day celebration of Passover. Shmini Atzeres is on the eighth day of the festival of Succot; Seven days for the nations, and the eighth day for the pious. There are eight days of Hanukkah. Anything dealing with 8 is otherworldly or supernatural. It means one beyond, eternal, infinite. The symbol of infinity is 8.

The Khet depiction is walling others out. It means the making a garment. It appears like a gateway where one runs and returns through. It is the first letter of the Hebrew word Khai which means life.

It has a most unique pronunciation like a German or Scottish person would pronounce words of their languages with a guttural throat clearing sound.

TET - Coiling Serpent,

Tet is the ninth letter with a numerical value of 9. It is composed of a Zayin attached to a Caf. It means potential; power released. It is the general symbol for goodness. Man longs for good life, good health, good business, etc.

It is shaped like a vessel hiding what is in it. It is like a womb hiding something precious for 9 months, then revealing the within. It is the first letter of the Hebrew word Tov which means goodness. The letter hides yet represents goodness within it. It is birth and renewal. It brings potential to actualization.

YOD - HAND

Yod is the tenth letter of the alphabet. It's numerical value is 10. The word Yod means hand. It is the smallest written letter yet represents the metaphysical. It is referred to as "the little that holds a lot." It represents the first step in an escalation to heights of spirituality. It is the symbol of the power that maintains creative and directed energy.

It is the first letter of God's true name; a powerful letter resembling an infinite God creating a finite world. All 22 Hebrew alphabet letters have a Yod in it.

It is the ending of the units and the beginning of the tens. Any number multiplied by 10 is it's full manifestation. In Bereshit (Genesis) there are 10 expressions, and 10 things that were created on the first day, 10 at dusk and on the sixth day. Abraham passed 10 tests, he inherited 10 nations. There is the 10 days period before Yom Kippur the holiest day of year. One is to give a 10th of income to charity, a 10th also given of crops. There are 10 sefirot. There were 10 plagues. And there are 10 commandments in which all mitzvahs are contained in.

CAF - PALM OF A HAND, CUPPED HAND.

Caf the eleventh in the alphabetical order with a numerical value of 20. This is a double letter. It also has a final letter which changes it's form at the end of a word. It is a curved Vav.

It is drawn like the shape of a cupped hand turned on side. Opened it represents the world. Closed it represents self.

It represents productivity and accomplishment, power and possession. It means the crown of *Torah*. It means potential, coaching, grabbing of opportunities. At the same time it also means to suppress that inclination of lower nature, the evil inclination. It is ending the bent. It is the potential to master primitive impulses with driving assistance, and thus the obligation to know *Torah* continually.

LAMED - OX-GOAD

Lamed is the twelfth letter of the alphabet with a numerical value of 30. It looks like a route drawn on a map. It is a Kuf with the Kuf's Vav moved to be on its roof. Kuf and Vav equal 26 the same gematria value of the shem hamephorash.

This letter denotes directions, goal, or purpose. The curving line of the letter symbolizes mans course in life. It Refers not only to learning, but also to teaching. It is the tallest of the letters. It is the only letter to goes above the other letters. It symbolizes the king of kings, the supreme ruler, the objective of your life. It means education, and learning the direction of your path; the goal, purpose (through learning). It means the aspiration of heart or what the heart longs for.

MEM - WATER

Mem is the thirteenth letter of the alphabet. It's numerical value is 40. It has a final letter form. This letter is symbolic of water. The top of the letter is shaped like a wave. The bottom has an opening in it denoting water pouring out. It has a Yod at the top denoting a small amount of water that flows down.

Mem reflects the female enclosing and nurturing values. It means a ripening process. Mem is attributed to the sefirah Binah. The *Zohar* states that it represents both Moses and the Messiah.

Mem has two forms, the nominative and the final. The nominative Mem an has opening in bottom meaning running streams of water. This open Mem is the revealed glory of God's actions. It is a constant outpouring of blessings. The final closed Mem, alludes to the celestial rule that is concealed. The closed Mem is the blessings being held back. It also means a closed body of water; ocean, lake. The spelling of the name of the letter Mem contains both a nominative Mem and a closed Mem, with a Yod for it's middle letter meaning a drop of water.

FORTY

Forty is the time necessary for a ripening process that leads to fruit. Forty represents a milestone of ones spiritual development. The flood of Noah rained for forty days. Moses lived in Egypt at Pharaoh's palace for forty years. Moses lived forty years in Midian. Moses was the leader of the Jewish people for forty years. Moses went up on Mount Sinai for forty days. Before Moses's second assent to Mount Sinai he fasted for 40 days. Then he again stayed on Mount Sinai for forty days for the second giving of the *Torah*. The scouts spying on Canaan took forty days, and hence the Israelites spent forty years in the desert. There are forty weeks of a pregnancy (fetus is in water). An embryo is established after forty days. King Solomon fasted forty days. A man's life milestone is forty years when he then attains insight.

Water covers 70% of the Earth. The body of an adult is 60% water. In the *Talmud* every mention of water in the *Torah* refers to the *Torah* itself. The *Torah* states that "Love" is like flowing water; a gematria value of 13. This alludes to the 13 aspects of compassion connected to love.

NUN - FISH

Nun is the fourteenth letter of the alphabet. It's numerical value is 50. It is constructed of a Vav with a Yod on the top and a flattened Yod at it's base. This letter has a final form when it is at the end of a word.

It symbolizes a man, or God, sitting on a throne as king. It symbolizes faithfulness, soul, emergence. Nun denotes continuity. As a word, it means endure. The final nun denotes the angels standing before God. The final nun distinguishes itself as an occasional act as opposed to a habitual act.

Nun represent a faithful servant, in Hebrew ne-eman, spelled with two nuns. It means bent over, humble. When the Messiah comes it is widely thought that his name will be "Ianun," spelled with two nuns (Psalm 72). Nun implies redemption, hope, and eventual resurrection.

It means eternal faithfulness. The aramaic word Nun means fish and reproductiveness. Two verses Numbers 10:35 & 36 describe the Holy Ark. These verses are so significant because they contain a reverse nun. As an isolated passage it is regarded as book all by itself. This means the nations downfall. In Psalm 145 the nun is omitted (the downfall).

The fiftieth year is the jubilee year of freedom where all indentured servants go free. It took fifty days to come out of Egypt.

SAMECH - PROP, SUPPORT

Samech is the fifteenth letter of the alphabet with a numerical value of 60. It is drawn with a completely empty inner area surrounded by an outer area. It is formed like a curved Vav with a completely closed interior.

It symbolizes support and protection. It has an inner core protected by a perimeter. The *Torah* is the inner area, surrounded by the teachings of the oral law. It represents a circle. Every point on circle is of an equal distance symbolizing that everyone is equal. Reincarnation is a circle that repeats. The Hebrew word Sovev means surround. There are two aspects of God. One aspect surrounds and one aspect fills. Samech represents the surrounding aspect.

SIXTY

Sixty symbolizes abundance. Sixty means nullification. Dreams are 1/60th of prophesy. Shabbat is 1/60th of the world to come. Fire 1/60th of Gehinmom (hell). Sleep is 1/60 of death. Honey is 1/60th of Manna. A person is either included or nullified by the age of sixty.

King Solomon's book in Ecclesiastes 12:13 has an enlarged Samech meaning reliance of God support. It means completion in time & space. The insides of a Samech represent the tabernacle. The outside roundness represents God. The line between them represents camps of Israel. It is an inner core protected by outer perimeter. God protects with a wall, no beginning or end. The hebrew word Samech means support and happiness (simha).

AYIN - Eye

Ayin is the sixteenth letter of the alphabet. It's value is 70. It is a sitting Vav with a Zayin attached. It means eye and also a spring of water. It depicts two eyes with a flow uniting from each to form a foundation. Ayin represents man's outlook and perception. It represents both a rich man, and a poor man.

The word Ayin means eye. The eye brings perception. It is the window of brain. The eyes reveals more to man that all of the other senses. It also means a spring of water. The eye sees the world. It is man's spiritual awareness. Man has two eyes for seeing, one for God one for his own shortcomings. Ayin represents light which makes vision possible. The Shema prayer has a large Ayin (Deut 6:4).

Seventy

The nature of spirituality has 70 facets. There were 70 nations from Noah. There were 70 souls that went into Egypt. God has 70 names, the *Torah* 70 names, Israel 70 names. 70 people went to Egypt from 70 nations. There are 70 holy days a year including Shabbat. The *Torah* was given to 70 elders. Sanhedrin has 70 sages. There are 70 facets of *Torah* that are translated into 70 languages and understood by 70 nations. The law was engraved on 70 stones. Jerusalem has 70 names. The holy temple had 70 pillars. On Succot there were 70 sacrifices for 70 nations which have 70 representatives of heavenly angels. 70 is a turning point in history. There were 70 languages at the Tower of Babel. There were 70 years of Babylon exile. 70 nations recognize the shem hamephorash as the ruler of world. 70 means to reveal secrets and it alludes to a high degree of secret meaning.

PEH - MOUTH

Peh is the seventeenth letter of the alphabet with a numerical value of 80. This is a double letter. It also changes its form at the end of a word. The Peh is composed of a Caf with a Yod hanging down. It depicts a speaking mouth with a tongue in it.

Intelligent speech separates man from animals. It symbolizes articulating mans insights and perceptions and communicating them to others. Speech is the basis of civilization.

The Peh symbolizes a closed mouth. The final Peh symbolizes an open mouth. There is a time for silence and a time for communication. God created the world with speech. Man creates or destroys with his speech. The Oral *Torah* is called the master of the mouth. The open mouth is to teach *Torah*. The closed mouth to learn it. The final Peh also symbolizes death.

The Mouth of God is described as giving the Torah, given from mouth of strength. The here and now is the power of speech. Inside the white space of the letter Peh is a shape like the letter Bet. This alludes to the mouth shows what is inside.

Man is a Speaking spirit whose mouth makes him able to fulfill his ultimate purpose and to communicate his soul's insights and concepts. Man's words, verbalized or not, are transformed into actions.

TZADI - Fish Hook

Tzadi is the eighteenth letter of the alphabet with a numerical value of 90. This is a letter that changes its form at the end of a word. The Tzadi, also called Tzadik, is constructed as a bent over Nun (servant) with two Yuds. They rest like a rider on the back of a horse. The Nun is bent in humbleness. It symbolizes two eyes coming together and forming a foundation.

The letter represents righteousness and humility. The letter is seen as its eyes elevated in readiness to do devotion. It represents a human being emulating God's righteousness and is unbiased by his personal interests. He is a tzadik, God's ambassador on the earth, devoid of injustice. A tzadik carries the whole world on his shoulders. The final Tzadi represents the final acceptance of a righteous person in the world to come.

It also means to hunt (tzud) as in hunting for one that needs redemption. Ninety is the age of Sara when she gave birth to her first and only child, Isaac. Man declines physically at the age of 90. The letter represents Sara, circumcision, and Abraham.

KUF - BACK OF THE HEAD

Kuf is the nineteenth letter. It's numerical value is 100. It depicts the back of a man's head. It is constructed of two letters, Caf and Vav, both adding to a value of 26, the same in gematria as the shem hamephorash.

It is the symbol for and means holiness, kedusha in Hebrew, which describes an object that is sanctified, forbidden to use for ordinary pleasures. Abstinence is a step towards kedusha; to refrain from evil talk, forbidden food, sexual immorality, etc. This abstinence results in self-discipline.

Kuf means cycles. God manifests himself in nature by creating cycles, indicating that there is a purpose to the universe. Hakuf in Hebrew means cycle, to go around. There are seven days in a week cycle; a seven year cycle, shemittah; seven seven's is a jubilee cycle; the Israelites circled Jericho seven times; on the festival of Succot the Lilav and Esrog circle the center of the worship area seven times.

It is the only letter that goes below the line, representing going down, as in the soul coming down to the body. It represents holiness and at the same time clipa, or shells. It means secret, strangeness of inner meaning, metaphysical.

The full pregnant (milui) spelling value in gematria is the same as the word omnipresent. It's concealed value, 86, is the same gematria as Elohim. Kuf has the same spelling as the word monkey, This was and example of a man at the time of Enoch. Man turned into an ape. And there was a second time for man at the tower of Babel.

REISH - HEAD

Reish is the twentieth letter of the alphabet. This is a double letter. It has a value of 200. The curved shape in the middle of the letter symbolizes a changing course from the original course; changing a course to greatness or degradation. It is similar to the letter Dalet. The difference is the right upper corner. The Reish accommodates itself smoothly to a new and perpendicular path. It bends to accommodate whims and idolatry.

The Reish means head or beginning or to inherit. It also means a wicked person. According Talmud, it means denying the sovereignty of God. It means intentionally becoming a non-believer by being unwilling to do the commandments.

SHIN - TOOTH

Shin is the twenty-first letter. It's value is 300. It is the most symmetrical of letters and one of its meanings is symmetrical. It's shape is made up of 3 Vavs as raised flames. It is composed of four Yods and three Vavs. The Vavs are the stems of the flames, three Vavs are on their tops, and the base is an elongated Yod.

Shin represents the element of fire. It looks like a fire with it's flames rising to the sky. The vocalization of Shin is also the sound of a fire, "shhhhhh."

The word shin itself means tooth. It's shape resembles a molar. It is an expansive, lively force. It is the transformation of the material into the heavens through extreme heat. If controlled beneficial. If not controlled, destructive. Its symbol of flames represents serenity, completeness. Its three heads represent a conflict with two people resolving to completeness, with God in the middle. Shin is related to the word sharpened. There is an enlarged shin in the song of Solomon.

It also denotes falsehood, sheker in Hebrew. The name sheker has consecutive alphabet letters going backward, the Shin, the Kuf, and the Resh. The Shin means falsehood, the Kuf means monkey, and the Resh means evil doer. Falsehood clothes itself in the appearance of truth so it has credibility. Falsehood is unreliable subjectivity.

TAV - Cross mark

Tav is the twenty-second letter, the last letter of the alphabet. It's value is 400. This is a double letter. The Tav is a composite of a Resh with an upsidedown Vav. The upsidedown Vav is reflective of the emotions in total control. Both the Resh and the Vav added together is ten in reduced gematria, reflecting the all, the ten sefirot.

Tav symbolizes everything in everything. It originally looked more like the symbol of an X. The cross symbolizes the four directions that encompasses everything. X marks the spot.

It means a seal, a stamp, an impression, God's stamp. It is a cleaning of up what has been left behind, an end. Every end starts a new beginning. Divine judicial pronouncement symbolizes divine perfection, body and soul being harmonious.

It is the symbol of truth and perfection. It is the final letter in the Hebrew word for truth, emet. Truth is obtained through effort. If the Alef is omitted from the word emet, its spells met, meaning death.

In Ezekiel's vision a Tav written in ink was on the foreheads of citizens of Jerusalem. Blood was used for the written Tav of the wicked. Abraham bought a burial place for Sara for 400 pieces of silver.

FINAL LETTERS

There are five letters that change their form when they appear as the last letter in a Hebrew word. Their pronunciations do not change. The reason for these letters changing is said to reflect mystical meanings. Their pronunciations don't change but their numerical values do change under certain value systems. Under the standard gematria value calculations their values are the same wherever they appear in a word, whether nominative or final.

Caf	ך	500
Mem	ם	600
Nun	ן	700
Tzadi	ץ	800
Peh	ף	900

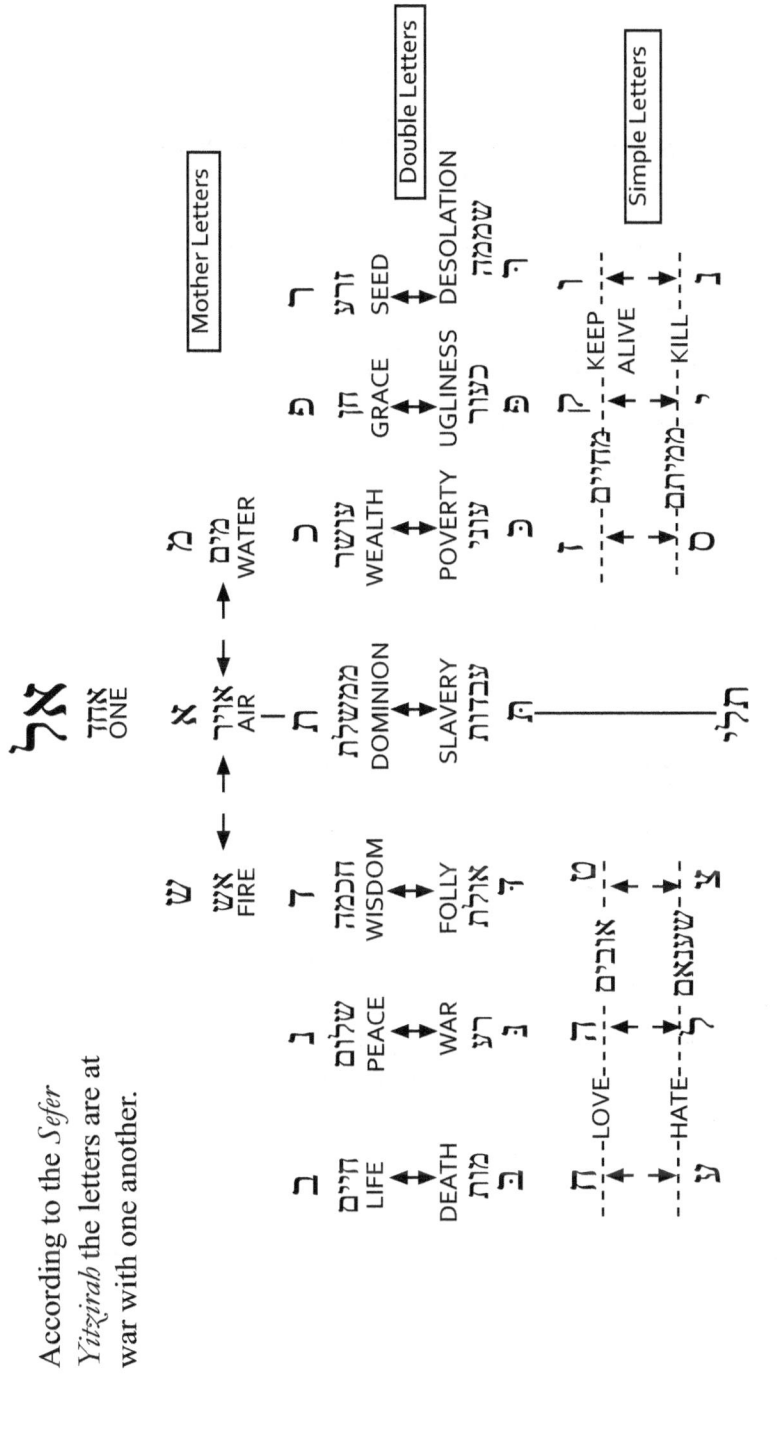

Alphabet in the Mouth

The Hebrew alphabet sounds are formed in five different parts of the mouth; the throat, palate, tongue, teeth, and lips.

Graphic	Name	Sound
א	Alef	ah
ה	Heh	h
ח	Khet	kh
ע	Ayin	aiy

Throat

Guttural. Aleph, Chet, Heh, and Ayin originate in the larynx. These are divided into four levels: Aleph is at the first level, close to the exit [the pharynx]; Heh is at the second level, for it is more internal; Khet is at the third level, further inside than the Heh and the Aleph. Ayin is at the fourth level, which is the most internal to all the letters and close to the inner sound, which is the innermost of all.

Graphic	Name	Sound
ג	Gimel	g
י	Yod	y
כ ך	Kaf	k, hard h
ק	Quof	q

Palate

Palatal. Gimel, Yod, Caf, Quf, are pronounced in five parts of the upper palate.

Graphic	Name	Sound
ד	Dalet	d
ט	Tet	t
ל	Lamed	l
נ	Nun	n
ת ת	Tav	t, th

Tongue

Lingual. Dalet, Tet, Lamed, Nun, Tav, are pronounced with the middle of the tongue.

Graphic	Name	Sound
ז	Zayin	z
ס	Samek	s
שׂ שׁ	Sin, Shin	s, sh
צ	Tzadi	tz
ר	Reish	r

Teeth

Dental. Zayin, Samech, Shin, Tzadi, Resh, are pronounced; these are from the tongue as it taps the taps between the teeth lightly.

Graphic	Name	Sound
בּ ב	Beit	b, v
ו	Vav	v
מ	Mem	m
פּ פ	Pey, Fey	p, f

Lips

Labial. Bet Vav Mem Peh are pronounced by the lips which are the external part of the mouth.

Hebrew Vowels Markings

In the Hebrew language, all alphabet letters are consonants. There are no vowels in the Hebrew alphabet. Vowels are separate markings. The vowels are like the soul of a word. Vowels set in motion the Hebrew alphabet consonant sounds.

In 600 A.D., a group of scribes in Tiberias called the Masoretes developed a system of writing the vowel marks (called nequdot) to indicate how the biblical text was traditionally suppose to be read. Since these scribes did not want to alter the consonantal text, they placed these markings under, above, or to the left of the Hebrew letters. In addition to these vowel markings, the scribes also created "cantonation" marks (ta'amim) to indicate how the text was to be inflected or sung.

The english letter "A" symbolizes any Hebrew alphabet letter (Aleph, Bet, Gimel, etc.) and the rectangular boxes above, below, and to the left of the letter symbolizes possible areas where a vowel notation is placed.

Most vowel notations are referred to as "simple" vowels because they are composed of only one identifying vowel notation attached in close proximity to a Hebrew letter. These notations are generally placed below the letter, except for; the Cholem notation which is located above to the left top of the letter Vav; and the Sureq which is to the left middle of the letter Vav.

The "full" vowels involve two Hebrew alphabet letters.

Note: the Kubutz and the Shuruk vowel symbols have the same sound, but one is said in a shorter time than the other, or more staccato. There is also one symbol, the Shewa, that denotes no sound.

הA 'A וA

"Full" or "Mixed" Hebrew Vowels

The above are examples of vowel types known as "full vowels" because the text includes an additional alphabet letter to compliment the vowel markings, although no additional sound is made.

Ah sound

ah sound

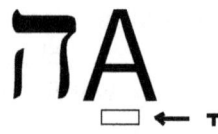

aoh sound
(Full vowel scripted)

Vowel	Name	Class
אָ	Qamets	Long
אַ	Patach	Short
אֲ	Chatepa Patach	Reduced

mat

Eh sound

eh sound

aeh sound
(Full vowel scripted)

Vowel	Name	Class
אֵ	Tsere	Long
אֶ	Segol	Short
אֱ	Chatepa Segol	Reduced

mae

Eeeh Sound

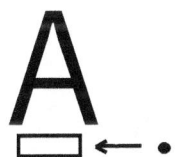 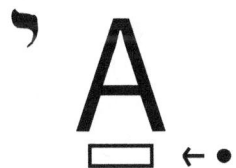

eeeh sound

eeeh sound
(Full vowel scripted)

Vowel	Name	Class
אִי	Chireq Yod	Long
אִ	Chireq	Short

meee

Owe Sound

owe sound

Full vowel scripted

Vowel	Name	Class
אֹ	Cholem	Long
אוֹ	Cholem Vav	Long
אֳ	Chateph Qamets	Reduced
אָ	Qamets Chatuph	Short (with special rule)

moe

oh — yome — y

m

Oow Sound

oow

oow sound
(Full vowel scripted)

Mark	Name	Class
אוּ	Sureq	Long
אֻ	Qibbuts	Short

oo — m — moo

v — sh — shoov — oo

No Sound

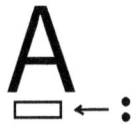

no sound

Shewa

Mark	Name	Class
אְ	Shewa	Silent

note: can be vocal under grammar rules

Hebrew Vowels Markings

	Comparative Chart				
Matres Lectionis	ה ה	י	י	ו	ו
Sound Category	a	e	i	o	u
Full	qamets heh הָ â ball	tsere yod יֵ ê they	hirek yod יִ î machine	holem vav וֹ ô open	shurek וּ û lure
Long	qamets ָ ā ball	tsere ֵ ē they	hirek ִ ī machine	holem ֹ (וֹ) ō open	shurek וּ ū lure
Short	patach ַ a ball	segol ֶ e bet	hirek ִ i hit	qametz hatuph ָ o on	qibbuts ֻ u under
Half/Reduced	hataph patach ֲ ă ball	hataph segol ֱ ĕ bet	sheva ְ e careen	hataph qaments ֳ ŏ on	blank

Vowels Linked to the Sefirot

Hebrew Name	Symbol	Sound	Sefirah
Kametz	אָ	aoh	Keter (Crown)
Patach	אַ	ah	Khochmah (Wisdom)
Tzeirei	אֵ	aeih	Binah (Understanding)
Segol	אֶ	aeh	Chesed (Kindness)
Shewa	אְ	staccato sound	Gevurah (Severity)
Holam	וֹ	oeh	Tiferet (Beauty)
Hirik	אִ	eeh	Netzach (Victory)
Kubutz *	וּ	ewh	Hod (Glory)
Shuruk *	אֻ	ewh	Yesod (Foundation)
No vowels	א	just breath out	Malkut (Kingship)

Hebrew Vowels Markings

* The pronunciation of Kubutz and Shuruk are indistinguishable in modern conversational Hebrew.

Linked to Amounts (Gematria)

Each Hebrew alphabet letter represents a numerical value. The numerical values of the letters in a word are added up and a value is derived for that word. This process is called gematria. The end objective of this process is to compare the different values of two or more words or phrases. When compared to other Hebrew words with the same numerical values the meanings of those words are spiritually closely related to each other. A typical practice in advanced tzeruf meditation to add up the numerical values of the letters in various words, and use these words with words of the same numerical values in various meditations.

Examples:

Blood in Hebrew is Dam. The numerical value for Dam is 44. The word child, which is Iled, and has a numerical value of 44. If you add the numerical values for the Hebrew words for father and mother together, the value is 44. Father is Av. Alef is 1 and Bet is 2, added together becomes three. Mother is Em. Alef is 1 and Mem is 40, added together is 41. The values from adding father and mother together is the same numerical value of blood, 44.

Gad means luck in Hebrew. Gimel value is 3 and Dalet value is 4. Adding them together is the lucky number 7. Mazal in Hebrew means good fortune. Mem value is 40, Zayin value is 7 and Lamed value is 30. All these letters add up to 77.

The following are several of the main ways of computing the various gematria of words.

Numerology

Numerology was derived from the practice of Gematria.

Absolute Value (in Hebrew: mispar hechrachi)

Also known as Normative value:

Each letter is assigned a value. Alef (the first letter of the alphabet) is given a value of 1. Beit (the second letter) value is 2, etc. The tenth letter, yud is is given the value 10. The successive letters after yud are increased by tens; 20, 30, 40, and up. The letter Kuf begins the hundreds and is valued at 100. The successive letters after the Kuf are increased by 100; 200 300, etc. The last letter of the alphabet, Tav, equals 400.

The letters which are the "final letter forms" (Kaf sofiet, Mem sofiet, Nun sofiet, Pei sofiet, and Tzadi sofiet), used when these letters conclude a word, generally are given the same numerical equivalent of the normally written (normative) letter forms. However, sometimes these final letters are also valued separately and given the high hundreds numerical values as seen in the gematria table.

Reduced value (in Hebrew: mispar katan aka Mispar Me'ugal) (modulus 9 in mathematical terminology)

Each digit of a letter's value is added together and reduced to one digit. For example, the Alef equals 1, Yud equals 10, Kuf equals 100. They separately all have a numerical value of 1. Beit equals 2, Kaf equals 20, and Reish equals 200. They separately all have a value of 2. The letters will only have values from one to nine, but when letters are added together the final sum may have a value of several digits.

In both the Ordinal and Reduced values, the five final Hebrew letters whose form changes when they are at the end of a word, are generally of equivalent value to the same value as they are given when they are written in other positions in a word. However, they are sometimes given their own values. For example, the ordinal value of the final Nun is at times considered 14, and is at times considered 25. At times it's reduced value is 5, and at other times, its reduced value 7. See Gematria Table.

	א	ב	ג	ד	ה	ו	ז	ח	ט
Absolute	1	2	3	4	5	6	7	8	9
Ordinal	1	2	3	4	5	6	7	8	9
Reduced	1	2	3	4	5	6	7	8	9

	י	כ	ל	מ	נ	ס	ע	פ	צ
Absolute	10	20	30	40	50	60	70	80	90
Ordinal	10	11	12	13	14	15	16	17	18
Reduced	1	2	3	4	5	6	7	8	9

	ק	ר	ש	ת	ך	ם	ן	ף	ץ
Absolute	100	200	300	400	500	600	700	800	900
Ordinal	19	20	21	22	23	24	25	26	27
Reduced	1	2	3	4	5	6	7	8	9

GEMATRIA TABLE

MANY METHODS

The practice of gematria analysis is a serious subject to many of those studying the *Torah*. In addition to the most commonly used methods detailed above, Moses Cordovero in his book *Pardes Rimonim* list only what are some of the additional methods;

> Mispar Gadol, Mispar Bone'eh, Mispar Kidmi aka Mispar Meshulash, Mispar P'rati aka Mispar ha-Merubah ha-Prati, Mispar ha-Merubah ha-Klali, Mispar Meshulash, Mispar ha-Akhor aka Mispar Meshulash, Mispar Mispari, Mispar Shemi, Mispar Ne'elam, Mispar Misafi, Kolel, Albam, Achbi, Ayak Bakar, Ofanim, Akhas Beta, Avgad.

The Sacred Hebrew Language

It is said that the Hebrew language is the language spoken in Heaven. The ancient sages have said that the source of all languages is the Hebrew language. The following examples are just a quick sampling of the many alignments and dimensions of the Hebrew letters to show their mystical sources.

Linked to Four Categories

There are four different categories of letters in the Hebrew alphabet. These four categories reflect the four levels of the soul.

First, there are three Mother letters; Alef, Mem, and Shin (air, water, and fire). These mother letters are linked to the most dominant areas of the seferot tree of Kabbalah.

The second category of the letters is called doubles. These are the seven alphabet letters that change sound if written with a dagesh, or dot, in the middle of the letter. They are the Bet, Gimel, Dalet, Kaph, Peh, Resh, and Tav.

In the third category there are five final letters that don't change their sound, but change their shape when they appear at the end of a word. They are the Kuf, Mem, Nun, Peh, and Tzadi.

In the fourth category, there are twelve remaining letters which are called simple letters. Nothing is distinct about them. They are the Tzadi, Vav, Zayin, Khet, Tet, Yod, Lamed, Nun, Samech, Ayin, Heh, Kuf.

Linked to Dimensions

The Kabbalah Cube is a depiction of Hebrew letters linked to the dimensions of space.

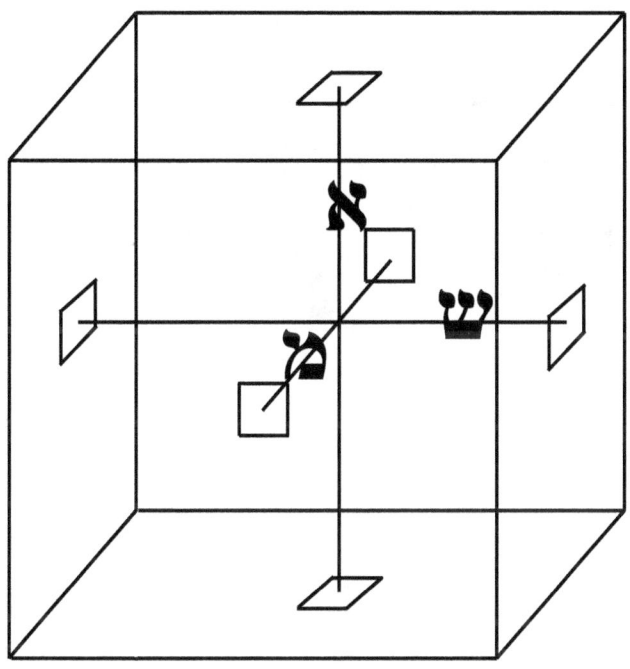

Cube 1

The height/depth line is the first dimension and represented by the mother letter Alelf.

The next dimension is the horizontal north/south dimension and is represented by the mother letter Shin.

The third dimension is the East/West dimension represented by the mother letter Mem.

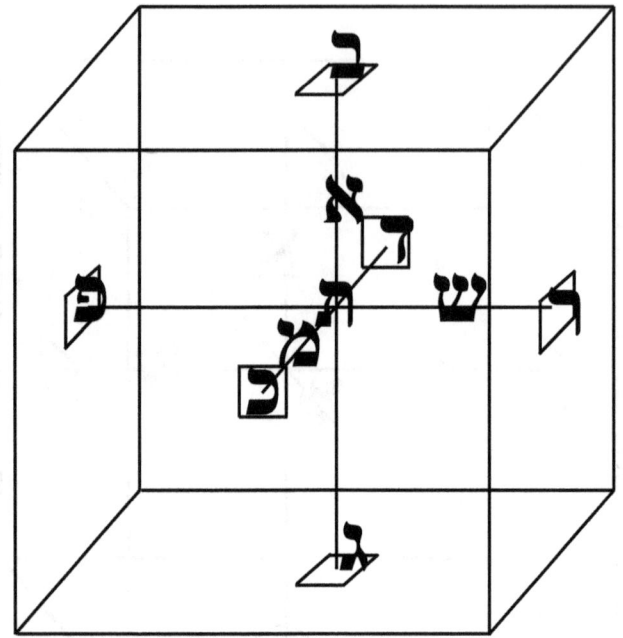

CUBE 2

The above cube shows other dimensions in addition to the mother letter directions. These dimensional outer planes along with the center point of the cube represent the double letters; Bet, Gimel, Dalet, Kaph, Pe, Resh, Tav.

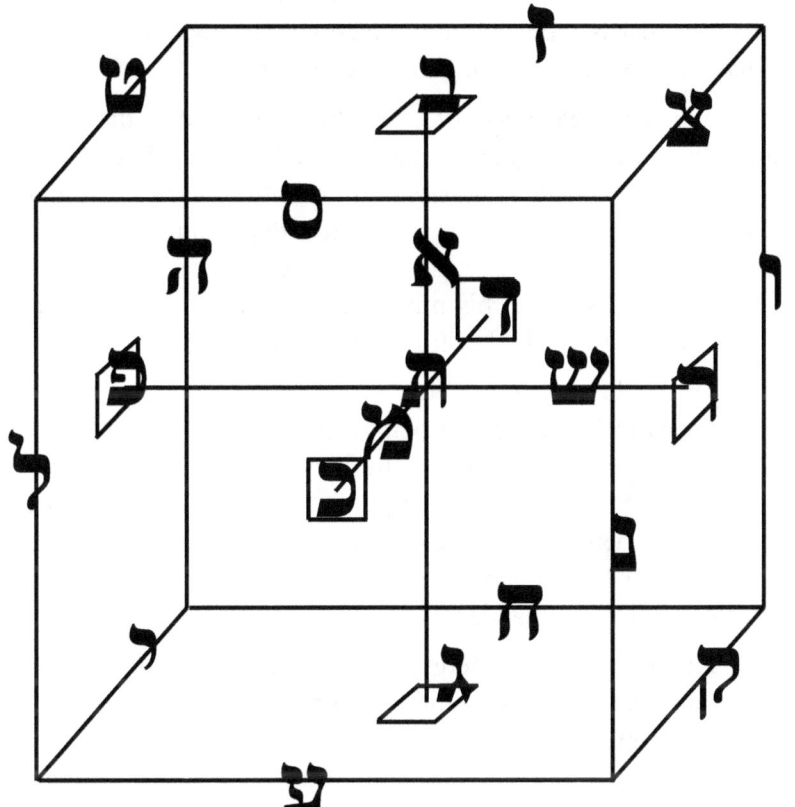

Cube 3

The twelve outer edges on the cube where the dimensional planes intersect, represent the twelve simple letters; Tzadi, Vav, Zayin, Khet, tet, Yod, Lamed, Nun, Samech, Ayin, Heh, Kuf.

Linked to a Sefirot Order

The Hebrew letters are linked to the paths between the sefirot on the sefirot tree. Sefirot is the plural, and sefirah is the singular. This sefirot tree, that is talked about extensively in Kabbalah, is the "order" of creation that is repeated in all creations, throughout our spiritual and material world, and throughout the universe.

A quick explanation of the sefirot tree is that there are ten sefirot that "Godly" energy must pass through before it becomes a creation or an action result. These ten different sefirot affect the amount and the type of energy released from a tree depending on the amount remaining in each sefirah and the mixing with other sefirot trees. The results of energies from this mixing of trees in the lowest form is physical matter. In the higher forms the energy result is life.

The highest sefirah Keter is the God emanation that is not even understandable to human beings. From there the energy flows to the other nine sefirot and they are divided into the upper and the lower sefirot The two upper sefirot, Chochma and Bina, formulate the design of this energy. The remaining lower seven sefirot are those that quantify and quality the amounts of different energies into a material result, but can be spiritual depending on the creation activity.

The main flow of energy down a tree is in a specific path, but each sefirah relates to other sefirah in their close proximity and is affected and is effected by them. This interaction is depicted as paths between sefirot, based on relative amount, quality, similarity, location, etc. to the other sefirot in it's relative influential area.

Each of the 22 paths between the sefirot are linked to a Hebrew letter, and each of the 10 sefirot are linked to many letters (except the sefirah Malkut). These paths can be used to achieve a more targeted and specific result in advanced tzeruf meditations. For example; the word for truth in Hebrew is emet (אמת). It is composed of the Alef, the Mem, and the Tav. On the sefirot tree this word stimulates the paths allowing the spiritual energies to mix between Chesed and Gevurah and to it's surrounding connectors, mix between Netzach and Hod and others connecting paths, and between Yesod and Malkut and to those connecting sefirot. When arranged in a tzeruf meditation this tends to create an effect similar to the concept of truth.

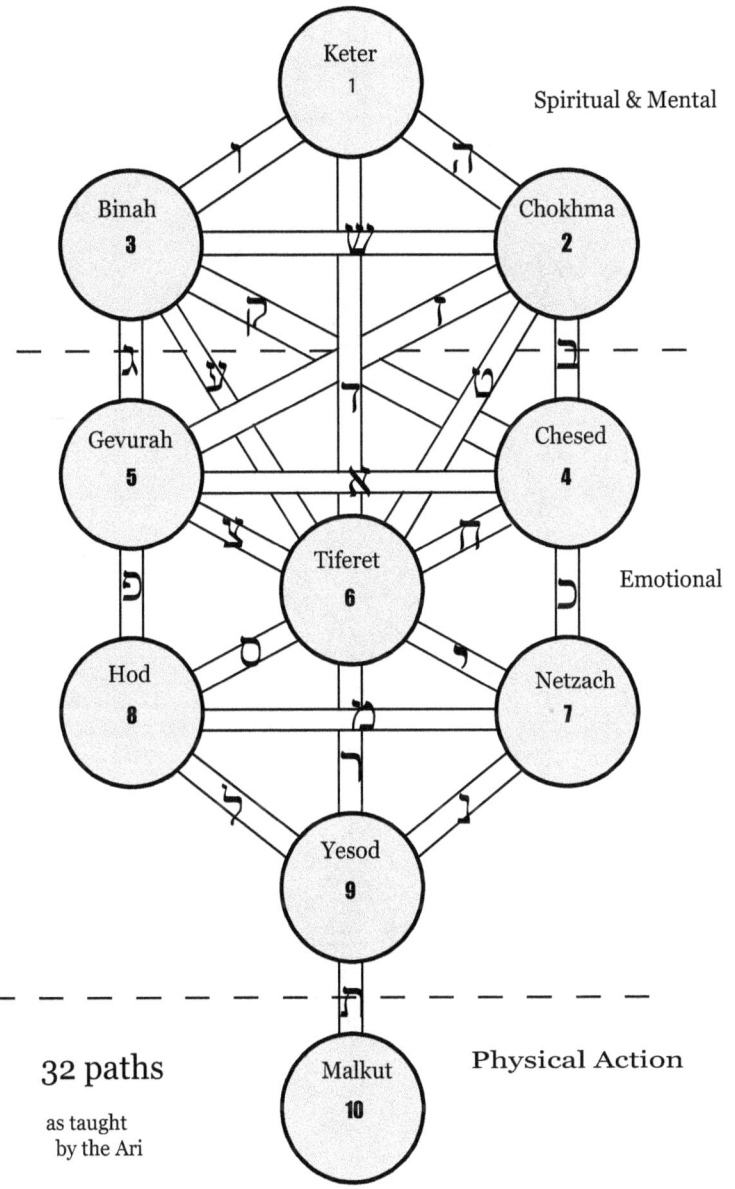

32 paths

as taught
by the Ari

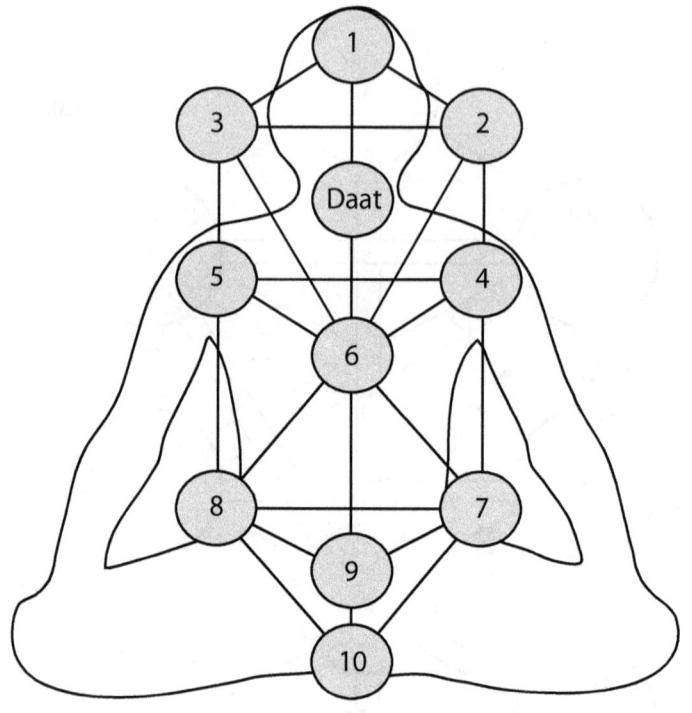

1. KETER
2. CHOKHMA
3. BINA
4. GEVURAH
5. CHESED
6. TIFERET
7. NETZACH
8. HOD
9. YESOD
10. MALKUT

Tarot & Playing Cards

Flash cards of the Hebrew alphabet letter meanings was the origin of today's playing cards. The name originates from the plural of the name Torah, Torot.

Tarot

Wands, Cups, Swords, and Disks, in ascending order, represent the 4 developmental levels of the soul each having ten cards representing each levels ten sefirot. Wands are the bottom level. Next is the Cups followed by the Swords. The top level is the Disks. The 16 court cards represent the 4 developmental levels on which each have 4 different soul levels. The 22 trump cards represent the 22 Hebrew letters.

Playing cards

Tarot Nouveau was the start of our modern day playing cards. The four suits represent the four ascending tree developmental levels and the numbers represent the ten sefirot steps. Clubs are the bottom level. Then the next level is hearts and then follows spades. The diamonds are the top level. The kings, queens, jacks and jokers represent the 4 developmental and the 4 soul levels of the sefirot There are no cards that reflect the Hebrew alphabet.

Fool	Aleph
Magus	Bet
High Priestess	Gimel
Empress	Dalet
Emperor	Heh
Hierophant	Vav
Lovers	Zayin
Chariot	Khet
Justice	Lamed
Hermit	Yod
Fortune	Caf
Lust	Tet
Hanged man	Mem
Death	Nun
Art	Sameck
Devil	Ayin
Tower	Peh
Star	Heh
Moon	Kuf
Sun	Resh
Aeon	Shin
Universe	Tav

Trump Cards represent the Hebrew Alphabet

> There is no intention here to endorse these sets of cards, but only to show their historical source.

LINKED TO THE BIBLE CODE

The Bible code is multifaceted and is intertwined throughout the letters and verses of the *Bible* on many levels. In the first chapter of Genesis one can see the depictions of the ten sefirot and the Hebrew letters showing the sefirot tree and it's 32 pathways of wisdom.

Each time God's name "Elohim" appears anywhere it is used to define some act of creation. The verses where God's name "Elohim" appears without the act of "said, saw or made", represents one of the twenty-two letters of the Hebrew language.

When a verse uses the word *"said"*, "and Elohim *said"*, this additional condition represents a sefirot. Thus there are ten *"Elohim said"* statements depicting the ten sefirot. Note that in the first verse "God created heaven and earth" it implies *"Elohim said."* There was nothing created yet.

When a verse states Elohim *"made"*, this additional condition represents one the three mother letters; Aleph, Mem, and Shin.

When a verse states Elohim *"saw"*, this additional condition represents the seven double letters in the Hebrew alphabet; Bet, Gimel, Dalet, Kaph, Peh, Resh, Tav.

The Bible code is depicted throughout the words and letters of the *Torah*. Each word in a verse represents a sefirah and has a numerical value. This value can be compared to other words with the same numerical value for a further understanding of the verse.

Letter sequences also occur at various places depicting a meaning. Letter sequences between words are part of the coding. Typically these sequences are found in a verse that alludes to a special meaning and are found at the first or last letter in a series of words. Sometimes it will be the middle letters in a series of words.

How was the Bible code developed? All the wise and learned Rabbis reply that the code is simply the shem hamephorish (יהוה) permuted many different and complicated ways.

Genesis Chapter 1

[פרשת בראשית]

בְּרֵאשִׁ֖ית	בָּרָ֣א	אֱלֹהִ֑ים	אֵ֥ת	הַשָּׁמַ֖יִם	וְאֵ֥ת	הָאָֽרֶץ׃
in beginning	**created**	Elohim	that	the heavens	and that	the earth

Keter

1 In the beginning God created the heaven and the earth.

וְהָאָ֗רֶץ הָיְתָ֥ה תֹ֨הוּ֙ וָבֹ֔הוּ וְחֹ֖שֶׁךְ עַל־פְּנֵ֣י תְה֑וֹם
and the earth / it was / without form / and void / and darkness / upon / face / deep

וְר֣וּחַ אֱלֹהִ֔ים מְרַחֶ֖פֶת עַל־פְּנֵ֥י הַמָּֽיִם׃
and spirit / **Elohim** / hovered / upon / face / the waters

Heh

2 And the earth was without form, and void; and darkness was upon the face of the deep. And the Spirit of God moved upon the face of the waters.

וַיֹּ֥אמֶר אֱלֹהִ֖ים יְהִ֣י א֑וֹר וַֽיְהִי־אֽוֹר׃
and he said / Elohim / let be / light / and let be / light

Chochma

3 And God said, Let there be light: and there was light.

וַיַּ֧רְא אֱלֹהִ֛ים אֶת־הָא֖וֹר כִּי־טֽוֹב
and he saw / **Elohim** / that / the light / like / good

Bet

וַיַּבְדֵּ֣ל אֱלֹהִ֔ים בֵּ֥ין הָא֖וֹר וּבֵ֥ין הַחֹֽשֶׁךְ׃
and he divided / **Elohim** / between / the light / and between / the darkness

Vav

4 And God saw the light, that it was good: and God divided the light from the darkness.

וַיִּקְרָ֨א אֱלֹהִ֤ים ׀ לָאוֹר֙ י֔וֹם וְלַחֹ֖שֶׁךְ קָ֣רָא לָ֑יְלָה
and he called / **Elohim** / to light / day / and to darkness / he called / night

Zayin

וַֽיְהִי־עֶ֥רֶב וַֽיְהִי־בֹ֖קֶר י֥וֹם אֶחָֽד׃
and it was / evening / and it was / morning / day / one

5 And God called the light Day, and the darkness he called Night. And evening and the morning were the first day.

פ

וַיֹּ֣אמֶר אֱלֹהִ֔ים יְהִ֥י רָקִ֖יעַ בְּת֣וֹךְ הַמָּ֑יִם
and he said / Elohim / let be / firmament / in midst / the waters

Binah

וִיהִ֣י מַבְדִּ֔יל בֵּ֥ין מַ֖יִם לָמָֽיִם׃
and let it / divide / between / water / to water

6 And God said, Let there be a firmament in the midst of the waters, and let it divide the waters from the waters.

וַיַּ֣עַשׂ אֱלֹהִים֮ אֶת־הָרָקִיעַ֒
and he made / Elohim / that / the firmament

Alef

וַיַּבְדֵּל בֵּין הַמַּיִם אֲשֶׁר מִתַּחַת לָרָקִיעַ
and he divided   between   the waters   which   beneath   to firmament

וּבֵין הַמַּיִם אֲשֶׁר מֵעַל לָרָקִיעַ וַיְהִי־כֵן׃
and between   the water   which   above   to firmament   and it was   so

7 And God made the firmament, and divided the waters which were under the firmament from the waters which were above the firmament: and it was so.

וַיִּקְרָא אֱלֹהִים לָרָקִיעַ שָׁמָיִם
and he called   Elohim   to firmament   heaven   — Khet

וַיְהִי־עֶרֶב וַיְהִי־בֹקֶר יוֹם שֵׁנִי׃
and it was   evening   and it was   morning   day   second

8 And God called the firmament Heaven. And the evening and the morning were the second day.

פ

וַיֹּאמֶר אֱלֹהִים
and he said   Elohim   — Chesed

יִקָּווּ הַמַּיִם מִתַּחַת הַשָּׁמַיִם אֶל־מָקוֹם אֶחָד
let gather   the water   beneath   the heavens   unto   place   one

וְתֵרָאֶה הַיַּבָּשָׁה וַיְהִי־כֵן׃
and it appear   the dry land   and it was   so

9 And God said, Let the waters under the heaven be gathered together unto one place, and let the dry land appear: and it was so.

וַיִּקְרָא אֱלֹהִים לַיַּבָּשָׁה אֶרֶץ
and he called   Elohim   to dry land   earth   — Tet

וּלְמִקְוֵה הַמַּיִם קָרָא יַמִּים
and to gathering   the water   he called   seas

וַיַּרְא אֱלֹהִים כִּי־טוֹב׃
and he saw   Elohim   like   good   — Gimel

10 And God called the dry land Earth; and the gathering together of the waters called he Seas: and God saw that it was good.

וַיֹּאמֶר אֱלֹהִים תַּדְשֵׁא הָאָרֶץ דֶּשֶׁא
and he said   Elohim   it vegetate   the earth   vegetation   — Gevurah

עֵשֶׂב מַזְרִיעַ זֶרַע עֵץ פְּרִי עֹשֶׂה פְּרִי לְמִינוֹ
plant   sprouting   seed   tree   fruit   making   fruit   to its kind

אֲשֶׁר זַרְעוֹ־בוֹ עַל־הָאָרֶץ וַיְהִי־כֵן׃
which   it's seed   in it   upon   the earth   and it was   so

11 And God said, Let the earth bring forth grass, the herb yielding seed, and the fruit tree yielding fruit after his kind, whose seed is in itself, upon

the earth: and it was so.

וַתּוֹצֵ֨א הָאָ֜רֶץ דֶּ֠שֶׁא עֵ֣שֶׂב מַזְרִ֤יעַ זֶ֙רַע֙ לְמִינֵ֔הוּ
and it bring forth the earth vegetation plant sprouting seed to it's kind

וְעֵ֧ץ עֹֽשֶׂה־פְּרִ֛י אֲשֶׁ֥ר זַרְעוֹ־ב֖וֹ לְמִינֵ֑הוּ
and tree making fruit which it's seed in it to it's kind

וַיַּ֥רְא אֱלֹהִ֖ים כִּי־טֽוֹב׃
and he saw Elohim like good   Dalet

12 And the earth brought forth grass, and herb yielding seed after his kind, and the tree yielding fruit, whose seed was in itself, after his kind: and God saw that it was good.

וַֽיְהִי־עֶ֥רֶב וַֽיְהִי־בֹ֖קֶר י֥וֹם שְׁלִישִֽׁי׃
and it was evening and it was morning day third

13 And the evening and the morning were the third day.

וַיֹּ֣אמֶר אֱלֹהִ֗ים יְהִ֤י מְאֹרֹת֙ בִּרְקִ֣יעַ הַשָּׁמַ֔יִם
and he said Elohim let be reflections in firmament the heavens   Tiferet

לְהַבְדִּ֕יל בֵּ֥ין הַיּ֖וֹם וּבֵ֣ין הַלָּ֑יְלָה
to the separation between the day and between the night

וְהָי֤וּ לְאֹתֹת֙ וּלְמ֣וֹעֲדִ֔ים וּלְיָמִ֖ים וְשָׁנִֽים׃
and they were to signs and to appointed times and to days and years

14 And God said, Let there be lights in the firmament of the heaven to divide the day from the night; and let them be for signs, and for seasons, and for days, and years:

פ

וְהָי֤וּ לִמְאוֹרֹת֙ בִּרְקִ֣יעַ הַשָּׁמַ֔יִם לְהָאִ֖יר עַל־הָאָ֑רֶץ
and they were to reflections in firmament the heavens to the shine upon the earth

וַֽיְהִי־כֵֽן׃
and it was so

15 And let them be for lights in the firmament of the heaven to give light upon the earth: and it was so.

וַיַּ֣עַשׂ אֱלֹהִ֔ים אֶת־שְׁנֵ֥י הַמְּאֹרֹ֖ת הַגְּדֹלִ֑ים
and he made Elohim that two the reflections the great ones   Mem

אֶת־הַמָּא֤וֹר הַגָּדֹל֙ לְמֶמְשֶׁ֣לֶת הַיּ֔וֹם
that the reflection the great to rule the day

וְאֶת־הַמָּא֤וֹר הַקָּטֹן֙ לְמֶמְשֶׁ֣לֶת הַלַּ֔יְלָה וְאֵ֖ת הַכּוֹכָבִֽים׃
and that the reflection the small to rule the night and that the stars

16 And God made two great lights; the greater light to rule the day, and the lesser light to rule the night: he made the stars also.

וַיִּתֵּן אֹתָם אֱלֹהִים בִּרְקִיעַ הַשָּׁמָיִם

Yod — and he gave / to them / Elohim / in firmament / the heavens

לְהָאִיר עַל הָאָרֶץ:

to the shine / upon / the earth

17 And God set them in the firmament of the heaven to give light upon the earth,

וְלִמְשֹׁל בַּיּוֹם וּבַלַּיְלָה

and to rule / in day / and in night

וּלְהַבְדִּיל בֵּין הָאוֹר וּבֵין הַחֹשֶׁךְ

and to the divide / between / the light / and between / the darkness

וַיַּרְא אֱלֹהִים כִּי טוֹב:

Kaf — and he saw / Elohim / like / good

18 And to rule over the day and over the night, and to divide the light from the darkness: and God saw that it was good.

וַיְהִי עֶרֶב וַיְהִי בֹקֶר יוֹם רְבִיעִי:

and it was / evening / and it was / morning / day / fourth

19 And the evening and the morning were the fourth day.

וַיֹּאמֶר אֱלֹהִים יִשְׁרְצוּ הַמַּיִם שֶׁרֶץ נֶפֶשׁ חַיָּה

Netzach — and he said / Elohim / they swarm / the water / swarm / soul / living

וְעוֹף יְעוֹפֵף עַל הָאָרֶץ עַל פְּנֵי רְקִיעַ הַשָּׁמָיִם:

and bird / flyer / upon / the earth / upon / face / firmament / the heavens

20 And God said, Let the waters bring forth abundantly the moving creature that hath life, and fowl that may fly above the earth in the open firmament of heaven.

פ

וַיִּבְרָא אֱלֹהִים אֶת הַתַּנִּינִם הַגְּדֹלִים

Lamed — and he created / Elohim / that / the sea giants / the big ones

וְאֵת כָּל נֶפֶשׁ הַחַיָּה הָרֹמֶשֶׂת

and that / all / soul / the living / the creepers

אֲשֶׁר שָׁרְצוּ הַמַּיִם לְמִינֵהֶם

which / they swarm / the water / to their kind

וְאֵת כָּל עוֹף כָּנָף לְמִינֵהוּ

and that / all / bird / winged / to it's kind

וַיַּרְא אֱלֹהִים כִּי טוֹב:

Peh — and he saw / Elohim / like / good

21 And God created great whales, and every living creature that moveth, which the waters brought forth abundantly, after their kind, and every winged fowl after his kind: and God saw that it was good.

וַיְבָ֣רֶךְ אֹתָ֛ם אֱלֹהִ֖ים לֵאמֹ֑ר פְּר֣וּ וּרְב֗וּ Nun
and you multiply you be fruitful to say Elohim to them and he blessed

וּמִלְא֤וּ אֶת־הַמַּ֙יִם֙ בַּיַּמִּ֔ים וְהָע֖וֹף יִ֥רֶב בָּאָֽרֶץ׃
in earth it multiply and the bird in seas the water that and you fill

22 And God blessed them, saying, Be fruitful, and multiply, and fill the waters in the seas, and let fowl multiply in the earth.

וַֽיְהִי־עֶ֥רֶב וַֽיְהִי־בֹ֖קֶר י֥וֹם חֲמִישִֽׁי׃
fifth day morning and it was evening and it was

23 And the evening and the morning were the fifth day.

וַיֹּ֣אמֶר אֱלֹהִ֗ים Hod
Elohim and he said

תּוֹצֵ֨א הָאָ֜רֶץ נֶ֤פֶשׁ חַיָּה֙ לְמִינָ֔הּ בְּהֵמָ֥ה
beast to it's kind living soul the earth bring forth

וָרֶ֛מֶשׂ וְחַֽיְתוֹ־אֶ֖רֶץ לְמִינָ֑הּ וַֽיְהִי־כֵֽן׃
so and it was to its kind earth and its life creeping things

24 And God said, Let the earth bring forth the living creature after his kind, cattle, and creeping thing, and beast of the earth after his kind: and it was so.

פ

וַיַּ֣עַשׂ אֱלֹהִים֩ אֶת־חַיַּ֨ת הָאָ֜רֶץ לְמִינָ֗הּ Shin
to its kind the earth living beings that Elohim and he made

וְאֶת־הַבְּהֵמָה֙ לְמִינָ֔הּ
to its kind the beast and that

וְאֵ֛ת כָּל־רֶ֥מֶשׂ הָֽאֲדָמָ֖ה לְמִינֵ֑הוּ
to its kind the ground creeping things all and that

וַיַּ֥רְא אֱלֹהִ֖ים כִּי־טֽוֹב׃ Reish
good like Elohim and he saw

25 And God made the beast of the earth after his kind, and cattle after their kind, and every thing that creepeth upon the earth after his kind: and God saw that it was good.

וַיֹּ֣אמֶר אֱלֹהִ֔ים נַֽעֲשֶׂ֥ה אָדָ֛ם בְּצַלְמֵ֖נוּ כִּדְמוּתֵ֑נוּ Yesod
like our image in our image Adam we make Elohim and he said

וְיִרְדּוּ֩ בִדְגַ֨ת הַיָּ֜ם וּבְע֣וֹף הַשָּׁמַ֗יִם
the heavens and in bird the sea in fish and they dominate

וּבַבְּהֵמָה֙ וּבְכָל־הָאָ֔רֶץ
the earth and in all and in beast

וּבְכָל־הָרֶ֖מֶשׂ הָֽרֹמֵ֥שׂ עַל־הָאָֽרֶץ׃
the earth upon the creeper the creeping and in all

70

26 And God said, Let us make man in our image, after our likeness: and let them have dominion over the fish of the sea, and over the fowl of the air, and over the cattle, and over all the earth, and over every creeping thing that creepeth upon the earth.

וַיִּבְרָ֨א אֱלֹהִ֤ים ׀ אֶת־הָֽאָדָם֙ בְּצַלְמ֔וֹ
and he created Elohim that the Adam in his image — Samekh

בְּצֶ֥לֶם אֱלֹהִ֖ים בָּרָ֣א אֹת֑וֹ זָכָ֥ר וּנְקֵבָ֖ה בָּרָ֥א אֹתָֽם׃
in image Elohim he created to him male and female he created to them — Ayin

27 So God created man in his own image, in the image of God created he him; male and female created he them.

וַיְבָ֣רֶךְ אֹתָם֮ אֱלֹהִים֒
and he blessed to them Elohim — Tzadi

וַיֹּ֨אמֶר לָהֶ֜ם אֱלֹהִ֗ים פְּר֥וּ וּרְב֛וּ
and he said to them Elohim you be fruitful and you multiply — Malkhut

וּמִלְא֥וּ אֶת־הָאָ֖רֶץ וְכִבְשֻׁ֑הָ
and you fill that the earth and subdue it

וּרְד֞וּ בִּדְגַ֤ת הַיָּם֙ וּבְע֣וֹף הַשָּׁמַ֔יִם
and you dominate in fish the sea and in bird the heavens

וּבְכָל־חַיָּ֖ה הָֽרֹמֶ֥שֶׂת עַל־הָאָֽרֶץ׃
and in all life the creeper upon the earth

28 And God blessed them, and God said unto them, Be fruitful, and multiply, and replenish the earth, and subdue it: and have dominion over the fish of the sea, and over the fowl of the air, and over every living thing that moveth upon the earth.

וַיֹּ֣אמֶר אֱלֹהִ֗ים הִנֵּה֩ נָתַ֨תִּי לָכֶ֜ם
and he said Elohim here I give to you — Kuf

אֶת־כָּל־עֵ֣שֶׂב ׀ זֹרֵ֣עַ זֶ֗רַע אֲשֶׁר֙ עַל־פְּנֵ֣י כָל־הָאָ֔רֶץ
that all plant seeder seed which upon face all the earth

וְאֶת־כָּל־הָעֵ֛ץ אֲשֶׁר־בּ֥וֹ פְרִי־עֵ֖ץ זֹרֵ֣עַ זָ֑רַע
and that all the tree which in it fruit tree seeder seed

לָכֶ֥ם יִֽהְיֶ֖ה לְאָכְלָֽה׃
to you it be to food

29 And God said, Behold, I have given you every herb bearing seed, which is upon the face of all the earth, and every tree, in the which is the fruit of a tree yielding seed; to you it shall be for meat.

וּֽלְכָל־חַיַּ֣ת הָ֠אָרֶץ וּלְכָל־ע֨וֹף הַשָּׁמַ֜יִם
and to all living things the earth and to all bird the heavens

וּלְכֹל רוֹמֵשׂ עַל הָאָרֶץ אֲשֶׁר־בּוֹ נֶפֶשׁ חַיָּה
and to all creeper upon the earth which in it soul life

אֶת־כָּל־יֶרֶק עֵשֶׂב לְאָכְלָה וַיְהִי־כֵן׃
that all green plants to food and it was so

30 And to every beast of the earth, and to every fowl of the air, and to every thing that creepeth upon the earth, wherein there is life, I have given every green herb for meat: and it was so.

 אֱלֹהִים אֶת־כָּל־אֲשֶׁר עָשָׂה וְהִנֵּה־טוֹב מְאֹד   Tav
and he saw Elohim that all which he made and it was good very

וַיְהִי־עֶרֶב וַיְהִי־בֹקֶר יוֹם הַשִּׁשִּׁי׃
and it was evening and it was morning day the sixth

31 And God saw every thing that he had made, and, behold, it was very good. And the evening and the morning were the sixth day.

פ

Letters Linked to Earth and the Planets

Each Hebrew alphabet letter is linked to an earthly element or to planets or to constellations. For Earth, it's the three mother letters.

Elements of Earth

א	Air
מ	Water
ש	Fire

Linked to Our Solar System

Double Letters (Bet, Gimel, Dalet, Kaph, Peh, Reish, Tav) are letters that change sound based on if it has a dot, called a dagesh, in the middle of the letter. They are linked to the main planets of our solar system.

ב	Mercury
ג	Moon
ד	Venus
כ	Jupiter
פ	Mars
ת	Saturn
ר	Sun

CONSTELLATIONS

The simple Letters (Tzadi, Vav, Zayin, Khet, Tet, Yod, Lamed, Nun, Samech, Ayin, Heh, Kuf) are each linked to a constellation. Since the lunar month and the names of the Tribes of Israel are also linked to the same letters they too are shown.

Letter	Constellation	Lunar Month	Tribe
ה	Aries	Nissan	Reuben
ו	Taurus	Iyar	Simon
ז	Gemini	Sivan	Levi
ח	Cancer	Tamuz	Judah
ט	Leo	Av	Issaschar
י	Virgo	Elul	Zebulun
ל	Libra	Tishrei	Benjamin
נ	Scorpio	Cheshvan	Dan
ס	Sagittarius	Kislev	Naphtali
ע	Capricorn	Tevet	Gad
צ	Aquarius	Shevat	Asher
ק	Pisces	Adar	Joseph

Letters linked to a Word's meaning

The letters contained in a Hebrew word reflect their characters and meanings into the word's meaning. The first letter is it's revealed meaning, and the others letters are the word's concealed meanings.

An example is the Hebrew word for fruit (pri) is made up of a Peh, a Reish, and a Yod. The letter Peh means mouth. The letter Reish means head. The letters Yod means hand.

There is a saying that you live by the fruit of your mouth. The first letter means the words from your mouth (Peh). The last letter means hand (Yod) or what you do. The middle letters stands for one's intention (head) that he had when he said the words.

Every Hebrew word is linked to one of the several sefirot and to one of the Hebrew names of God.

Mystical Powers of the Names of God

This concept of the letters reflecting into the word's meaning also applies even more so to the Hebrew names of God. The order of the letters also gives a mystical power to a word, especially the names of God. This order of the letters has a logical meaning to a name of God when you analyze it.

The most mystical word in the *Torah*, and in the Hebrew language, and in the universe, is the shem hamephorash, God's true name. This is why most of the seeding is done with this name. The other mostly used names for seeding are Ehieh and Elohim. However commonly used words can also be used for seeded or seeding names in advanced meditations.

THE DIFFERENT NAMES OF GOD

IHVH (יהוה)

Hebrew is the only language to be able to write out God's true name. It is the ultimate word of all languages. It consists of three individual letters in which one letter is repeated twice. The shem hamephorash is used 6832 times in the Tanach. The shem hameforash יהוה, is the ineffable name. "Hayah, hoveh, yi'yeh" he was, he is, he will be. This is the level where past, present, and future are one.

IHVH (יהוה) the shem hamephorash is the only name of all the names of God which represents the full and true substance of God.

English texts translate all of the various Hebrew names of God as "God" or "Lord." This skips much towards understanding the *Bible*. In some places written is shem hamephorash, yet it is to be pronounced differently. The other Hebrew names of God are merely predicates of the shem hamephorash's divine attributes. The names are direct forces which emanate from the sacred name the shem hamephorash. These other names are used for a more directed meditation in advanced tzeruf.

The letter spelling of the name is Yod (י), Heh (ה), Vav, (ו) Heh (ה). The first yod represents wisdom (male). The second letter Heh represents understanding (female) or more specifically wisdom in the breadth and depth of understanding. The third letter Vav is written with a point that is drawn downward (male) in a line representing the birth of the 6 emotional sefirot, in their pregnant state of Understanding. The fourth letter and second Hei (a female vessel) represents the revelation of all the previous sefirot into the level of action, of Malkut.

The three letters of the Tetragrammaton, Yod (י), Heh (ה), and Yav (ו), can also serve as suffixes and prefixes for personal pronouns. As suffixes the Yod means "me," Heh means "her," and Vav means "him or you." When a suffix Vav is combined with a prefix Yod the meaning becomes "they." In prefixes the Vav means "and," the

Names of God Associated with Each Sefirah

Sefirah	Name
Keter	Ehyeh Asher Ehyeh
Chochma	Yah
Binah	ihvh (read Elohim)
Chesed	El
Gevurah	Elohim
Tiferet	ihvh (read Adonai)
Netzach	Elohim Tzevaot
Hod	Adonai Tzevaot
Yesod	El Shadai (El Chai)
Malkut	Adonai

Yod means "he," and the Heh means "the."

TRADITION

The stated tradition is that the only person allowed to pronounce the sacred name was the high priest when the sacred temple stood in Jerusalem. This tradition states that the only time permitted for the high priest to say this sacred name was inside the holy of holies room during the temple services on the most holiest day of the year, Yom Kippur.

Many people say a person will suffer one of the many creatively put forth punishments from God on account of violating the prohibition of pronouncing the shem hamephorash out loud, including getting struck by an unexplainable force (lightning?).

WHY THE DON'T PRONOUNCE

Nothing in the *Torah* prohibits a person from pronouncing the shem hamephorash. It is evident from scripture and ancient writings that God's true name was pronounced routinely on the Temple grounds. Many common Hebrew names contain "Yah" or "Yahu," which is the upper half of the shem hamephorash. The sacred Name was pronounced as part of the daily services in the Temple. The Mishnah confirms that there was no prohibition against the pronouncing of the shem hamephorash. Historian Flavius Josephus, who was born a Kohein (priestly status) at a time when the pronunciation of the shem hamephorash name was still known, said that the correct pronunciation had four vowels (War of the Jews, Book V, Chapter 5).

One explanation for not pronouncing today the sacred name comes from the revered Kabbalist Rabbi Nachman. Since there is no Temple in Jerusalem the Shekina (a mystical God presence) has fled. He says that the shekina and spiritual nature of the world today is in the materialistic level of Malkut and very impure. This level is controlled by the many nations of the world run by corrupt people and corrupt governments headed by forces with great cruel selfish interests. Rabbi Nachman gives the explanation that by saying out loud the name of the shem hamephorash, this causes a strengthening of the other side, the side of evil. By pronouncing the sacred name in prayer, one is bringing down to the shekina in Malkut spiritual energies which strengthen these corrupt nation governments and furthers their objectives.

The pronouncing of the Shem Hamephorash is a very complicated subject. Only very learned, wise, and spiritually pure know the correct circumstances and the different pronunciations of the sacred name. These are the teachings of the Ari, Vital, Luzzatto, and others. Anyone else saying God's name will undoubtedly do it with incorrect vocalizations and in incorrect circumstances such that it will cause a negative effect, even severe, to the world and to the pronouncing person because of impurities.

Those that are wise and learned in this area are referred to as the "Baalai Shem" or masters of the name. Advanced tzeruf practitioners incorporate various constructions of the names of God depending on the correct circumstances.

When the Messiah comes, everyone will know the correct pronunciation of God's sacred name (Pesachim 50a). The Messiah will be called by a new name with which he will redeem Israel and the world.

Substituted Pronunciation

When reading the name of the shem hamephorash (יהוה) in prayer, the vocalization applied to the sacred name is to be the same as the vocalization of the word Adonai (אדני), which is also a sub-name or cognitive of God attached to the sefirah Malkut. By visualizing the written sacred name of the shem hamephorash while vocalizing the sound Adonai at the same time, a channel opens and allows spiritual energy to flow from the sefirah Tiferet (representing your heart, where the shem hamephorash is attached) down to the sefirah Malkut (the physical level where the name "Adonai" is attached). So, by looking at the sacred name and pronouncing verbally Adonai, spiritual energy descends from Tiferet down to Malkut. In this way the shem hamephorash is not pronounced in prayers but causes a positive effect of helping the influx descend to action.

In Conversation

When people make reference to the sacred name the shem hamephorash in conversation, a substituted name is used. The most common is "Havaya." This is the sacred name rearranged so that there is no possibility of pronouncing the sacred name correctly. The word "Ha Shem" which means "the name" is also frequently used as a substituted conversational name.

When the shem hamephorash is written as it should be but is

vocalized Elohim, this is actually derives from a different sefirah force which draws from the sefirah Binah and flows to Malkut. For example if the shem hamephorash is immediately followed by the name Adonai, it is pronounced Elohim.

EHIeH - אהיה

Exodus 3:14

וַיֹּאמֶר אֱלֹהִים אֶל־מֹשֶׁה אֶהְיֶה אֲשֶׁר אֶהְיֶה
and he said   Elohim   Moses – unto   I am   which   I am

וַיֹּאמֶר כֹּה תֹאמַר לִבְנֵי יִשְׂרָאֵל אֶהְיֶה שְׁלָחַנִי אֲלֵיכֶם׃
and he said   thus   you say   to sons   Israel   Ehieh   sent me   unto you

14 And God said unto Moses, I AM THAT I AM: and he said, Thus shalt thou say unto the children of Israel, I AM hath sent me unto you.

Ehyeh asher ehyeh (אהיה אשר אהיה) is the sole response given to Moses when he asks God what name shall he say to the Israelites as to whom has sent him (Exodus 3:13). The King James version of the *Bible* translates the Hebrew as "I am that I am." Yet the word "I am" is used as a proper name for God.

Ehyeh is the first-person singular imperfect form of *hayah*, "to be". *Ehyeh* is usually translated "I will be," since the imperfect tense in Hebrew denotes actions that are not yet completed (e.g. Exodus 3:12, "Certainly I will be [ehyeh] with thee.") The Qal imperfect first person form of the Hebrew verb hayah translates "I will be."

Asher is an ambiguous pronoun which can mean, depending on context, "that", "who", "which", or "where."

Therefore, although Ehyeh Asher Ehyeh is generally rendered in English "I am that I am." Better translations might be "I will be what I will be" or "I will be who I will be", or even "I will be because I will be." In these renderings, the phrase becomes an open-ended mystery on God's promise in Exodus 3:12 regarding "certainly I will be with thee." Other translations have been: "I will be that I will be," "I will become whatsoever I please," "I am The Being," "I am The Existing One" or, "I am Who I am."

The name takes the foundation name of Yah (Yod and Heh) from the shem hamephorash, and adds an Alef and a He to the front of it.

The next verse after this mystical declaration states "this is my

80

name forever."

Exodus 3:15

וַיֹּאמֶר עוֹד אֱלֹהִים אֶל־מֹשֶׁה כֹּה תֹאמַר אֶל־בְּנֵי יִשְׂרָאֵל
Israel   sons - unto   you say   thus   Moses – unto   Elohim   again   and he said

יְהוָה אֱלֹהֵי אֲבֹתֵיכֶם
your fathers   Elohim   ihvh

אֱלֹהֵי אַבְרָהָם אֱלֹהֵי יִצְחָק וֵאלֹהֵי יַעֲקֹב
Jacob   and Elohim   Isaac   Elohim   Abraham   Elohim

שְׁלָחַנִי אֲלֵיכֶם זֶה־שְּׁמִי לְעֹלָם
to forever   my name – thus   unto you   sent me

וְזֶה זִכְרִי לְדֹר דֹּר:
generation   to generation   memorial   and this

15 And God said moreover unto Moses, Thus shalt thou say unto the children of Israel, The LORD God of your fathers, the God of Abraham, the God of Isaac, and the God of Jacob, hath sent me unto you: this is my name forever, and this is my memorial unto all generations.

Deut 31:23

אֲשֶׁר־נִשְׁבַּעְתִּי לָהֶם וְאָנֹכִי אֶהְיֶה עִמָּךְ:
with you   "Ehieh"   and I am   to them   I swore - which

23....which I sware unto them: and I will be with thee.

The Aramaic Targum Onkelos leaves the phrase untranslated and is so quoted in the Talmud (B. B. 73a).

The name is not mentioned in the *Torah* except in three places, and then it talks about redemption alone. Neither is it mentioned in the prophet writings (Ketuvim).

Elohim

Elohim is the Name of God depicted as the stern Judge of the universe. The name implies strength, power, and justice. When I judge the creatures I am Elohim (Exodus Rabbah 3:6). This is further shown in the verse "Judgment is for Elohim" (Deuteronomy 1:17). Elohim is also the source of testing for it is written, "and Elohim tested Abraham" (Genesis 22:1)

Elohim is the name used exclusively in the creation story showing the 32 paths of creation (Gen 1:1 to 2:4). This story is actually about judgments of the prior life forms before creating the creatures in the physical. Since the shem hamephorash is not used, one can infer that God used one of his arms of creation to do this (angels, aliens?).

Variations on this name include Eloha, Elohai (my God) and Elohaynu (our God). Though it may appear so, other nation's gods are not called Elohim.

"The Holy One, Blessed be He, said to those, You want to know my name? I am called according to my actions. When I judge the creatures I am Elohim, and when I have mercy with My world, I am named YHVH" (Ex R. 3:6).

Yah

This name occurs about 50 times in the Tanach. First used in Exodus 15:2.

It is the first half the shem hamephorash name representing the spiritual upper sefirot, Keter, Chocma and Bina. Saying this name is saying the essence of the shem hamephorash. In it's pregnant form (milui) with the letter names spelled out, Yod Vav Dalet and Heh Alef, it's gematria is equivalent to the shem hamephorash, 26.

This name excludes the physical realm or the lower seven sefirot which are dependant on the upper three sefirot. The last half of the shem hamephorash name is never used by itself since it's sustenance relies on the upper three sefirot.

The Talmud states that God used the letter Yod to create the world to come and the Hey to create the present world. The sages derive this idea from the Yah found in Isaiah 26:4.

El

El is the name of God that depicts compassion and mercy from harsh judgments given by the attribute named Elohim. This attribute either pardons, reduces or postpones severe punishment.

El does not stand for a shortened version of the name Elohim.

Ihvh Tzvaot / Elohim Tzavot

Tzvaot means forces. These names do not appear in the *Torah* (the five books written by Moses). They appear primarily in the prophetic books of Isaiah, Jeremiah, Haggai, Zechariah and Malachi, as well as many times in the Psalms.

Ihvh Tzvaot is source of the visions of the Prophets and is

a jealous force. Elohim Tzvaot is connected to wars and wages war. Because Tzvaot is written in the plural both names are inseparable and the forces act as a legion or army.

EL SHADAI

This name occurs 48 times in the Tanakh. The root word "shadad" (שדד) means "to overpower" or "to destroy" All miracles in the *Torah* whereby the natural order is overpowered without causing noticeable change in the normal scheme of things are miracles [using the name Shaddai].

In Genesis 17:1, YHVH said to Abram: "I am El Shaddai. Walk before me and be perfect." Then this name is used in the next verse when it refers to multiplying Abraham's offspring (Gen. 17:2).

"I am El Shaddai. Be fruitful and increase in number" (Gen. 28:3) (Gen. 35:11). "By El Shaddai who will bless you with blessings of heaven above, blessings of the deep that lies beneath, blessings of the breasts [shadayim] and of the womb [racham]" (Gen. 49:25).

The word "dai" which means "enough." God is called Shadai because it is that aspect of God that told the world "enough!" That is the name or aspect of God that set boundaries to this world, causing it to be finite and limited unlike many of the spiritual worlds (Talmud tractate Chagigah 12a and Midrash Berishit Rabbah 5:8).

Elohim spoke to Moses saying that he is the ihvh (the shem hamephorash), and further states that he appeared as El Shaddai to the three great patriarchs: Abraham, Isaac, and Jacob:

EXODUS 6:2-3

וַיְדַבֵּר אֱלֹהִים אֶל־מֹשֶׁה וַיֹּאמֶר אֵלָיו אֲנִי יְהוָה׃
ihvh | I | unto him | and he said | Moses - unto | Elohim | and he spoke

2 And God spake unto Moses, and said unto him, I am the LORD:

וָאֵרָא אֶל־אַבְרָהָם אֶל־יִצְחָק וְאֶל־יַעֲקֹב בְּאֵל שַׁדָּי
Shadi | in El | Jacob – and unto | and to Isaac - unto | Abraham - unto | and I appeared

וּשְׁמִי יְהוָה לֹא נוֹדַעְתִּי לָהֶם׃
to them | I made known | not | ihvh | and my name

3 And I appeared unto Abraham, unto Isaac, and unto Jacob, by the name of God Almighty, but by my name JEHOVAH was I not known to them.

ADONAI

This name occurs about 300 times in the Tanach. This name

is associated with the sefirah Malkut.

This is God's name that is closest to creatures that have been created. It is the lowest level of the divine names. The hierarchy of main names of God is Ehieh at the top (Keter), Ihvh in the middle (Tiferet), and Adonai at the bottom (Malkut). In order to cleave to the shem hamephorash, the name other names are derived from, one has to enter through the name Adonai.

There are some people that also use a variation of it's pronunciation as a substitute pronunciation instead of saying out loud the name Adonai. It is pronounced as ayohav (אֲיָהוֹ) which is said to be an adaptation of the name Ehyeh.

GOD WORKING THROUGH OTHER PEOPLE AND FORCES.

When a verse talks about an God doing an action naming God by the shem hamephorash or one of it's cognitive names, like Elohim, it doesn't mean that God by himself alone did this action. God works through people, and nature all the time. If God makes a person carry out a judgement on a particular someone this is an example of Elohim giving judgment. The person executing this judgment is then called Elohim. These names are forces, arms of God and do actions using other people, nature, chance, self-destruction, and so on. Most think of judgment as a negative act, but it can also be a positive act.

Learning Hebrew

There is only one main reason to learn Hebrew. It is to truly read and fully understand the *Torah* (the *Bible*).

Biblical Hebrew has a very small root vocabulary. It's 1/4 the amount of words used by Shakespeare. It's vocabulary is approximately 1% the amount of the over 660,000 words contained in the Oxford English Dictionary). Also, of the Hebrew words used in the *Bible*, many only occur once or are proper names. Hebrew has no formal recognizable cases (like Greek, Latin or German, with their nominative, accusative, genitive, dative etc.) and has a very simple word order which can be rearranged for emphasis. Hebrew is read right to left, opposite that of English. The alphabet has just 22 letters - all are consonants, and all letters consist of one case. The additional vowel marks were added by the Masoretes.

Masoretes

The Masoretes (בעלי המסורה) felt the need to preserve the correct way to read the *Torah*. Their system is called masora from Hebrew words massoreh (tradition) and masar (to hand down). The masoretes devised the vowel notation system for Hebrew (masoretic points) as well as the trope symbols used in the cantillation of the verses.

Biblical Hebrew vs Modern Hebrew

Biblical Hebrew is different from the modern day Hebrew as it is spoken today in Israel. Modern Hebrew verb conjugations of past present and future generally do not apply to Biblical Hebrew. The verbs tenses of Biblical Hebrew are written according to the voice (active, passive, middle), kind of action (simple, intensive, causal) etc.

Before doing any reading in Hebrew or any vocalizations of tzeruf meditation, it's best to get a Hebrew language audio course in order to hear and understand the specifics of pronunciation and how the sentences are spoken.

The Best Way to Learn Hebrew

Since the objective of learning Hebrew is to read the *Torah*, the

Torah is the best place to start. When the Pilgrims settled in America, they learned to read English from the *King James Bible*. The best way to learn Hebrew is by reading an interlinear *Torah*, with the English translation of the Hebrew words directly below the Hebrew *Torah* text. Your mind will see a Hebrew word and an English translation directly underneath it at the same time. One's subconscious will automatically start developing a vocabulary.

An excellent place to start one's Hebrew reading comprehension is an interlinear translation of *King Solomon's Books of Wisdom*. These wisdom books are *Ecclesiastes, Proverbs, and the Song of Songs*. King Solomon was the wisest man ever to have lived. Not only will you be gaining wisdom from the King of Wisdom, you will also be learning Hebrew at the same time. Also very important, read it out loud so your soul will be nourished by effects of the sounds of the Hebrew letters as well as the Bible code arraignment in the verses.

When incorporating the modern Hebrew language into your learning, there are available excellent beginner and intermediate newspapers describing current events in simplified Hebrew sentences and words.

In order to learn Hebrew, one needs to read Hebrew everyday. Also one needs to have the language come out of him or her from the inside to the outside, by speaking numerous sentences in Hebrew everyday. In doing this one will learn the language very quickly.

THE TORAH

The *Torah* is the most mystical book on the planet (Hebrew version only). NO other book even comes close. It is made up exclusively of the sacred mystical Hebrew letters, 304,805 letters to be exact.

One of the main objectives of this book is to have one realize the significance of reading and learning *Torah* (IN HEBREW).

THE TORAH EFFECT

If you read the *Torah* (*Bible*) in English, your soul only receives about one tenth of the total spiritual effect that is possible. Reading the *Torah* in Hebrew feeds the soul a spiritual nourishment that any English translation can't come close to. The *Bible* code, which is the mystical arrangement of the Hebrew letters and words, feeds a spiritual food directly into your soul. This code greatly magnifies the effect that letters alone would have. Only after reading the *Torah* for some time does a person notice it's effects such as spiritual thoughts, perceptions, protections, opportunities, etc. This is in addition to the information gleaned from the intellectual concepts.

THE FOUR LEVELS OF UNDERSTANDING IN THE TORAH

"If you believe exactly what is written in the *Torah*, better you were never born." This expression is designed to shock one into thinking. It means there is a lot more to the story behind the simple written text of the *Torah*.

There are four levels of understanding that reflect the four levels of the soul. The acronym for the four different levels is פרדס, pronounced PaRDeS, translated as orchards. The acronym stands for P=Peshat, R=Remez, D=Derush, S=Sod.

1. Peshat.

Plain meaning, simple. This is the lowest level of understanding. It is what is understood by the plain words. If the final interpretation diverges from or contradicts the Peshat, that final interpretation can be considered flawed. The *Talmud* affirms this, stating, "A verse cannot depart from its plain meaning." [1] This level parallels the Mishna and the creation level of Asiyah.

2. Remez

Hint, Allusion. These are typically found in the gematria of the Hebrew words involved. It parallels the Gemara and the creation level of Yetzirah.

3. Derush

Means Search. Derivation via analogy, metaphor. [2] Parallels the Midrash and the creation level of Beriyah.

4. Sod

Means secret or hidden meaning. a Kabalistic explanation as found in the mystical book of the *Zohar*, meaning radiance.

1. Rashi's commentary is written at this level.
2. Example: Esau selling his birthright for a bowl of food happened on the day of the death of Abraham when an oath was no longer in effect. Actually sold was the Berakah. The "bowl of soup" contained much more than what was eaten.
Example: Adam & Eve & Serpent story is about a dual pregnancy. Cain is not in the genealogy of Adam.

The *Tikunei Zohar* gives seventy interpretations of the first word of the *Torah* "Bereshit." This parallels the creation level of Atzilut.

The Mystical Kabbalah

The name Kabbalah derives from the Hebrew word Kabel which translates as receive. Kabbalah is hidden mystical knowledge that is received, and hence revealing Gods nature in the world. It is the understanding the rules in which God operates his world.

Kabbalist Yehuda Ashlag (Baal HaSulam) who wrote an extensive commentary in his leading mystical treatise of the *Zohar*, provides this definition:

This wisdom is no more and no less than a sequence of roots, which hang down by way of cause and effect, in fixed, determined rules, interweaving to a single, exalted goal described as, "the revelation of His Godliness to His creatures in this world."

Torah Books

The *Torah* is specifically the five books of Moses (the *Pentateuch*). The name *Torah* is used throughout these five books. The English names attributed to the five books of Moses are actually Greek names. The Hebrew name for each book of the *Torah* is the same word as the first word appearing in that book.

However, in general people also use the name *Torah* to refer to all of the books of the *Bible*, including the Nevi'im (Prophets) and the Ketuvim (Writings). All of these Hebrew books together (24 total) are called the "Tanach." The books of the Tanach were established by the "Men of the Great Assembly" around 450 BCE.

The word Tanach is actually an acronym: "T" is for *Torah*, "N" is for *Nevi'iim* (Prophets) and "Ch" is for *Ketuvim* (Writings).

The five books of Moses are by far the most powerful and mystical of all the *Bible* books. The *Writings* and the *Prophets* are also powerful and mystical and contain the Bible code but to a lesser degree. One is not considered spiritual until they have read all of these 24 books.

1. (בראשית / **Bereshit**) - **Genesis**

    The Creation, Fall, Flood, the spread of the nations. Abraham, Isaac, Jacob, and Joseph. Israelites move to Egypt.

2. (שמות / **Shemot**) - **Exodus**

    Enslavement, Moses, 10 plagues, Passover, Leaving Egypt, Red Sea Crossing, Mt. Sinai and the 10 Commandments.

3. (ויקרא / **Vayikra**) - **Leviticus**

    Instructions on sacrificial system and the priesthood. Instructions on moral purity.

4. (במדבר / **Bamidbar**) - **Numbers**

    Still at Mt. Sinai, people make false idol, punishment, 40 years wandering begins.

5. (דברים / **Devarim**) - **Deuteronomy**

    Moses' discourses on God's Acts for Israel, the Ten Commandments, the ceremonial, civil, and social Laws, and covenant ratification.

The Prophet Books, Nevi'iim (נביאים)

6. (יהושע / **Y'hoshua**) - **Joshua**

    First half of Joshua describes the seven year conquest of the Land of Promise. The last half deals with partitioning the lands to the people.

7. (שופטים / **Shophtim**) - **Judges**

    The Israelites did not drive out all the inhabitants of Canaan and began to take part in their idolatry. Seven cycles of foreign oppression, repentance, and deliverance. In the end, the people failed to learn their lesson.

8. (שמואל / **Sh'muel**) - **Samuel (I & II)**

    Samuel influences Israel from Judges to King Saul and David as King, adultery, and murder.

9. (מלכים) / M'lakhim) - Kings (I & II)

Solomon, powerful Israel. Solomon dies, then division of tribes: 10 to the north and 2 to the south. All 19 kings of Israel were bad; therefore, captivity in Assyria.

10. (ישעיה) / Y'shayahu) - Isaiah

Looks at the sin of Judah and proclaims God's judgment. Hezekiah. Coming restoration and blessing.

11. (ירמיה) / Yir'mi'yahu) - Jeremiah

Called by God to proclaim the news of judgment to Judah. God establishes a New Covenant.

12. (יחזקאל) / Y'khezqel) - Ezekiel

He ministered to the Jews in Captivity in Babylon. Describes the end times.

13. The Twelve Prophets (תרי עשר)

A. (הושע) / Hoshea) - Hosea

Story of Hosea and his unfaithful wife, Gomer. Represents God's love and faithfulness and Israel's spiritual adultery. Israel will be judged and restored.

B. (יואל) / Yo'el) - Joel

Proclaims a terrifying future using the imagery of locusts. Judgment will come but blessing will follow.

C. (עמוס) / Amos) - Amos

He warned Israel of its coming judgment. Israel rejects God's warning.

D. (עובדיה) / Ovadyah) - Obadiah

A proclamation against Edom, a neighboring nation of Israel that gloated over Jerusalem's judgments. Prophecy of its utter destruction.

E. (יונה / Yonah) - Jonah

Jonah proclaims a coming judgment upon the people of Nineveh. But they repented and judgment was spared.

F. (מיכה / Mikhah) - Micah

Description of the complete moral decay at all levels of Israel. God will judge but will forgive and restore.

G. (נחום / Nakhum) - Nahum

Nineveh has gone into apostasy (approximately 125 years after Jonah lived) and will be destroyed.

H. (חבקוק / Havakuk) - Habakkuk

Near the end of the kingdom of Judah, Habakkuk asks God why He is not dealing with Judah's sins. God says He will use the Babylonians. Habakkuk asks how God can use a nation that is even worse than Judah.

I. (צפניה / Ts'phanyah) - Zephaniah

The theme is developed of the Day of the Lord and His judgment with a coming blessing. Judah will not repent, except for a remnant, which will be restored.

J. (חגי / Khagai) - Haggai

The people failed to put God first, by building their houses before they finished God's temple. Therefore, they had no prosperity.

K. (זכריה / Z'kharyah) - Zechariah

Zechariah encourages the Jews to complete the temple. Many messianic prophecies.

L. (מלאכי / Mal'akhi) - Malachi

God's people are lax in their duty to God. Growing distant from God. Moral compromise. Proclamation of coming judgment.

The Writings, Ketuvim (כתובים)

-- The Books of Truth (Sifrei Emet) --

14. (תהלים / Tehillim) - Psalms

Consists of five divisions. Worship with specific prayer.

15. (משלי / Mishlei) - Proverbs

Practical wisdom for everyday life by King Solomon.

16. (איוב / Iyov) - Job

A righteous man tested by God. Deals with God's sovereignty.

-- The Five Scrolls (Megillot) --

17. (שיר השירים / Shir Hashirim) - Song of Songs

A song between King Solomon and his Shulammite bride, portraying love between a man and a woman.

18. (רות / Rut) - Ruth

Kinsman redeemer in Boaz, redeeming Ruth, a Moabitess. Speaks of righteousness, love, and faithfulness to the Lord.

19. (איכה / Eikhah) - Lamentations

Five lament poems. Description of defeat and fall of Jerusalem.

20. (קהלת / Kohelet) - Ecclesiastes

The simple wisdom of King Solomon.

21. (אסתר / Esther) - Esther

Took place during chapters 6 and 7 of Ezra. Mordecai. Plot to kill the Jewish people.

-- The rest of the "Writings" --

22. (דניאל / Dani'el) - Daniel

Many visions of the future for the Gentiles and the Jews.

23. (עזרא ונחמיה / Ezra v'Nechemia) - Ezra & Nehemiah

Ezra - Cyrus let most of the Jews return to their land of Israel. Zerubbabel led the people (539 B.C.). Ezra returned later with more Jews (458 B.C.) Built the temple.

Nehemiah - Building the walls of Jerusalem. Nehemiah got permission from the king of Persia to rebuild the walls (444 B.C.). Revival in the land.

24. (דברי הימים / Divrei Hayamim) - Chronicles (I & II)

A recounting of the history of Israel to the time of Solomon. continued recounting of the life of Solomon, building of temple, to the captivity. History of Judah only.

Concentrating the Torah Power

The whole purpose of tzeruf meditation is to concentrate the mystical power of the *Torah*. The *Torah* is the most mystical and powerful book in existence. Tzeruf meditation uses verses and words from the *Torah* that are considered as the most powerful, or that focus on a specific aspect of life. Then these are transformed using mystical techniques that are based on the principles of Kabbalah, causing a resulting increased and concentrated effect.

Your Neighbor

Why all this ... the Hebrew letters, the *Torah*, etc.??? What is the greatest law in the *Torah*??? Love your neighbor as yourself. The rest is commentary.

Do you know what love is??? Can you explain it in detail.???

What are your detailed definitions of your different levels of friendship???

וְאָהַבְתָּ לְרֵעֲךָ כָּמוֹךָ

AND YOU LOVE YOUR NEIGHBOR
LIKE YOURSELF

Rabbi Isaac Luria

had the ability to analyze the character of an individual, by detecting and interpreting the Hebrew letters evident to him on the forehead of the person. Chaim Vital, a disciple of Luria, writes in his *Sha'ar Ruach ha-Kodesh* regarding his master's psychic abilities saying: Concerning his attainments, it is impossible for one to relate them just in general terms, let alone in detail.

He knew how to make a future soul appear before him, as well as the soul of a living or deceased person, from among the early as well as later sages. He could inquire of them whatever he wished concerning knowledge of the future and secret mysteries of the *Torah*. The prophet Elijah would also appear to him and teach him. He could recognize the letters on the forehead and was expert at the science of physiognomy, as well as at seeing the lights that are upon the skin and body of an individual. He could also see the lights in the hair, understand the language of chirping birds and the language of trees and plants. He even understood the speech of inanimate objects, as Scripture says:

> "For the stone shall cry out of the wall and the beam out of the timber shall answer it" (Habakuk 2:11).

He was able to see the angels who announce all the proclamations from the higher realm and he was able to converse with them. His was an expert concerning all the plants and their genuine remedies. There are many other such things which ordinary people cannot even relate to. Those who hear of these feats will not even believe them. Vital stated, "I have recorded that which my eyes have seen in all truth."

The Basics

Intro to the Soul

One must have a solid foundation in order to get the most from the descending "influx," a spiritual energy derived from your *Torah* reading, your good actions, your prayers, and from your tzeruf meditations. This foundation involves the four levels or aspects of your soul. All levels must be correctly functioning or your tzeruf meditation results will be in disarray, or worse, have negative results.

The following are the four levels or aspects of one's soul, starting from the top;

1. Spiritual, level   (Chaiya)
2. Mental level   (Neshama)
3. Emotional level   (Ruach)
4. Physical level.   (Nephesh)

There is actually a fifth and highest level which is the result after one has reached perfection of all four levels. This is called Yehida, meaning unity with God or enlightenment.

These soul levels mirror the physical levels of creation or existence;

1. Atzilut   (Nearness)
2. Beriyah   (Creation)
3. Yetzirah (Formation)
4. Asiyah   (Making)

The Four Soul Levels

The four soul levels are a simplification of the 10 sefirot levels on the seferot tree.

The top sefirah, Keter, comprises of extreme divinity. It can not be understood by man.

The next sefirah down, Chokhma, is on the spiritual level.

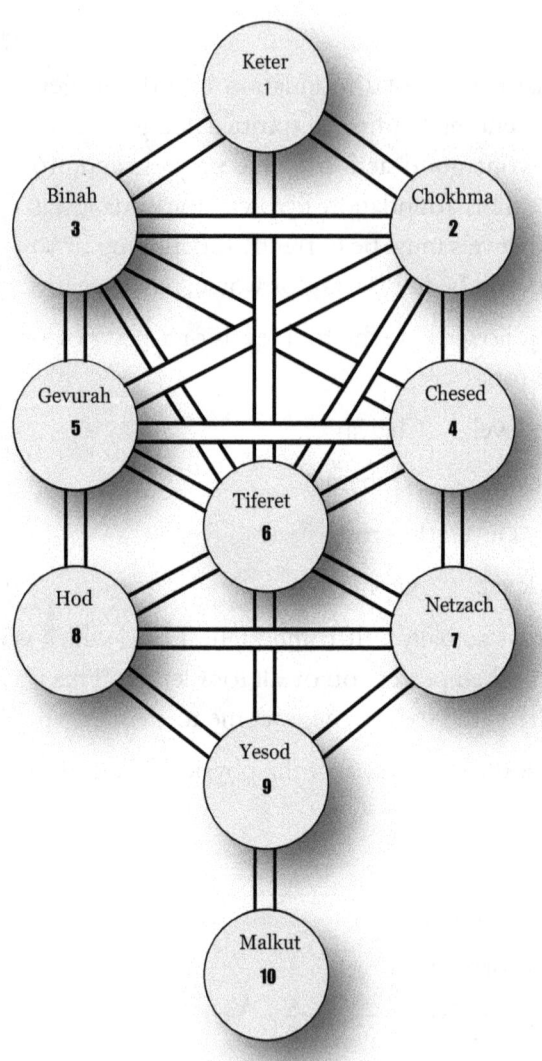

THE TREE OF SEFIROT

Chokhma would be the subconscious mind and it is mainly perceived as a mental flash. This flash is derived from prior learnings, prior judgments and events that have been stored in the brain. It is where the spiritual energy, the influx, first manifests as it descends from Keter. Dreams are manifested at this level.

The next sefirah descending down the sefirot tree is Bina. This is the mental level that involves one's logical mental functions. This includes the visualizations of images.

The next level down is the emotional level and it is comprised of six sefirot; Chesed, Gevurah, Tiferet, Hod, Netzach, and Yesod. By these six sefirot the soul starts reflecting itself into the physical world.

The last level is the physical action level, the sefirah Malkut. This where the mental thoughts transcend down to and manifest into actions.

There are no tangible physical qualities to these sefirot. They are all spiritual stages between a thought and a final action stage that moves the physical world.

The influx flows down the sefirot tree, originating in Keter and starts flowing down into Chochma and Bina of the mental level. Then it continues descending through the six emotional sefirot, and finally manifests results in Malkut. It flows from the start, a flash of thought, through all the sefirot below it, to become action.

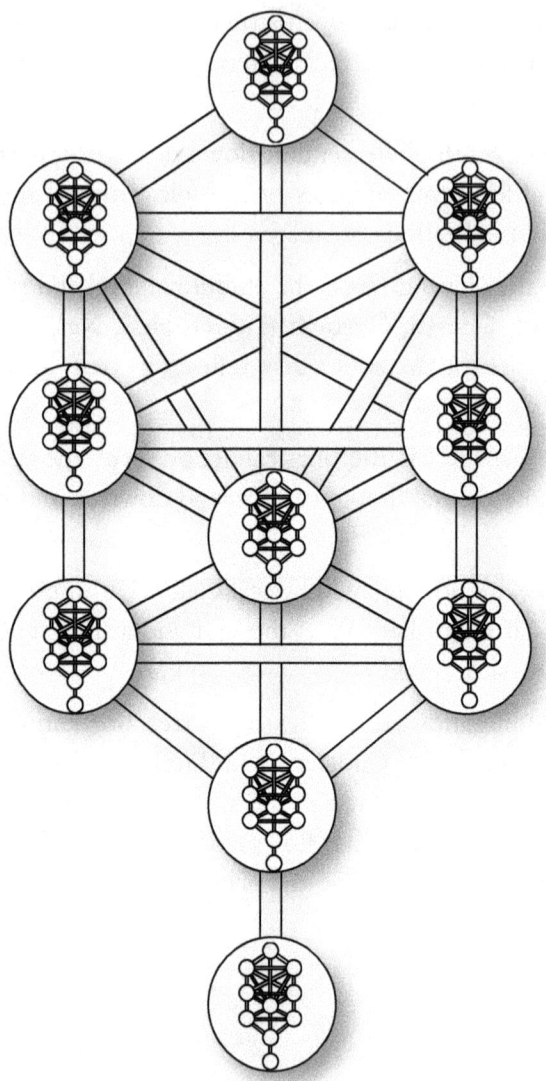

TREES WITHIN THE TREE

Within each sefirah tree there are ten sefirot. Within each sefirah on a tree, there is contained inside the sefirah another sub sefirot tree. Thus a sefirah tree has it's ten main sefirot, and there are 10 sub sefirot in each main seriah, making 100 sub sefirot. This goes on numerous times.

Creating a Vessel in Yesod

First one needs to create a "vessel" to effectively receive the descending spiritual energy or influx. This is the establishing of a foundation and is done at the foundation sefirah, Yesod, in the seferot tree. This is the second to the last sefirah which is before the physical action level. An adequate vessel or spiritual "body temple" is needed to receive the influx, otherwise it will be ineffective or worse have negative effects. The receiving vessel is your physical body prepared specifically to maximise the effects of the meditations.

Water

Pure water is a must. The water that comes from the tap in the U.S. generally has no germs, but is loaded with very harmful chemicals, metals, and minerals. Many of the chemicals can't be filtered out. The government authorities (that control the water supply) deliberately add to the water supply many of these chemicals. These authorities in the U.S. add about 125 different chemicals to water supply. The only added chemical the government doesn't mind disclosing is the stated fluoride (sodium fluoride) which the government alleges is good for your teeth. Sodium fluoride has no independent scientific basis for bettering the teeth.

The first known use of Fluoride was in the Nazi concentration camps of WWII (I. G. Farben Co.). It was given to the prisoners in the water supply to pacify them. Sigmund Freud is know as the father of psychology. His nephew, Edward Bernays, stated to be one of the most influential people of the 20th century, is known as the father of mass psychology (*Propaganda* by Bernays). This nephew advocated to governments that they should put fluoride in the water to help pacify their citizens.

Other known uses -- Sodium Fluoride (a by product of the manufacture of aluminum) is also one of the basic ingredients in both PROZAC (FLUoxetene Hydrochloride) and Sarin Nerve Gas (Isopropyl-Methyl-Phosphoryl FLUORIDE). Sodium Fluoride by itself is known and is widely used as a rat poison.

To avoid the effects of the numerous chemicals that are deliberately put into the water supply, as well as avoid any possible cancer and other diseases that may develop from these chemicals (also add the recent radiation isotopes), it is best to use distilled water for drinking and cooking.

It is best to have your own water distiller, if nothing else for emergencies when the water supply becomes tainted. This enables you to distill pond water if necessary. The infrastructures of city water and sewer pipes are failing constantly because of excessive age. Contamination has occurred many times in numerous cities. Further, natural disasters are increasing, like floods, etc., where the affected governments put out "boil only" orders. This boiling has no effect on the chemical pollutants found in the water in disaster areas. A water distiller is easy and inexpensive to make.

A distiller can also be used to also distill alcohol spirits (moonshine), and even make alcohol as a fuel. You can also use the large distilling pot for canning, or also for making large amounts of soup.

If one lives in a humid area one can use a dehumidifier to extract distilled water from the air. However this needs electrical power and would be useless in a power out disaster.

Food

Man originally was not allowed to eat animals.

Genesis 2:29-30

וַיֹּאמֶר אֱלֹהִים הִנֵּה נָתַתִּי לָכֶם
and he said Elohim here I give to you

אֶת כָּל עֵשֶׂב זֹרֵעַ זֶרַע אֲשֶׁר עַל פְּנֵי כָל הָאָרֶץ
that all plant seeder seed which upon face all the earth

וְאֶת כָּל הָעֵץ אֲשֶׁר בּוֹ פְרִי עֵץ זֹרֵעַ זָרַע
and that all the tree which in it fruit tree seeder seed

לָכֶם יִהְיֶה לְאָכְלָה:
to you it will be to food

29 And God said, Behold, I have given you every herb bearing seed, which is upon the face of all the earth, and every tree, in the which is the fruit of a tree yielding seed; to you it shall be for meat.

וּלְכָל חַיַּת הָאָרֶץ וּלְכָל עוֹף הַשָּׁמַיִם
and to all living things the earth and to all bird the heavens

וּלְכֹל רוֹמֵשׂ עַל הָאָרֶץ אֲשֶׁר בּוֹ נֶפֶשׁ חַיָּה
and to all creeper upon the earth which in it soul life

אֶת כָּל יֶרֶק עֵשֶׂב לְאָכְלָה וַיְהִי כֵן:
that all green plants to food and it was so

30 And to every beast of the earth, and to every fowl of the air, and to every thing that creepeth upon the earth, wherein there is life, I have given every green herb for meat: and it was so.

It was only after the flood that permission was given for man to eat meat. However there was a requirement that the blood would be totally removed from the animal so no blood would be consumed.

Genesis 9:3

כָּל־רֶמֶשׂ אֲשֶׁר הוּא־חַי לָכֶם יִהְיֶה לְאָכְלָה
crawling - all which liveth - it to you it will be to food

כְּיֶרֶק עֵשֶׂב נָתַתִּי לָכֶם אֶת־כֹּל:
like green plant I give to you all – that

3 Every moving thing that liveth shall be meat for you; even as the green herb have I given you all things.

104

flesh - but	in his soul body	his blood	not	you will eat it
אַךְ־בָּשָׂר	בְּנַפְשׁוֹ	דָמוֹ	לֹא	תֹאכֵלוּ׃

4 But flesh with the life thereof, which is the blood thereof, shall ye not eat.

THE HUMAN BODY IS BY NATURE A VEGETARIAN.

With carnivores, their jaws only open up and down, not side to side. They have two large front canine teeth for ripping and tearing the flesh of the prey that they eat. Their saliva aids very little in the digestion of their meat. They have short alimentary canals, approximately one third the length of a vegetarian animal. They have three times more digestive acid in their stomach. The majority of their digestion occurs in stomach. They take a short time to digest the meat they eat.

With herbivores, including humans, they have teeth that go side to side with molars to grind in all directions their food of plant matter and grain. Their saliva starts digesting the food right away. They have a long alimentary canal three times longer that carnivores. Most of their food is digested in small intestines. Some herbivores have four stomachs to break down their food before going to their long small intestines. The biggest animals in the jungle are herbivores, sustaining a huge muscular body from only plant matter.

In the *Bible*, God wanted the Israelites to be vegetarians. After the Israelites left Egypt and went to live in the desert, God gave them manna to eat, that fell with the dew in the early morning. It was such a spiritual food that it would taste like anything that you wanted it to taste like. It also did not produce a bowel movement. But, the people cried out that they wanted meat, and that they had meat in Egypt, and that they should return there for the good eats. God was angry and gave them meat in the form of quails. However while the meat was still in their teeth, God struck the people down with a severe plague. They buried many people from this plague there at Kibroth-hattaavah (the graves of lust).

God allowed man to eat only certain kinds of meat. The *Bible* prohibits man from eating animals and fowl that prey on other creatures or that eat the bodies of creatures that are already dead.

The only mammal types that are acceptable for man to eat are the ones that chew the cud (four stomachs) and have hoofs. These are animals that are vegetarians. The fowl acceptable to eat are ones that don't prey on other animals or fowl, or that eat from dead bodies. Fish are unique and are considered not to have blood, and are acceptable to eat only if they have scales and fins. These acceptable fish are coincidently the only ones that are alkaline positive.

ALKALINE VERSES ACIDIC

Foods that humans eat are either alkaline or acidic. All Plant matter is alkaline positive on the alkaline/acidic scale (up to plus 40 for alkaline, and up to a minus 40 for acidic). All living creatures (except fish with fins and scales), have negative alkalinity in the vicinity of negative 40. Red meat is the maximum of the negative side of the scale at a minus 40. On the positive side, plant matter with a lot of chlorophyll is at the maximum of the positive side of the scale at a plus 40.

The human body is designed to eat alkaline foods. Germs can not live in a highly alkaline environment. Further, the red and white blood cells become healthy looking with a positive charge on their exterior of their cell wall and bounce off the walls of the blood vessels and other cells. On the other hand, germs love and thrive in an acidic environment. In an acidic environment the red and white blood cells look withered and stick to other cells and blood vessels.

Humans are designed to be at their peak by eating vegetables and alkaline fish. In an extreme example, there are world champion MMA cage fighters that eat nothing but fish and fresh vegetables (no highly starchy vegetables) to get in peak conditioning before a title bout.

With alkaline blood, your face will become rosy, any acne will disappear, your eye sight will improve, cuts will heal fast. You will have more endurance, your breath and body odor won't smell bad, and many more positive effects comes from an alkaline positive diet.

The most excellent alkaline food is wheat grass because of it's high concentration of chlorophyll. It has 60 per cent more chlorophyll than spinach, which is the second best. Cucumber is also very high. One needs to get a chart on the alkaline vegetables and the alkaline fish (with fins and scales). Chlorella from sea plants is also excellent because of it's high chlorophyll content. However in order to get to the chlorophyll the plants must have the cell walls broken by an involved process.

For the typical American the quintessential meal is a grilled, two inch thick 16 oz. filet mignon steak (Kobe beef if possible). Since you may be one of those who are crying (like the Israelites) for a mesquite grilled freshly cut steak (grain fed free range Texas Longhorn or Angus), or a fresh ground steak grilled hamburger, you need not panic. It's not that bad to eat such a meat meal if its only done once or twice a month. The American Heart Association recommends eating NO meat. They further say that if one insists on eating meat, one should have ONLY three, 6 oz. meat portions a WEEK. In layman's terms that's a maximum total weekly meat allowance .... equivalent to three regular sized hamburgers. And that is what is NOT recommended.

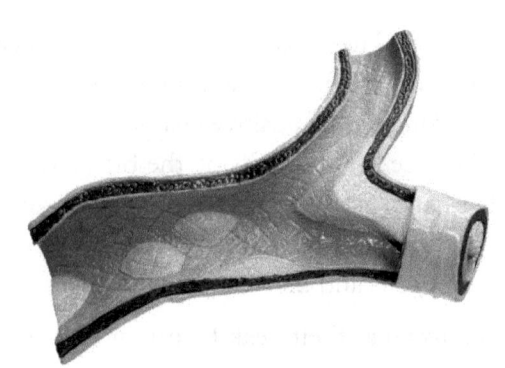

CLOGGED ARTERY

It is best to have any meat that you are going to eat come from an animal that has been properly slaughtered. This is done when the animal is not afraid and killed so the animal looses consciousness within one to two seconds. This is done by totally cutting the carotid artery and quickly stopping the flow of blood to the brain. Then all the blood of the animal needs to be drained and afterwards any blood residue left is salted out. This is the definition of kosher meat.

Keep in mind that eating meat makes your body release cholesterol. Plus you ingest cholesterol that is already within the meat itself. Some of the smaller cholesterol particles sticks to the walls of the blood vessels particularly at certain spots. This builds up over time in your blood vessels and blocks the blood flow. There is none of this build up with alkaline foods.

The former President Clinton found this out the hard way. He underwent a quadruple by-bass heart surgery. Not much later he needed a stent and had one put in. In order to prevent having another stent, he disciplined himself to eat only plant derived foods and a little portion of fish. He now states that the cholesterol that had built up in his heart is currently breaking down and is being removed by his body's healing processes.

In conclusion, we are designed to function best as vegetarians. The only non-plant-life our bodies should eat is fish with fins and scales. The reason for eating alkaline foods is because it significantly heightens and sensitizes your body vessel for easier spiritual perceptions which comes from the influx that descends on account of the tzeruf meditations.

Dangers in Food

In the U.S., beef and chicken when growing and maturing are loaded up with steroids as they rapidly grow and this is the reason why these animals can grow so big. They are also given large amounts of penicillin to prevent disease. They are given especially high doses of steroids to fatten them up several days before being weighted for slaughter. These chemicals are lodged in the muscle cells and organs of the animals and are transferred to humans when eaten. The processed canned and boxed foods are loaded with chemical preservatives such as MSG, and other hard to pronounce laboratory made chemicals. All the soda drinks and other foods are loaded with high fructose corn sugar. This high fructose is shocking the body into bad health, which was not seen before when the sodas contained cane sugar in them. Many high fructose corn sugar products have been found by the FDA to contain mercury. Mercury is a metal on the periodic table and cannot be created.

The worst are the diet colas. There is a chemical in diet colas that makes holes in the brain (Washington U, and others). The pictures of lab mice demonstrating this are easily available on the web. This subject is not exposed to the public by Doctors because of the fear of litigation.

EXERCISE

Exercise helps bridge the flow of influx from the emotional level to the physical action level. It strengthens your receiving vessel body and becomes a foundation for the emotional level. By strengthening your physical body you open the flow through this bridge. It helps you control your reactive emotions.

Plain rote exercise is boring. One needs to make it interesting. Exercising does not have to be a stressful effort. Tai Chi and Yoga activate circulation without the stress and are easy and interesting to do. Tai Chi activates the meridians several times by doing one form, and this can be done in 15 minutes. Yoga squeezes out the lactic acid in the muscles and can also be done in 15 minutes. Jogging and other cardio workouts are great if you are entertained while doing the exercises such as listening to music or vocal instruction with a mp3 player.

PHYSICAL ENVIRONMENT

When meditating, seek a warm and dry and clean comfortable room that is secluded, quiet, with no background sounds like TV. Turn off all cell phones. No disturbances for the duration of the meditation. And this is most important; the room must be such that no one can hear you as you vocalize.

POST A DECLARATION

It's best to have a small written declaration (in Hebrew) rolled up into a tube on a door post (Mezuzah) of all the entrances to the house. This has been commanded in the *Bible*.

DEUTERONOMY 6:9

וּכְתַבְתָּם　עַל־מְזֻזוֹת　בֵּיתֶךָ　וּבִשְׁעָרֶיךָ:
and you write them　door posts - upon　your house　and your gates

9 And thou shalt write them upon the posts of thy house, and on thy gates.

DEUTERONOMY 11:20

וּכְתַבְתָּם　עַל־מְזוּזוֹת　בֵּיתֶךָ　וּבִשְׁעָרֶיךָ:
and you write them　door posts - upon　your house　and your gates

20 And thou shalt write them upon the door posts of thine house, and upon

thy gates:

Why would this matter? By posting a declaration, bad influencing and untrustworthy spirits stay out of your residence. This establishes a peaceful environment where there are no roaming spirits deliberately sending thoughts of incorrect wisdom and selfish thoughts generated by them to penetrate and cause chaos to any person. When one becomes more spiritual one will notice receiving these foreign and extraneous thoughts when one is around certain people who posses a bad character.

When one falls asleep, these posted declarations keep bad spirits from entering the residence and being present when one falls asleep. This is talked about in *Gates of Light* and the *Zohar*. After falling asleep, one's soul travels to higher dimensions. Between the lower dimension of the body location and the higher dimension where the soul goes after falling asleep, there is an intermediate area that your soul passes through. In this intermediate area there are many spirits roaming. These spirits are mostly trying to deceive the soul of the sleeper, especially when he is coming back to his body, about what he has learned in those higher dimensions. When the sleeper descends to the physical plane, these spirits in this intermediate area try to confuse and change the meanings the sleeper gleaned from his or her dreams.

The posting of a declaration at the entrances of your home is abhorrent to these bad spirits, and they will not come into the posted area. You will notice a very peaceful feeling inside your posted area.

Time

Think ahead and block out enough time. Once meditation is started, stopping in the middle significantly reduces the meditation's effectiveness and becomes a time drain. Most meditations are dependent on all parts.

The Room

There should be no fluctuations of temperature or unpleasant blowing air. Your chair must be very comfortable. It's best to have plants around the room. Have physical items that are pleasant to you around the room. Lighting large candles helps the mood. Rabbi

Abulafia recommends lighting many candles to brighten up the room with candlelight. The flame burning is a symbol of the physical transforming into the spiritual. Sitting is best but lying down in a reclining position is acceptable. Light classical music or other slow paced instrumental music played at a low volume is ideal.

You should have some liquid to drink, like water. It's nice to drink green tea, hot or cold. Have whatever liquid you prefer to keep your mouth from getting dry from any lengthy quantity of vocalizing needed to be done.

Washing

Immersing yourself totally in a pool of water, called a mikvah, is ideal when done before a meditation session. A shower is second best. This washing clears negative charges that are on the body. If these are not practical at the time, it is essential that you at least wash your hands before meditation. The sages of old emphasized the importance of washing the hands, especially right after you arise in the morning after a nights sleep. This clears away the klipot, a negative spiritual energy, that attaches and remains on the hands particularly after sleeping.

Clothing

You can dress in whatever is comfortable preferably loose fitting. Sages of old recommended white clothing that has been freshly cleaned. They recommended a full length one piece robe that was typical of that time period.

One note about the clothes that you wear. Your garments should not contain a combination of animal and plant fibers. It has been said that this has to do with disrupting the flow of electricity on the surface of the skin known as meridians. This is commanded from the *Bible*.

Leviticus 19:19

וּבֶגֶד כִּלְאַיִם שַׁעַטְנֵז לֹא יַעֲלֶה עָלֶיךָ׃
and garment   mingled   linen & wool   not   it ascend   upon you

19 ... neither shall a garment mingled of linen and woolen come upon thee.

DEUTERONOMY 22:11

לֹא תִלְבַּשׁ שַׁעַטְנֵז צֶמֶר וּפִשְׁתִּים יַחְדָּו:
not   you wear   mixed garment   woollen   and linen   together

11 Thou shalt not wear a garment of divers sorts, as of woollen and linen together.

FRONTLET & RING

The *Bible* commands you to bind a sign on your hand, and on your forehead.

DEUTERONOMY 6:8

וּקְשַׁרְתָּם לְאוֹת עַל־יָדֶךָ
and will bind them   to sign   your hand – upon

וְהָיוּ לְטֹטָפֹת בֵּין עֵינֶיךָ:
and they will be   to frontlets   between   your eyes

8 And you shall bind them for a sign upon your hand, and they shall be as frontlets between your eyes.

DEUTERONOMY 11:18

וְשַׂמְתֶּם אֶת־דְּבָרַי אֵלֶּה עַל־לְבַבְכֶם וְעַל־נַפְשְׁכֶם
and put them   my speakings – that   these   your heart – upon   your soul – and upon

וּקְשַׁרְתֶּם אֹתָם לְאוֹת עַל־יֶדְכֶם
and you bind   to them   to sign   your hand – upon

וְהָיוּ לְטוֹטָפֹת בֵּין עֵינֵיכֶם:
and they will be   to frontlets   between   your eyes

18 Therefore shall you lay up these my words in your heart and in your soul, and bind them for a sign upon your hand, that they may be as frontlets between your eyes.

This is ultimately an allegory referring to a spiritual meaning, but since heaven and earth need to be in alignment, one should have this commandment fulfilled also on the physical plane. Phylacteries as seen in the photo are traditionally worn to satisfy these verses. Their true purpose is to keep open the path to the upper worlds where they are directing their prayers and

PRAYER SHAWL AND PHYLACTERIES

keep away the destructive spirits. It's the scrolls inside the phylacteries that those spirits hate.

The "between your eyes" is referring to the vision you see with your eyes and the vision you create in your brain. Physically your brain is between your eyes as their connections attach to the brain.

Ring

A ring would be a sign on your hand. It should be solid gold (min 22 carat) but can be silver, not hollowed out, and weigh a substantial amount like 2 ounces for a man. It must have the name of the shem hamephorish (יהוה) written on it. Also acceptable would be the written words in Hebrew,

HOLINESS TO THE LORD --> קֹדֶשׁ לַיהוָה.

Frontlet

What is specifically more suited to meditation is wearing a metal plate on the forehead. This frontlet is the same frontlet as worn by the high priest of the holy Temple. It was also was worn by other priests and pious ones in ancient times.

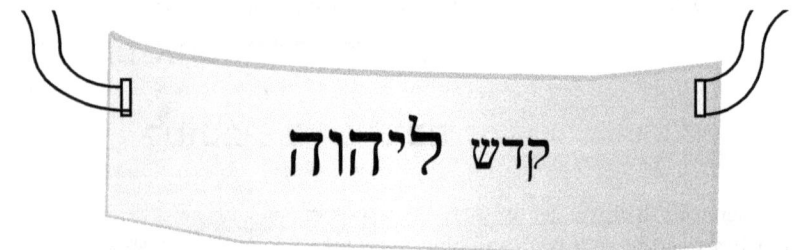

Frontlet worn on the forehead

The frontlet as a sign between your eyes, as worn by the high priest, is described by the *Bible*. It is a thick sheet of pure gold that covers the forehead. It is between 2 to 3 finger-breaths in height. It's width extends ear to ear. It is suspended on the forehead by light blue ribbons around the head. On the front of the frontlet is written in raised Hebrew letters -

HOLINESS TO THE LORD --> קֹדֶשׁ לַיהוָה.

One can enhance his or her meditations by wearing a frontlet. This should be made of solid gold. Since this would be extremely

HIGH PRIEST FRONTLET

EXODUS. 28:36-38

זָהָב טָהוֹר וּפִתַּחְתָּ עָלָיו פִּתּוּחֵי חֹתָם קֹדֶשׁ לַיהוָה:
gold pure and you will engrave upon it fancy it's engravings holy to ihvh

36 And thou shalt make a plate of pure gold, and grave upon it, like the engravings of a signet, HOLINESS TO THE LORD.

וְשַׂמְתָּ אֹתוֹ עַל־פְּתִיל תְּכֵלֶת
and you put to it upon - lace light blue

וְהָיָה עַל־הַמִּצְנֶפֶת אֶל־מוּל פְּנֵי־הַמִּצְנֶפֶת יִהְיֶה:
and it be mitre - upon forefront - unto the mitre - face it will be

37 And thou shalt put it on a blue lace, that it may be upon the mitre; upon the forefront of the mitre it shall be.

וְהָיָה עַל־מֵצַח אַהֲרֹן
and it be forehead - upon Aaron

וְנָשָׂא אַהֲרֹן אֶת־עֲוֹן הַקֳּדָשִׁים
and bear Aaron that - iniquity the holy things

אֲשֶׁר יַקְדִּישׁוּ בְּנֵי יִשְׂרָאֵל לְכָל־מַתְּנֹת קָדְשֵׁיהֶם
which they hallow sons Israel to all - gifts their holy

וְהָיָה עַל־מִצְחוֹ תָּמִיד לְרָצוֹן לָהֶם לִפְנֵי יְהוָה:
and will it be his forehead - upon always to accepted to them before ihvh

38 And it shall be upon Aaron's forehead, that Aaron may bear the iniquity of the holy things, which the children of Israel shall hallow in all their holy gifts; and it shall be always upon his forehead, that they may be accepted before the LORD.

THE HIGH PRIEST FRONTLET

expensive, one should consider alternative constructions.

One alternative would be a very thin solid rolled sheet of gold with raised lettering. Another substitute would be solid silver. This silver would be best if plated with a thick electroplating of gold.

This meditation headpiece seems to enlarge and extend the mind out of the body. There is no doubt the mood is pronounced when a frontlet is put on the forehead for a meditation session. It is also an aid when doing your visualizations.

Prayer Shawl

Commanded in the *Bible* is to put on tzitzit, or hanging strings, onto garments.

Numbers 15:38-40

דַּבֵּר אֶל־בְּנֵי יִשְׂרָאֵל וְאָמַרְתָּ אֲלֵהֶם
speak — sons-upon — Israel — and you say — unto them

וְעָשׂוּ לָהֶם צִיצִת עַל־כַּנְפֵי בִגְדֵיהֶם לְדֹרֹתָם
and you make — to them — tsitsit — corners-upon — their garments — to their generations

וְנָתְנוּ עַל־צִיצִת הַכָּנָף פְּתִיל תְּכֵלֶת׃
and you give — tsitsit-upon — the corners — thick thread — blue

38 Speak to the people of Israel, and bid them that they make them fringes in the borders of their garments throughout their generations, and that they put upon the fringe of the borders a thread of blue;

וְהָיָה לָכֶם לְצִיצִת וּרְאִיתֶם אֹתוֹ
and it will be — to you — to tsitsit — and you see them — to it

וּזְכַרְתֶּם אֶת־כָּל־מִצְוֹת יְהוָה וַעֲשִׂיתֶם אֹתָם
and you remember — that - all - commandments — ihvh — and you do them — to them

וְלֹא תָתֻרוּ אַחֲרֵי לְבַבְכֶם וְאַחֲרֵי עֵינֵיכֶם
and not — you stray — after — your hearts — and after — your eyes

אֲשֶׁר־אַתֶּם זֹנִים אַחֲרֵיהֶם׃
which – to you — straings — after them

39 And it shall be to you for a fringe, that you may look upon it, and remember all the commandments of the Lord, and do them; and that you seek not after your own heart and your own eyes, which incline you to go astray;

Deuteronomy (22:12)

גְדִלִים תַּעֲשֶׂה־לָּךְ עַל־אַרְבַּע כַּנְפוֹת כְּסוּתְךָ
fringes   to you - you make   four - upon   quarters   your vesture

אֲשֶׁר תְּכַסֶּה־בָּהּ׃
which   in it - you cover

12 Thou shalt make thee fringes upon the four quarters of thy vesture, wherewith thou coverest thyself.

These fringes have to be placed only on a four cornered garment. Wearing a prayer shawl helps set the mood when meditating especially as a substitution when not changing into meditation clothes.

Amulets

Amulets (Kame'ot) are a piece of jewelry hung around a neck, a key chain, or on a purse, whereby a small scroll can be inserted. Inside a scroll is written with a saying that repels negative spirits. The same writing that is on the high priest frontlet would be acceptable. This writing states your allegiance to "the one and correct" God. This writing is to be in Hebrew using the name shem haMephorish (יהוה). These negative spirits hate this declaration on the piece of paper and will totally avoid such a person and will feel it's futile to influence their thoughts. This is the same effect that the declaration on your door posts has upon these negative spirits.

Gold

Gold has an attractive property to it, both physically and spiritually. In Kabbalah gold is said to be God's metal. Opportunities come to a person that has large amounts of gold stored.

King Solomon knew the power of gold. He would trade anything for gold and then he would hoard it. The amount of gold that came to him from numerous sources every year was approximately 50 tones. When King Nebuchadnezzar conquered Israel, he took just **a portion** of King Solomon's gold and erected an obelisk style image of himself in pure solid gold that was 100 feet tall (more than an eight story building) (Daniel 3:1).

Today, modern countries and banks still recognize the innate spiritual power of possessing large amounts of gold. People will fol-

SOLID GOLD BUDDHA

Similar to what Nebuchadnezzar created is the statute in Wat Traimit, Bangkok, Thailand, a 900 years old graven image of Buddha. It is today's largest known pure solid gold object. It measures 16 feet (five metres) in height and weighs five and a half tons.

low and believe in someone who owns a large amount of gold.

Conclusion of Preparing the Shell

This past section covered the preparation of the vessel to receive the influx descending from the top levels. These preparations are important, or any meditation efforts will be minimized or ineffective.

The levels following will start at the top spiritual level and follow the path of the influx as it descends through the levels to the shell in the foundation sefirah Yesod, then manifesting in Malkut, or physical action.

Level 4 - Spiritual

The highest sefirah of the spiritual level is called Keter. It is the level called Nothingness (Ayin). This is where God's creative energy originates. Keter's nature is such that man can not understand it. It is on this highest point of this level that the laws of nature cease to exist, and can therefore be altered. Keter is where the influx is generated. This influx starts it's descent down the sefirot tree to the first manifestation of being, the sefirah of Chochma, the start of man's spiritual level.

Chochma

Chochma is referred to as the subconscious. From this sefirah originates a thought flash. This is the where one's automatic decisions reside and one's wisdom. Dreams happen at this level. It is the level of prophesy. As it is written, "Who is wise (Chochma)? He who perceives the future."

Wisdom, past, present and future have not yet been separated at this level. Hence one perfecting this level can see the future just like the past and present.

Commandments

At the various spiritual levels your past actions, good or bad, directs what events are going to occur to you based on your prior merit.

There are 613 commandments (called in the plural mitzvot), that are enumerated in the *Torah*. There are 248 are positive and 365 negative commandments. All these 613 commandments are extensions of the ten commandments. Torah in gematria equals 611. This infers that the Torah is to enumerate 611 laws to the people and God personally enumerates two of the laws. Some of the commandments are not able to be performed today since there is no holy temple in Jerusalem. But for the most part these commandments direct a person to what is, and what is not acceptable actions.

In all actions there is cause and effect. Your objective is to have your actions, the cause, result in a beneficial effect being returned to you. By following the commandments and instructions of the written and oral laws of the *Bible*, there is no uncertainty as to your actions being correct and thus with a beneficial yield to you.

Mitzvah

Doing a moral deed performed as a religious duty is called a mitzvah. It is a positive act of doing a good deed that betters the world. These good deeds build up as spiritual merit. Merit is like depositing money in a savings account. It protects you and comes back to you when you ask for it, or when you least expect it. But more importantly, it establishes your character (your soul).

Since the word mitzvot specifically denotes all of the 613 commandments, the negative commandments are also included in this definition. The negative commandments require discipline in not to doing a certain act. This takes effort and merit is also gained when one avoids doing those acts.

Violations of Torah Law

If you have done a wrong deed, just wait around, the effect is coming, you can count on that. You will not escape it. It takes a while to come back to you. If for example, you stole something. The *Bible* states that you must repay 4 or 5 times what you stole depending on how the stealing was done.

To correct a wrong already done, there is the remedy of repenting the wrong action. Repenting is deciding you don't want your soul to be that way in the future and that you sincerely resolve not do that type of action again. But to prove the resolution, one needs to make a restitution. The restitution has to be backed up by deeds or money, a sacrificial offering to God that costs you, and demonstrates your sincerity.

A general remedy called the Tikun Haklali was developed by Rabbi Nachman, a famous Rabbi noted for his simplification of explaining the spiritual elements of life. It helps mitigate decrees from prior bad actions that are being repented.

You must have a spiritually pure soul. Otherwise negativity will continue to come to you. Further, when you meditate with an impure soul, the positive effects will be diminished by this negativity.

Money

Idol worship was extremely prevalent among the common people of Israel during the period of the first and second temple. This is the reason why both temples were destroyed. After the second temple destruction, many of the top Rabbis made an agreement that they would constantly pray so that the urge of the people for idol worship would cease. They prayed vigorously and constantly until God changed this urge from the worshiping of idols, to the worshiping of money.

As a famous comedian said, "Money alone................that doesn't mean a thing to me......................Love.................... now that means something to me.............................I LOVE Money."

He who Loves money will never have enough. He does so to increase his or her immediate pleasure which is self idolization. It makes one impersonal towards others and makes a person regard others as objects to manipulate.

People are to be loved. Money is to be directed by action to create a return for the better good of all and to further establish one's own character. The people who worshiped the Golden Calf were all killed by the tribe of the Levities, the only tribe that didn't have any participants. Prove that money is not your idol, give of your assets, but only to worthy recipients.

Charity

"Giving charity is the way to guarantee your own prosperity."

This giving will benefit you in ways you wouldn't believe. That is....only if it is done correctly.

You aren't able to give any money? You can always give. You can give your time. You can give your labor. You can give your knowledge. Make it your socializing time instead of hanging out with a friend. You can give SOME money. You can't afford not to give. Have you known a person that just always seems to be lucky?

Giving incorrectly will hurt you. If you are not wise, you could give to someone from your assets and at the same time the giving would be detrimental to you. Giving (sefirah Chesed) must be tempered with stern judgment (sefirah Gevurah). Giving to the wrong people can cause your spiritual decline. You would be furthering wrong doing. You are responsible for furthering of any good or bad result if you could have reasonably perceived this result at the time of your giving. Make sure you give to further the good in life.

Those that are poor consider what Rabbi Nachman said (Likutey Moharan #4). One is poor because the cause of poverty is idle chatter (flattery, falsehood, slander, self-praise), gossip, and pride (anger, haughtiness, hatred). By giving charity one negates these qualities and gains wealth. Poverty is a sign of a haughty spirit. Haughtiness is an akin to idolatry (Sotah 4b).

Idol Worship

Genesis 20:3

לֹא־יִהְיֶה לְךָ אֱלֹהִים אֲחֵרִים עַל־פָּנָי׃

my face - upon   other ones   Elohim   to you   there will be - not

3 Thou shalt have no other gods before me.

In God's eyes, the worst act a person could do is worshiping an idol. The first and second holy temples were destroyed because of idol worship.

The majority of Christians believe that the "New" testament replaced the "Old" Testament. This is not so. Jesus was a Jew who abided by the *Torah*, the stated by some "Old Testament." He was called up to the *Torah* scroll during the temple services to read from the *Torah*. Jesus specifically stated;

> Matthew 5:17 "Think not that I am come to destroy the law (*Torah*), or the prophets: I am not come to destroy, but to fulfil.
>
> 5:18 For verily I say unto you, Till heaven and earth pass, one jot or one tittle shall in no wise pass from the law (*Torah*), till all be fulfilled.

Jesus has stated in the *New Testament* that there were things that he was not able to do, that only his Father in Heaven (God) was able to do. The doctrine of Jesus himself being "God in the flesh" was developed at the time of Constantine. Constantine worshiped the Sun.

"Yio-Zeus" in Greek means "Dawn of Zeus." Zeus was the king of gods. Is this name a close resemblance to the sound of the name "Jesus"? [People don't like pronouncing double vowels] Coincidence? Jesus is not a Hebrew name. Today a large number of Christians admit that the name is "mis-translation." Based on Psalm 72:17 many sages believe that the name of the Messiah will be Ianun.

Constantine was uniting his kingdom by establishing a highbred religion at Constantine's Council of Nicaea in A.D. 325. He did this to prevent his kingdom from disintegrating. Constantine decreed the day of worship to be Sunday not Saturday (against one of the ten commandments) in order to honor a pagan god of the Sun. Around

RUINS OF ZEUS TEMPLE

that time the Christian doctrine changed, and the new doctrine became "Jesus was God in the flesh." The quotations by Jesus himself in the *New Testament* have never even hinted that he was God. In his dialogs Jesus refers many times to his Father in Heaven as God. Further Constantine commissioned fifty *Bibles,* each including the *New Testament,* as master copies from which all other *Bibles* were to be copied from.

It has been predicted in ancient writings that there would be two Messiahs; a suffering Messiah, and later a Messiah of peace. But believing that Jesus was "God in the flesh" begs the question for believers to ask themselves. "Am I just a regurgitater? Can this belief be construed as me doing idol worship? Have I been conned by the great con Constantine?"

The kabbalah texts state that the highest spiritual level attainable by man is called "Ruah HaKodesh." This is literally translated word for word as "spirit the holy." This is a state where one reaches the sefirah keter, the mental state of God consciousness. The Bud-

124

dhists refer to this state as enlightenment. But when one attains this level, one does not become God.

Genesis 23:13 states that one should not mention other gods upon one's mouth. The Hebrew word translated as mention means in the sense of memorializing or giving credence as to it's powers.

On a final note, is God's second personal commandment. Any graven image used to help idolize a spiritual power is forbidden by one of the ten commandments (a cross?).

Saturday

The Seventh Day

One of the ten commandments of the *Bible* is "keep my Sabbath." How many different times is this stated in the *Bible*? And it doesn't say to keep my "Sundayath." And many times after this commandment the next verse that follows is, "I am ihvh (יהוה) your God."

Exodus 20:8

זָכוֹר אֶת־יוֹם הַשַּׁבָּת לְקַדְּשׁוֹ:
remember that – day   the sabbath   to it's holiness

8 Remember the sabbath day, to keep it holy.

שֵׁשֶׁת יָמִים תַּעֲבֹד וְעָשִׂיתָ כָּל־מְלַאכְתֶּךָ:
six   days   you will work   and you do   all - your work

9 Six days shalt thou labour, and do all thy work:

וְיוֹם הַשְּׁבִיעִי שַׁבָּת לַיהוָה אֱלֹהֶיךָ
your Elohim   to ihvh   sabbath   the seventh   and day

לֹא־תַעֲשֶׂה כָל־מְלָאכָה
work - all   you will do - not

אַתָּה וּבִנְךָ וּבִתֶּךָ עַבְדְּךָ וַאֲמָתְךָ וּבְהֶמְתֶּךָ
and your beasts   and your maids   and your servant   and your daughter   and your son   you

וְגֵרְךָ אֲשֶׁר בִּשְׁעָרֶיךָ׃
in your gates   which   and your stranger

10 But the seventh day *is* the sabbath of the LORD thy God: *in it* thou shalt not do any work, thou, nor thy son, nor thy daughter, thy manservant, nor thy maidservant, nor thy cattle, nor thy stranger that *is* within thy gates:

כִּי שֵׁשֶׁת־יָמִים עָשָׂה יְהוָה אֶת־הַשָּׁמַיִם וְאֶת־הָאָרֶץ
the earth - and that   the heavens - that   ihvh   made   days - six   like

אֶת־הַיָּם וְאֶת־כָּל־אֲשֶׁר־בָּם
in them - which - all - and that   the sea - that

וַיָּנַח בַּיּוֹם הַשְּׁבִיעִי
the seventh   in day   and he rested

עַל־כֵּן בֵּרַךְ יְהוָה אֶת־יוֹם הַשַּׁבָּת וַיְקַדְּשֵׁהוּ׃
and he hallowed it   the sabbath   day - that   ihvh   blessed   thus - upon

11 For in six days the LORD made heaven and earth, the sea, and all that in them is, and rested the seventh day: wherefore the LORD blessed the sabbath day, and hallowed it.

The Sabbath day is so important that it was made one of the ten commandments. An extra offering sacrifice was required on the sabbath when the Temple stood. When honoring the Sabbath one should spend twice the time on prayer and meditation than one would do during the other days of the week.

Meditations and Prayers

Tzeruf meditation, Hebrew prayers and good deeds are what generate influx, or descending spiritual energy. Tzeruf meditation has been said to be more powerful than prayers. Tzeruf is an initiator creating and starting the descent of the influx flowing down the sefirot tree, eventually to a physical manifestation as an action effect of your creation.

One of the highest forms of prayer are the Hebrew Psalms. The Psalms were written mostly by King David to be used for specific results. In Psalms 145 and 119, a basic tzeruf permutation appears more recognizable because each verse starts with a different alphabet letter.

Each word in a Hebrew prayer reflects a sefirah and also has a significant numerical value. Through extensive analysis one can only get a glimpse of how the Bible code is constructed to produce effects. Few people in a generation understands it.

Torah

One should read the *Torah* (in Hebrew) every day. This not only teaches one the standards by which to live but also brings down a great deal of influx created from the mystical Hebrew letters and their arraignment. The 5 books of the *Torah* are broken down into 54 portions. A portion is named in Hebrew a Parashah. One portion is designated to be read every week of the year. Some shorter portions are doubled up for one week's reading. Each weekly reading division is further divided into seven parts, called Aliahs. Each day one should read the appropriate Aliah for that day. On Friday read a double portion, two Aliahs. On Saturday read the whole designated weekly reading portion again. You will notice the influx effect in a short time.

Most people know about the *Written Bible*, but don't know about the *Oral Bible*, AKA the *Talmud*. The *Oral Bible* was given to Moses at the same time the *Written Bible* was given to him on Mount Sinai. This *Oral Bible* is what further explains the stories and laws of the *Written Bible*. This is a set of books which is typically comprised of approximately 63 large sized volumes, 5,422 pages. Study groups typically take seven years to read through all of the volumes of the *Talmud*. It is a huge intellectual undertaking.

One also needs to read the commentaries by famous Scholars, that explain the many deeper meanings of the *Torah* verses. These commentaries are also considered part of the *Oral Bible*.

Conclusion

You have to die someday (one of the 903 types of death). You are here as a life on this earth to establish your character and to fulfill a spiritual purpose. You will have trials, and bad things will happen to you. It must be so. How else would you be tested? As you become more advanced spiritually, you will realize that even the bad is from God and that you can become wise from the evil that exists life. Evil is given to you so that you will learn and change for the better. Don't be depressed by it. The opportunities that come out of a terrible event are much greater than if everything were normal. This is from the teachings of the renown Kabbalist the Baal Shem Tov.

You may have been allotted only a normal life because of your prior merit that you earned before being born. This does not preclude you from living a mystically enhanced life by pursuing your spiritual path and enhancing and increasing that which you were allotted. What is wealth? One who is happy with their portion and uses it well.

Level 3 - Mental

This mental level represents the sefirah Binah on the sefirot tree. At this level concepts are delineated and defined as separated objects. It involves recalling and interrelating information that your brain has stored in your subconscious mind from the spiritual level, the sefirah Chokhma. When a mental image is formed, it is directed down through the remaining lower sefirot.

One constantly has thoughts. Try to stop them. You can't. According to the National Foundation of Science it is estimated that a normal person has 12,000 thoughts a day and a mental person has around 50,000 thoughts a day. The quick thoughts are mostly from the Chochma sefirah and the thoughts you consider for more than a flash are at the Bina sefirah level.

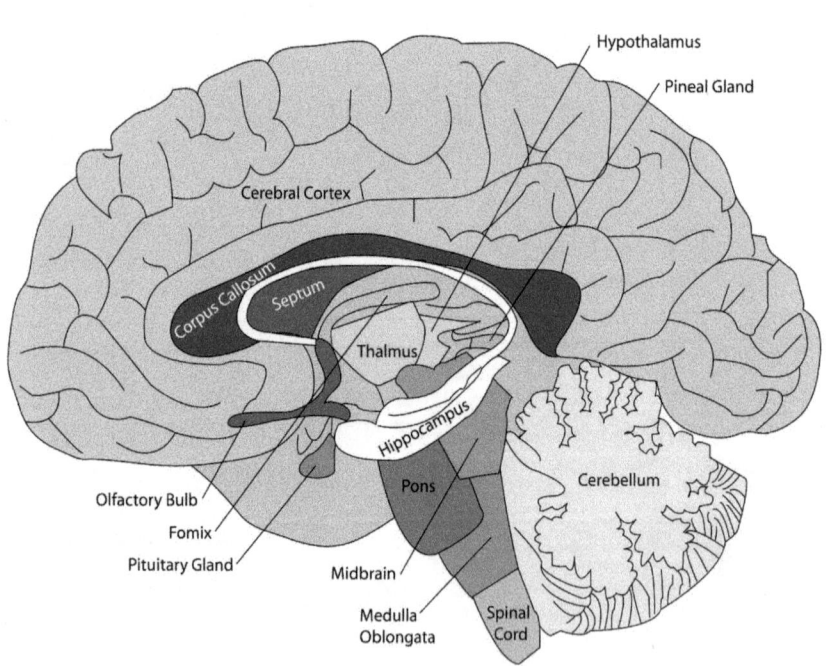

When one is awake his mind visualizes what his eyes are seeing. Then at times one greatly reduces the awareness of what the eyes are seeing and concentrates his or her energy on visualizing with his imagination a visualization which overrides what his or her eyes are seeing. The mind is always visualizing something.

At this mental level, one is forming and visualizing images, making calculations, formulating a plan, and deciding on an action. This is a feminine aspect of receiving flash thoughts from the upper spiritual level Chokhma, expanding and processing the thoughts, then sending them down the tree eventually to the physical level for resulting actions.

Unfocused

If you are not focused in your mental visualizations, then you are in a pure reactive state where your future is determined by whatever events come along. Then the behaviors that are in control of you are your instinctive reactions to situations of pain and pleasure, not your directed intellect.

Focused

Your life has become what it is now because of the images you have focused on in your daily visualizations. These visualizations are produced in the brain as an energy that when nurtured eventually manifests into reality. It descends down from the mental level through the emotional level and then to the physical action level of the material world and becomes your character. The brain influences this energy flow based on the brain's stored knowledge and the remembered emotions attached to those images.

Spiritual influx energy gained from tzeruf meditation and praying will magnify this energy flow through all of the sefirot and thus increases the results of this mental focusing into action at the final physical level of Malkut. This gained influx energy is of a much higher quality since it has stimulated the soul with the concepts of creation through the uniting of sight and sounds of the Hebrew letters with the shem hamephorash or other names of God.

Continuous Visualizations of Desired Future

By consciously visualizing a scene where you are an actor interacting in a scene (the scene is your desired results for the future) you attract the elemental concepts from the world that are needed to bring this visualization into a reality. Your subconscious identifies and attracts these needed elements (RAS, Reticular Activating System). Your tzeruf meditations will be increasing the attraction through accentuating spiritual concepts which will bring you opportunities that would not have otherwise been presented to you.

All Levels of the Soul are Linked

Thoughts of past events are linked to the spiritual, mental and emotional levels as memories. A memory contains facts and emotions linked to it from the event based on a mental perception of the physical effects it had on him or her at that time.

All the levels of your soul will attract opportunities to you that consist of the different elements you need to actualize your desired visualization. The how of it happening is always a mystery.

How to Visualize

All soul levels need to be aligned while doing a directed visualization. The spiritual level must be aligned by right actions as was discussed in the spiritual level. The mental level needs to properly direct the visualizations. The emotional level must be aligned at the same time by feeling the future emotional effects.

At this mental level you need to visualize what you want the physical action level to look like in the future. Visualize a very vividly colorized movie with you as the main actor in it. This movie is to have numerous scenes with you performing your desired future actions. Have the scenes very detailed. Include the five senses, touch, taste, smell, hearing, and you seeing lots of color with lots of details. See yourself doing the all actions that you will do once the visualized seed starts to grow.

Your breathing while doing this can assist. As you visualize seeing your end result, breath in slowly till you have taken in a large breath and finished one aspect of your vision. Breathe out. Then visualize the next aspect of your goal always breathing in as you see the images.

Using the emotions by feeling what will happen while visualizing is essential for realizing any results, otherwise it will just remain thoughts. There are six sefirot in the emotional level that need to be stimulated while doing these visualizations. A detailed explanation on including these necessary six sefirot in your visualizations is explained in the next segment on the emotional level.

WRITE IT

Write out in paragraphs the movie scenes and get as detailed as possible. It should be at least several long paragraphs to be an effective effort. See yourself as living this desired life and see yourself as if you already have attained it. Believe that this scene is in the process of coming true.

Statements like "I am an airplane pilot flying a 757 plane" is a positive statement but not true. Though this statement will help you, your spiritual level knows this is not true and will give you resistance. It's best to write the statement as "I am in the process of becoming....." It is best to have the statements you use be true. However while visualizing, act and feel with the surface of your skin as if you are already are receiving and living the scene.

You will never raise higher than you see yourself. Your life follows your vision.

"I DON'T WANT"

Your supernal mind doesn't know the difference between negative and positive statements, it just sees a visualization. If you focus on a negative statement or desire, such as "I don't want XYZ", your mind will be focusing on XYZ and thus will attract this negative result "XYZ" that you don't want. Then you will have the condition "what you resist persists."

Focus only on what you DO want.

Daat

Daat is the process of spiritual energy transcending from the upper mental level to the lower emotional level comprised of the six sefirot. It is a significant transition, but not as material as to be one of the sefirot. This area acts as a bridge between both of these realms. It is the last of the intellect influence and the first of the emotions and the start of the physical manifestations of the soul.

According to the Zohar, the influences to the lower levels by the Daat gate are referred to as "the key that includes six." The "key" Daat, opens all six chambers (emotional level sefirot) of the heart and fills them with life force. Each of these six chambers, when filled with Daat, is referred to as a particular dei'ah ("attitude") of the soul that has been shaped by the upper sefirot of Chochmah and Binah.

The voice is considered related to this concept. It is the verbalization of thought into the physical. Tzeruf meditation facilitates the use of this bridge extensively by using the voice as the main component in opening the flow of influx from the upper realm of the mind, to the lower realm of the start of physicality by creating the appropriate sounds.

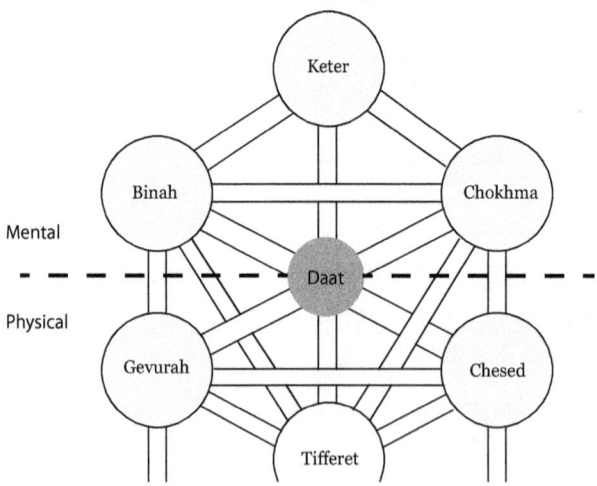

Counting the Omer

This is an excellent meditation that is closely related to Daat and exemplifies it's concept. This is a daily meditation that is commanded to be done right after passover by the *Bible*. One contemplates at the mental level about the mixing of two sefirot from the lower emotional levels and derives a meaning from this mixing and decides on what his or her future actions would be.

This meditation is called Counting the Omer. An omer is a unit of measurement of wheat or barley. The day after eating the passover meal, an omer of barley was brought to the temple as an offering. This starts the counting which continues for 49 days. The 50th day was the day when the *Torah* was given to the world on top of mount Sinai.

This counting is for a seven week period. Each week represents one of the lower seven sefirot and is called the base sefirah. Each day in the base sefirah's week represents one of the lower seven sefirot physical levels inside the base sefirah. During each of these 49 days one meditates on the meaning of the weekly base sefirah and it's relationship to one of it's seven levels of emotion. One analyses these two mixed sefirot concepts and thinks about what actions these produce. One thinks about how he or she relates with those emotions to other people and what he or she should do to improve his or her actions in the future.

Counting the Omer Verses

Leviticus 23:15-16

וּסְפַרְתֶּם לָכֶם מִמָּחֳרַת הַשַּׁבָּת
and you will count to them from tomorrow the sabbath

מִיּוֹם הֲבִיאֲכֶם אֶת־עֹמֶר הַתְּנוּפָה
from day the bringing you that - omer the sheaf

שֶׁבַע שַׁבָּתוֹת תְּמִימֹת תִּהְיֶינָה׃
seven sabbaths it will be complete it will be so

15 And ye shall count unto you from the morrow after the sabbath, from the day that ye brought the sheaf of the wave offering; seven sabbaths shall be complete:

עַד מִמָּחֳרַת הַשַּׁבָּת הַשְּׁבִיעִת תִּסְפְּרוּ חֲמִשִּׁים יוֹם
day   fifty   you will number it   the seventh   the sabbath   from tomorrow   till

וְהִקְרַבְתֶּם מִנְחָה חֲדָשָׁה לַיהוָה:
to ihvh   new   offering   you will sacrifice

16 Even unto the morrow after the seventh sabbath shall ye number fifty days; and ye shall offer a new meat offering unto the LORD.

Deuteronomy 16:9-10

שִׁבְעָה שָׁבֻעֹת תִּסְפָּר־לָךְ
to you - you number   weeks   seven

מֵהָחֵל חֶרְמֵשׁ בַּקָּמָה
in corn   sickle   from the beginning

תָּחֵל לִסְפֹּר שִׁבְעָה שָׁבֻעוֹת:
weeks   seven   to number   begin

9 Seven weeks shalt thou number unto thee: begin to number the seven weeks from such time as thou beginnest to put the sickle to the corn.

וְעָשִׂיתָ חַג שָׁבֻעוֹת לַיהוָה אֱלֹהֶיךָ
your Elohim   to ihvh   weeks   feast   and you do

מִסַּת נִדְבַת יָדְךָ אֲשֶׁר תִּתֵּן
you will give   which   your hand   freewill offering   tribute

כַּאֲשֶׁר יְבָרֶכְךָ יְהוָה אֱלֹהֶיךָ:
your Elohim   ihvh   he will bless you   when

10 And thou shalt keep the feast of weeks unto the LORD thy God with a tribute of a freewill offering of thine hand, which thou shalt give unto the LORD thy God, according as the LORD thy God hath blessed thee:

Level 3 - Mental

Day	Meditation	Day	Meditation
1	Chesed of Chesed	26	Hod of Netzach
2	Gevurah of Chesed	27	Yesod of Netzach
3	Tiferet of Chesed	28	Malkut of Netzach
4	Netzach of Chesed	29	Chesed of Hod
5	Hod of Chesed	30	Gevurah of Hod
6	Yesod of Chesed	31	Tiferet of Hod
7	Malkut of Chesed	32	Netzach of Hod
8	Chesed of Gevurah	33	Hod of Hod
9	Gevurah of Gevurah	34	Yesod of Hod
10	Tiferet of Gevurah	35	Malkut of Hod
11	Netzach of Gevurah	36	Chesed of Yesod
12	Hod of Gevurah	37	Gevurah of Yesod
13	Yesod of Gevurah	38	Tiferet of Yesod
14	Malkut of Gevurah	39	Netzach of Yesod
15	Chesed of Tiferet	40	Hod of Yesod
16	Gevurah of Tiferet	41	Yesod of Yesod
17	Tiferet of Tiferet	42	Malkut of Yesod
18	Netzach of Tiferet	43	Chesed of Malkut
19	Hod of Tiferet	44	Gevurah of Malkut
20	Yesod of Tiferet	45	Tiferet of Malkut
21	Malkut of Tiferet	46	Netzach of Malkut
22	Chesed of Netzach	47	Hod of Malkut
23	Gevurah of Netzach	48	Yesod of Malkut
24	Tiferet of Netzach	49	Malkut of Malkut
25	Netzach of Netzach		

Level 2 - Emotional

This emotional level, from a Kabbalistic view, encompasses six sefirot and involves many aspects. This emotional level is a transitional state where the mental level shines into the physical level before any action. There is much to be said about these six sefirot. Suffice it to say that this is the level where one's physicalness interfaces with one's soul as it relates to other people.

As the influx leaves the mental level and descends through these emotional level seferot it does this in a prescribed order; Chesed, Gevurah, Tiferet, Netzach, Hod, and Yesod. After flowing through these six sefirot, it leaves last sefirot of the emotional level, Yesod (foundation), to Malkut, the last of the ten sefirot.

Uniting Upper Mental and Lower Emotional Levels

All levels, the upper world sefirot, the spiritual and mental, must align with the lower world sefirot, the emotional, to produce the desired results at the last sefirah of action Malkut. While using the up-

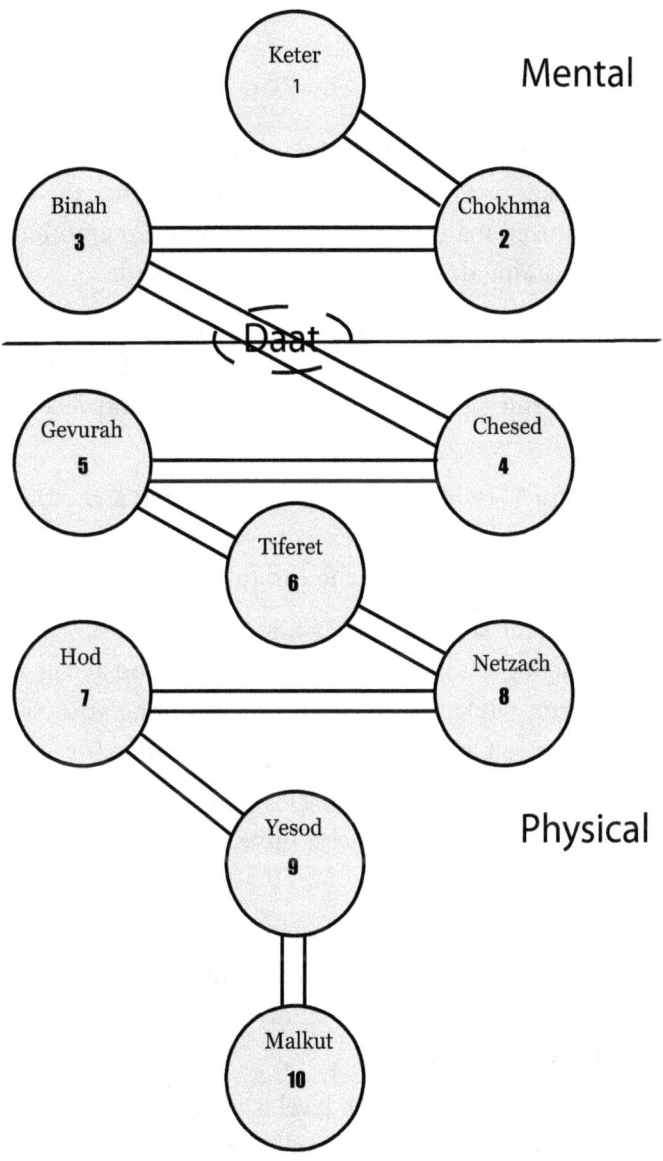

PATH OF THE INFLUX THROUGH THE TREE

per mental levels to visualize your desired future outcome, you must feel positive lower emotions of these six sefirah in order to manifest the desired action.

Visualize with Feelings

Each aspect of the different six sefirot should be emphasized in your visualizations to stimulate feelings to influence the influx. Do this in an organized manner starting at the top most emotional sefirah Chesed, and working down to the last sefirah Yesod.

For Chesed, see yourself much larger than others around you and you dominating the scene with your large size. See yourself giving many different and significant aspects to others and feel their emotional reactions to you.

Then for Gevurah, see yourself gathering and storing power and money, having the ability to execute your tasks instantly by making correct discerning judgments being careful not to be wasteful.

The Tiferet sefirah is the source of the work. See and feel yourself interacting with everyone and everything on a daily basis, producing your fruit while you perform tasks to bring you your desired results. Feel yourself involved in the detailed work.

For Netzach, feel the obstacles that you are overcoming and note others who are associated with these challenges that are assisting you.

For Hod, feel yourself enjoying the glamor and pleasure of others admiring you by seeing and hearing their reactions especially of people close to you. Feel opportunities coming easily to you because of what you are accomplishing.

The Yesod or foundation level is your office, desk, cell phone, etc., the tools you need. You can be aligned with this sefirah by having objects around that will be needed or will remind you of your desired future. Mount related pictures on a magnetic board and hand it on the wall. Put on it statements and motivational words. You will look daily at this board to remind you to focus on your desired future results.

What you are doing is feeling through each of the six sefirot. The important part is that you do as much as you can to activate the sefirot in the emotional level. This allows the descending influx to be felt by the soul and descend into the resulting action and not just remain as thoughts.

Chesed – see and feel yourself giving ....

Gevurah – see and feel yourself storing up and making limiting decisions

Tiferet – see and feel yourself doing the work and tasks of ....

Netzach – see and feel yourself overcoming the challenges of ....

Hod – see and feel yourself enjoying the glamor of ....

Yesod – see and feel yourself having a solid foundation ......

Go through each of the six sefirot visualizing and feeling. It is imperative that one needs to visualize while feeling the positive emotions you are linking to, and, that you truly believe that these visualized images will manifest into action. This is the "allowing" of the spiritual energy to flow down to manifest in the physical action level.

ALLOWING

This is a very important overlooked aspect because your emotions can easily prevent you from achieving your desired results.

From your prior decisions and actions you formulated judgments and conclusions which have become established beliefs. A belief is a feeling of certainty that your judgment on an aspect of life is true. Whether real or imagined, accurate or inaccurate, this belief is regarded by you as the truth. A belief that you cannot achieve your visualizations will affect the spiritual energy descending to limit or even negate any results.

You need to change the reasoning you assigned to a prior judgment that is preventing you from accepting a positive and certain feeling. Change the negative reasoning to a believable rationalization that makes the belief either inapplicable or positive and in agreement with your current visualizations. This changes the belief and thus changes any prohibitive emotion that you "don't deserve" the results.

When the "light" starts coming on strong, and it will, there is a natural tendency to feel you don't deserve it. Self destructive behavior is very common.

Remember to emotionally "Allow" your visualizations. You have to work at it. Justify it.

How to Eliminate Limiting Beliefs

A limiting belief is not thinking you can accomplish something. This holding back can be broken by seeing this belief as giving you a horrendous outcome and personal grief or pain from the failure. Decide to take action and substitute the limiting images with desired fabulous action images and see it bringing pleasure as if you are at a great party. The associated hold back feelings must be replaced with new linked positive feelings. Nothing changes unless new feelings are linked to the desired action.

When replacing old visualizations with new visualizations, scramble the old image, or destroy it by blowing it up or melting it. Then substitute it with a new desired pleasurable image coming out of a fog. also allow this image by positive reasoning and seeing yourself earning it and deserving it.

Many limiting beliefs about yourself are simply wrong. You may have accepted this belief because someone other than yourself has stated it to you. You may even know that it is not true but you accept it as true for various reasons.

Substitute this limiting painful feeling with a positive pleasurable feeling.

Visualizing to Change a Bad Habit

A bad habit is nothing more than a negative belief. There is an emotion in between the thought and the repetitive manifested "bad" action. It is an incorrect emotional attachment to this thought.

When you have bad habits you need to be serious about changing, you need lots of reasons and strong reasons. Eighty per cent of change is not the how but the why. The why is your new path of thought and action.

When you see yourself doing the wrong habit action, stop, and interrupt the thought. If it has proceeded to action stage, stop in the middle of the action. Consciously think of the reasons why you need to do a changed behavior, and substitute that new emotion along with a new visualization right then. Then after that, do the desired new action.

Disintegrate and dissolve a visualization of the habit as old and grungy and painful, and replace it with a beautiful new pleasurable image of the new desired outcome. Do this change from negative to positive visualization as it is done in the movies with a scene transition while feeling the good emotions changing to a positive as you change the action.

Talk to your subconscious self to change prior limiting beliefs and bad habits. To do this as a 100% effort, you need to recite a prepared paragraph or two. Write it down. Say it every morning upon waking and every night before sleeping. Or you could say it at every meal you before you eat. Keep it in your mind as much as possible. Then all of a sudden, it will be gone.

Reinforce

Repetition is the mother of all skill. This is reflective of the Yesod (foundation) sefirah, the last sefirot before descending into the physical action level.

Reinforcement is accomplished by repetition of visualizations to strengthen the conditioning of your mind. Do you ever find yourself waiting? Use that time for reinforcement.

Verification Log

When you start seeing results, write down the results in a journal as reinforcing proof to yourself that your visualizations are coming into action. Soon you will see yourself starting to live your desired movie.

LITTLE STEPS ADD UP

Spend at least half of your time, if not more, visualizing the steps along the way that you must make to realize your big vision. These smaller steps are much easier to visualize and implement into action.

Put the most important task at the top of your list and do it next. With each listed item put with it a time needed to complete and any materials needed. Gather all the materials and block out enough time so you will know there will be nothing preventing the accomplishment but you.

Reward yourself when you have finished an important milestone. Treat yourself to a fabulous celebratory meal in a great restaurant. Have a "talk time" about the milestone and about what went into accomplishing it. It works wonders on your subconscious (Pavlov's dog).

Set weekly objectives. Make them Sunday morning and such that they are reasonably possible to be completed in six days. Then six days later on the Sabbath, recall and celebrate the goals that you have accomplished in the past week.

> Thoughts lead to words, words lead to actions, actions lead to character, character leads to DESTINY.

Level 1 - Physical Action

Malkut means sovereignty. It's like you know that there is a king yet you have never seen him, but you see his power all around.

This is the results or action level. This is the realization of the sought after goal. The start of one's motivation to seek pleasure begins at Keter the top of the sefirot tree. The sefirot tree has gathered and executed effects to the influx as it descended from the top serfirah and ending at this final sefirah level Malkut.

The decent of this spiritual energy culminates into action, whether good or bad. This sefirah is feminine in nature for it is simply a culmination of receiving what has happened prior. It is the leaving of the womb of all the preceding sefirot. It is the revealed ending.

Berakah of Food

We are commanded to make a berakah regarding the food at a meal. A barakah is commonly translated as a blessing. This is a mistranslation. Typically a blessing is commonly thought to be someone imparting a spiritual quality to an object or person. A berakah is a "bending of the knee" to God in humility, by thanking and appreciating the meal and all that had to happen prior so that you could eat it. It is the appreciation all the labor and materials involved in the planting, the growing, the harvesting, the processing, the bringing to market, you buying, preparing and then you eating it. When you make a berakah at every meal, food will take on a totally different meaning for you.

Deut 8:10

וְאָכַלְתָּ וְשָׂבָעְתָּ וּבֵרַכְתָּ אֶת־יְהֹוָה אֱלֹהֶיךָ
and you eat / and you are satisfied / and you will bend knee / ihvh - that / your Elohim

עַל־הָאָרֶץ הַטֹּבָה אֲשֶׁר נָתַן־לָךְ:
to you - given which the good the land - upon

10 When thou hast eaten and art full, then thou shalt bless the LORD thy God for the good land which he hath given thee.

הִשָּׁמֶר לְךָ פֶּן־תִּשְׁכַּח אֶת־יְהוָה אֱלֹהֶיךָ
your Elohim ihvh - that you forget - thus to you be careful

לְבִלְתִּי שְׁמֹר מִצְוֺתָיו וּמִשְׁפָּטָיו וְחֻקֹּתָיו
and his decrees and his judgments his commandments he heeds to without

אֲשֶׁר אָנֹכִי מְצַוְּךָ הַיּוֹם:
the day commanding you I am which

11 Beware that thou forget not the LORD thy God, in not keeping his commandments, and his judgments, and his statutes, which I command thee this day:

פֶּן־תֹּאכַל וְשָׂבָעְתָּ וּבָתִּים טֹבִים תִּבְנֶה וְיָשָׁבְתָּ:
and you settle you build best ones and houses and you satisfied you eat - thus

12 Lest when thou hast eaten and art full, and hast built goodly houses, and dwelt therein;

וּבְקָרְךָ וְצֹאנְךָ יִרְבְּיֻן
they multiply and your flock and your cattle

וְכֶסֶף וְזָהָב יִרְבֶּה־לָּךְ וְכֹל אֲשֶׁר־לְךָ יִרְבֶּה:
it multiplied to you - which and all to you - it increases and gold and silver

13 And when thy herds and thy flocks multiply, and thy silver and thy gold is multiplied, and all that thou hast is multiplied;

וְרָם לְבָבֶךָ וְשָׁכַחְתָּ אֶת־יְהוָה אֱלֹהֶיךָ
your Elohim ihvh - that and you forget your heart and high

הַמּוֹצִיאֲךָ מֵאֶרֶץ מִצְרַיִם מִבֵּית עֲבָדִים:
slaveries from house Egypt form land your bringer out

14 Then thine heart be lifted up, and thou forget the LORD thy God, which brought thee forth out of the land of Egypt, from the house of bondage;

הַמּוֹלִיכְךָ בַּמִּדְבָּר הַגָּדֹל וְהַנּוֹרָא
and the awesome the great in wilderness the one leading you

נָחָשׁ שָׂרָף וְעַקְרָב וְצִמָּאוֹן אֲשֶׁר אֵין־מָיִם
waters - isn't where and drought and scorpion venomous snake

הַמּוֹצִיא לְךָ מַיִם מִצּוּר הַחַלָּמִישׁ:
the flint from rock water to you the bringer out

15 Who led thee through that great and terrible wilderness, wherein were fiery serpents, and scorpions, and drought, where there was no water; who brought thee

forth water out of the rock of flint;

הַמַּאֲכִלְךָ מָן בַּמִּדְבָּר אֲשֶׁר לֹא־יָדְעוּן אֲבֹתֶיךָ
your fathers   he knew - not   which   in wilderness   manna   the feeder of you

לְמַעַן עַנֹּתְךָ וּלְמַעַן נַסֹּתֶךָ לְהֵיטִבְךָ בְּאַחֲרִיתֶךָ׃
in your afterwards   to do you good   prove to you   and to end   humbled you   to end

16 Who fed thee in the wilderness with manna, which thy fathers knew not, that he might humble thee, and that he might prove thee, to do thee good at thy latter end;

וְאָמַרְתָּ בִּלְבָבֶךָ כֹּחִי וְעֹצֶם יָדִי עָשָׂה לִי אֶת־הַחַיִל הַזֶּה׃
the this   the wealth - that   to me   done   my hand   and strength   my power   in your heart   and you say

17 And thou say in thine heart, My power and the might of mine hand hath gotten me this wealth.

וְזָכַרְתָּ אֶת־יְהוָה אֱלֹהֶיךָ
your Elohim   ihvh - that   and you remember

כִּי הוּא הַנֹּתֵן לְךָ כֹּחַ לַעֲשׂוֹת חָיִל
wealth   to produce   power   to you   the giver   he   like

לְמַעַן הָקִים אֶת־בְּרִיתוֹ
his covenant - that   establishing   to end

אֲשֶׁר־נִשְׁבַּע לַאֲבֹתֶיךָ כַּיּוֹם הַזֶּה׃
the this   like day   to your fathers   he swore - which

18 But thou shalt remember the LORD thy God: for it is he that giveth thee power to get wealth, that he may establish his covenant which he sware unto thy fathers, as it is this day.

וְהָיָה אִם־שָׁכֹחַ תִּשְׁכַּח אֶת־יְהוָה אֱלֹהֶיךָ
your Elohim   ihvh - that   you forget   forget - if   and it will be

וְהָלַכְתָּ אַחֲרֵי אֱלֹהִים אֲחֵרִים
other ones   elohim   after   and you walk

וַעֲבַדְתָּם וְהִשְׁתַּחֲוִיתָ לָהֶם
to them   and you worship   and serve them

הַעִדֹתִי בָכֶם הַיּוֹם כִּי אָבֹד תֹּאבֵדוּן׃
you will perish   perish   like   the day   in you   I the testify

19 And it shall be, if thou do at all forget the LORD thy God, and walk after other gods, and serve them, and worship them, I testify against you this day that ye shall surely perish.

כַּגּוֹיִם אֲשֶׁר יְהוָה מַאֲבִיד מִפְּנֵיכֶם
from before you   destroyed   ihvh   which   like nations

LEVEL 1 - PHYSICAL ACTION

146

כֵּן תֹּאבֵדוּן	עֵקֶב	לֹא	תִשְׁמְעוּן	בְּקוֹל	יְהֹוָה	אֱלֹהֵיכֶם:
thus you will perish	reason	not	you heeded	in voice	ihvh	your Elohim

20 As the nations which the LORD destroyeth before your face, so shall ye perish; because ye would not be obedient unto the voice of the LORD your God.

In the higher interpretations of these verses the meaning is seen as an allegory applying to any wealth gained from the labors of others in the land in which you have been satisfied by. Whenever you feel satisfied from what you are experiencing, give a berakah or an acknowledgment of thanks to the creator of the universe for the fabulous orchestration coming together for you.

Be Grateful

You want to attract more? The law of increase is based on you thanking and praising the good you have. It changes your perceptions to positive. What you thank about, you bring more about. And it all starts with food....

> One should say 100 barakas a day so that 10 will nourish to your Ruach (middle) soul and 1 will nourish to your Neshama (higher) soul.

Soul Development

The Souls of a Person

Every person at birth has the capacity of obtaining five souls. From the bottom to the top they are; Nefesh, Ruach, Neshamah, Chiyah, and Yechidah. They translate as Rest, Wind, Breath, Life-Force, and Singular. At present the upper worlds of Chiyah and Yechidah are generally inaccessible. These levels are the top levels involving prophesy and enlightenment. Therefore generally, Kabbalah texts refer to the workings of the three lower levels; Nefesh, Ruach, and Neshamah. Each person must master each of their souls to achieve completion or fulfillment of their soul and their life's destiny.

Acquiring Souls

All of these three souls are not acquired at one time. When one is born, he or she is has a Nefesh soul. Around puberty, at the end of the thirteenth year of a young man, a Ruach soul will enter him. This is why a bar mitzvah is performed at a boy's thirteenth year. In time if he is worthy and has completed his twentieth year, his Neshamah soul will enter him (Zohar, Mishpatim 94b). Heavenly judgements are not made against a person until he or she has completed their 20th year.

When a person is born, his first soul consist only of a Nefesh soul which controls the body. A person acquires the other completed souls of Ruach and Neshama, only if he or she is sufficiently developed spiritually. However, if a person has not developed and does not complete and rectify his first Nefesh soul, a Ruach soul will not develop in him. If during one's lifetime one has not rectified their first Nefesh soul, he will reincarnate and come back to rectify this Nefesh soul before he can rectify the next additional soul of Ruach. One must then rectify the Ruach soul to finally be able to complete the rectification of the final Neshama soul. When he rectifies the Neshama soul he can achieve completeness or fulfillment, and he will not have to reincarnate.

In rectifying a soul one must correct blemishes from incorrect actions that are associated with the various ten sefirot of that soul level. There is no order in rectifying the sefirot on that level. Only if one is very spiritual can he acquire all three souls and rectify them in the first incarnation. If one only rectified his Nefesh soul, he will have to reincarnate to rectify his next higher soul. Subsequent reincarnations can only rectify one soul. Many non-spiritual people take numerous lifetimes to rectify one soul.

The Developmental Levels

We are born to accomplish a spiritual objective in our lifetime. This can be seen when someone is powerfully drawn to a particular mitzvah (good deed or duty) or a cause or job, and made it the focus of his or her entire life's work.

There are actually four developmental levels each having a sefirot tree. As one progresses spiritually in one's lifetime, he or she ascends from the first sefirah tree and on to another sefirah tree at the next higher developmental level. These four levels reflect the levels of creation; Atzilut, Beriyah, Yetzirah, and Assiya. Generally theses reflect the stages in life as adolescence, pairing of male and female and having small children, mid age, and old age.

One has to learn the lessons relating to the sefirot of a developmental level before he or she matures from that level and climbs up the next developmental level's sefirot tree. There is an endless amount to learn at each level.

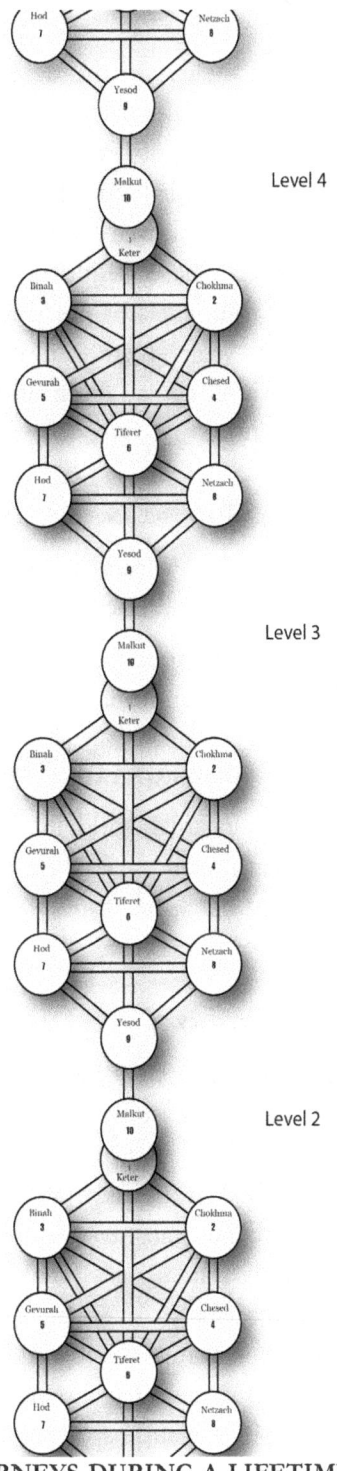

40 JOURNEYS DURING A LIFETIME

42 Journeys

Just like the Israelites in the desert took 42 journeys during their 38 years in the wilderness (the forty year sentence was shortened by two years), so too each person takes 42 journeys in their lifetime (Baal Shem Tov). Besides birth and death journeys, there are 40 journeys towards a person's promised land, or the completion of his lifetime spiritual purpose. These 40 journeys are divided into four sets of ten mirroring the four levels of creation and the four major ageing cycles of a persons life. Each Keter sefirah from a lower level overlaps and transitions into the Malkut sefirah on the next higher level as depicted in the illustration.

The Last of the 42 Journeys - Death

"And the dust returns to the earth as it was, and the spirit returns to God, who gave it.." Kohelet (Ecclesiastes)

After death, one's soul detaches from the body and it goes either to Gan Eden to Gehinnom, or to Shoel.

Gan Eden (the "Garden of Eden", or Paradise)

Gan Eden is a spiritual world, inhabited by souls without physical bodies. After death, your mitzvot and positive actions will be your exquisite pleasure in Gan Eden forever. From there one will enter other worlds and dimensions.

Gehinnom ("Purgatory")

One's destructiveness of his actions through his lapses and transgressions in this world are rectified by his going through the excruciating pain of Gehinnom. One minute will seem like an hour of torture. If one has been extremely evil because of severe violations of the *Torah*, before entering into Gehinnom, that person may first be reincarnated as an animal or a plant. However, once he enters into Gehinnom, the sages say even the most wicked of souls (a few exceptions) experience at most twelve months in Gehinnom. This is followed by either reincarnating again, or by a life detached of reincarnation in Gan Eden if that time spent in Gehinnom has rectified his last soul.

The effects of Gehinnom can be mitigated by the good actions of one's children. After death the soul of a parent continues to watch over the lives of his/her children more deeply and more meaningfully than before.

Sheol & Reincarnation (Gilgul neshamot)

Sheol is a gathering place of all the deceased souls, a waiting place before reincarnation. One must fulfill his or her designated spiritual purpose while living on earth. If one doesn't succeed in doing this during one's lifetime, he or she must reincarnate to perfect all his souls.

The overwhelming majority of us are reincarnated souls and have returned to earth to perfect the imperfections left from a previous lifetime. A "new" soul is a rarity.

The World to Come (Ha Olam HaBa)

When one is reincarnated he brings with him the souls he perfected in his last life and reincarnates at a root sefirah in his highest acquired soul. This is a very complicated area involving things like another soul entering a person to help, or one soul being attached to two different bodies, etc. Male and female reincarnations are different (reincarnations are mostly about men).

The period of reincarnations will end at some point. At some time in the future of existence a person's body will be regenerated and restored to him because the World to Come will be a physical world, inhabited by souls with physical bodies.

The world as we know it will be destroyed before the Hebrew calendar year 6000 according to the many ancient texts. In April 2012 the Hebrew calendar year was 5772. In our highly nuclear armed violent civilization and with severe global changes this doomsday prediction seems very plausible with including the words "before the year 6000."

The destruction of the physical world as we know it will be replaced by a new existence, a physical world, which is referred to as the World to Come. "Death will be eradicated forever" and "the world will be filled with the knowledge of God as the water covers the seas."

Tasting the World to Come

Through tzeruf meditation and a great spiritual lifestyle, one enters the advanced dream states. These dreams become constant and more vivid. Their meanings become clear and questions asked are answered. Eventually during sleep, one breaks through the Rakia, to a higher dimension similar to the world to come.

Aliens?

In many places the *Bible* talks about the Nephilim and their descendents. The direct English translation for Nephilim is "the ones that fell" (from the sky) [the descendents of Shamchazi and Azael, who fell in the generation of Enosh]. They have various names in the *Bible*. The Anakim, descended from Anak (Numbers 13:28). The Rephaim, descended from Rapha. There were the Zamzummims, the Emims, the Avims, etc.

The offspring of these Nephilim were giants that stood as high as 13 feet tall. The height of the average man living in those times was 5'6". These giants were the most decadent of people. Og was a prominent figure who ruled the kingdom Bashan, called the land of the giants. The bed of Og was was 18 feet long, and 8 feet wide (Deut 3:11).

King David ran and knocked down to the ground a giant named Goliath (approximately 11 feet in height). There were many giants in the land of Canaan and that is why most of the spies advised the Israelites not to conquer the land, and hence God's decree of not permitting the Israelites to enter their promised land till all men of that generation who were of fighting age died (38 years).

The Tzeruf Tables

Intro to the Meditations

When is the best time to meditate? Your meditations should reflect what the daily temple sacrifices were when the holy temple stood. One sacrifice was done in the morning and one sacrifice was done in the evening. Further on the sabbath and holidays an extra sacrifice was done in addition to the two regular daily sacrifices. So your meditation schedule should be similar.

Morning. The best time to do tzeruf meditation is at sunrise in the morning when you first get up. This effect is what you need to infuse your day. As soon as you get up, wash your hands to remove negative energies. Make yourself something hot or cold to drink to help you wake up while you are doing your meditations. It's a great way to start your day. After finishing, recite your prepared paragraph and do your visualizations of your desired future.

Nighttime. The second best time in the day to meditate is before you go to sleep. This also is an excellent time to do relaxation yoga. Doing these things at this time greatly increases your chances of having vivid dreams that impart meanings with them.

Midnight. The long magnetic plume from the earth is formed because of the sun's photons hitting the earth. This makes the magnetic field opposite the sun about five times stronger at midnight. Since ancient times the sages have said that one's spiritual awareness is the greatest at the midnight hour. Psalm 111 has traditionally been said at midnight and is an included psalm for those who rise at midnight to do meditation or *Torah* study.

Other Times. There are days and times that are most conducive to your prayers, meditations and study. These are based on solar, lunar and personal influences. However any time is a great time to meditate and pray. For certain and positive results do it consistently, every day.

Time Allotted

According to Rabbi Nachman, one should spend the morning praying and meditating before starting the day. He stated one must be very diligent and accustom himself to spending at least **one hour** in the morning in such meditations. He stated that following this meditation session, the rest of the day will then be a state of joy and ecstasy for you.

Make sure you have allotted the amount of time needed to fully complete your meditations and without any interruptions.

Direction to Face

When doing your meditations you should face east where the sun rises and the upper and lower energies of nature start to infuse into the world. This natural release of energies is a reason that the best time to meditate is in the early dawn hours as you experience the sun coming up.

Vowel sounds

There are two ways to pronounce vowels in meditations;

1. Natural vowel sound

In Tzeruf meditations when no vowel pointings are depicted under the Hebrew letter, one has to know which vowel sound he or she should say with the letter in order to pronounce the letter. A letters natural vowel sound is the first vowel sound that is vocalized when saying the letter's name. For an Alef the natural vowel sound is assigned an "ah." For a Bet the natural vowel sound would be an "eh." Gimel would be "ih." The same goes for the rest of the alphabet letters.

2. Notareikoon

נוֹטָרִיקוּן Notareikoon is the name for the procedure of vowel permutations. This is where the five different vowel sounds are depicted under an alphabet letter by permutation. This vowel permutation method is permuted in some tzeruf meditations in addition to the permutations of the letters. A word or name contains the vowels according to those designated by way of vowel permutations.

Consonant sounds

When doing tzeruf meditation, the consonant sound is to be the main emphasis. It should be drawn out longer than the vowel sound being used with it. The ratio of time drawing out the consonant sound verses drawing out the attached vowel sound would be somewhere between 75%/25% to 66%/33%. Do what is comfortable. What is important is to accent the consonants in time and in volume. This is in line with the male/female principal. [Advanced] (Demut, male, of Chomer, substance, and the vowel is Tzurah, female form and spiritual force acting upon the Chomer).

Remember the Yod, Alef and Ayin are consonants even though their consonant sound is like that of a vowel. For example the natural vowel sound of an Yod is "yee" so one would pronounce and draw out the Yod consonant "yee" sound, take a slight pause and then pronounce it's natural vowel "oh." If in a meditation a hiruk, "eeh" sound is to be the attached vowel on a Yod consonant, pronounce the "yee" sound of the consonant Yod, take a slight pause, then pronounce the "eeh" sound of the attached vowel, hiruk. If as you do this you run both sounds together it doesn't really matter. But try to make the sound as long in time as you would another letter sound combined with it's vowel sound.

The consonant sound for the Alef is "ah." In the Hebrew grammar the Aleph is actually a silent consonant and all that is pronounced when read is the vowel sound that is accompanying it. However in tzeruf meditation the consonant sound is an "ah," and the natural vowel sound is an "ah." This reasoning can be seen by using the "ah" vowel sound place holder as the natural vowel of Alef; it's meaning is then one. Using the "eh" as the vowel sound placeholder would make it's meaning be 1,000.

When doing tzeruf meditation with the Alef, one needs to distinguish the difference between the consonant "ah" and the natural vowel "ah" by putting a brief pause between the two "ah" sounds, i.e. "ah, ah."

The consonant sound for the Ayin is "ay." The natural vowel sound for Ayin is the next sound an "eeh."

Be sure to watch for the Khet. It's appearance is close to that of a Heh. Don't look at it casually and pronounce it as a Heh. And remember to make it's sound very guttural (see Hebrew pronunciation).

Letter Sounds with their Natural Vowels

א   Alef = ah   The **Aleph**. Being a place holder consonant for a vowel, the natural vowel sound is also given an "ah" sound.

ב   Bet = be   The **Bet** for meditation purposes is pronounced with the "beh" sound even though in conversational speaking it can sometimes be pronounced "veh."

ג   Gimel = gi

ד   Dalet = da

ה   Heh = hae

ו   Vav = vah

ז   Zayin = za

ח   Khet = khae   The **Khet** is a guttural sound much like a cat's angry hiss with a low tone. It's like a Heh with a low deep throat guttural roll.

ט   Tet = tae

Standard Vocalizations of tables

Hebrew is read from right to left, the opposite of English. The meditation tables are also read, starting at the top right, from right to left, and continuing the same on the next line and down the page.

When a cell of a table containing two letters, there should be four sounds. Two for the first consonant and it's attached vowel, and two for the second consonant and it's attached vowel sound. There are two ways of breathing with this vocalization.

The first is to vocalize the first consonant and it's vowel sound with one exhaled breath. That would be 75% of the breath would be pronouncing the consonant sound and 25% would be pronouncing the vowel sound. Then the same is done with the second letter in the cell.

The second way is to vocalize both consonants and their attached vowel sounds in one exhaled breath. This allots half an exhaled breath to each consonant and it's attached vowel. The consonants still should be emphasized and a ratio close to 75%/25% should be maintained.

The breathing is regulated by the continuous discipline of the vocalizing of each cell of the tables in a rhythmic manner. One breathes at the same constant pace throughout the tables as they vocalize. Breathe comfortably. The pace should be consistent while making sure to clearly enunciate the letters and the vowels.

On tables where a name is seeded with the shem hamephorish like on the 72 names table, one can try to emphasize the consonants of the name being seeded as much as possible. Since one is making so many sounds in a single exhalation the main priority should be on clearly enunciating all of the consonant sounds.

Vocalizations for the Seeded Shem Hamephorash

The Abulafia method applies the natural vowel sounds to all consonant letters in cells that do not have assigned vowels through a notakeikoon permutation. Under his basic system seeded letters of the shem hamephorash also use their natural vowel sounds. The sounds that are the most important and essential are the consonant sounds.

In more advanced meditations ehieh (אהי״ה) and other names

י	Yod = yo	the "y" sound is the consonant sound and the "o" is the natural vowel sound.
כ	Caf = ka	The **Caf** is pronounced two different ways, one soft and one hard. When meditating pronounce it as a hard sound Ka as in Cafe.
ל	Lamed = la	
מ	Mem = mei	
נ	Nun = nu	
ס	Samec = sa	
ע	Ayin = ayi	The **Ayin**. The a and the y sound "ay" as the first consonant. These two sounds are said together. The following "eeh" sound would be the natural vowel sound.
פ	Pe = pae	
צ	Tzadi = tza	The **Tzadi**. The t and the z are pronounced at the same time as one sound, "tz."
ק	Kuf = ku	

are also used for seeding. Further there are special vocal pointings for the shem hamephorash depending on a sefirah targeted, current lunar month, and so on. Also there are advanced meditations when the order of the letters are also permuted during the seeding.

The last table of the 72 names has an advanced pointing to the names that is found in many ancient texts. An example of an advance meditation when the seeding the shem hamephorash has special pointing instead of using the natural vowels, would be;

יְהֹוָה (Malkut)

Separator Phrase

Your inhaled breath between your exhalation vocalizing is regarded as a separator. Generally sages of old when vocalizing cells that contain many letters like the one depicted in the 72 names meditation would use a separator phrase (tashegiviva toveda yah tzuruva). This is helpful by telling the subconscious mind of the separate sections.

The subconscious mind will more easily recognize and reorganize the sections into sentences using the mind's logical and creative hemispheres. This is part of the process of the creation of the influx energy.

Stilling the Mind

After doing the tzeruf vocalizations for many sessions, they will start to have a boring feel to them. This is what places the mind in a meditative "no thinking" state. Don't try to think of anything while vocalizing. This quieting state of mind (boring) lets the letter visualizations and letter and vowel sounds into the subconscious. One gets used to it after a while and accepts it.

Advanced Breathing

There are advanced ways of breathing while vocalizing. An example method is called Khedvah breathing. This is done by breathing in for 8 counts, holding it for 4, exhaling while vocalizing for 6 counts, then holding the exhale for 5 counts. This ratio is based on the first verse of the Shema prayer and found echoed in numerous other verses in the *Bible*.

ר   Resh = rae

שׁ   Shin = shi   The **Shin** can be pronounced as Sin if the dot is on the top left of the letter. In tzeruf meditation the shin is pronounced as if the dot was at the top right of the letter and thus the "sh" sound is used.

ת   Tav = ta

DIFFERENT PRONUNCIATIONS

There are different dialects or ways to pronounce the Hebrew alphabet. There is the dialects of the Ashkenazi, the Sephardi, the Moroccan. Tzeruf meditation natural vowel sounds goes by the pronunciations made by the different parts of the mouth as described in Sefer Yitzerah. Abulafia in his books also follows this method of pronunciation.

Another advanced way is to breathe in 2 units of time, hold your breath for 8 units of time, then vocalize as you breathe out for 4 units of time. The ratio is 1:4:2 (2:8:4). This is to be done at whatever pace is most comfortable. After a while these breathing ratios become ones natural breathing while vocalizing.

Mistakes

Restate the letters in the box if you make a mistake. Abulafia suggests if you have made a mistake in a cell, you should go to the beginning of the line of cells that you are at in the table, and restart the vocalizations from the beginning of that line. This advice is found to be necessary when used in conjunction with the ultimate meditation where one has memorized the table and is mentally visualizing the all letters.

Pointer

To keep track where you currently are in the meditation tables, you may need to have is a pointer like a pen keeping track of your current cell location.

Head movements

Head movements help further align the physical level with the meditations. There are five directions in which one moves their head.

As an example when pronouncing a Cholam vowel you will begin with your head positioned normal, facing east, raise your head

Cholam	Begin straight ahead and move head upwards
Kametz	Begin with head close to right shoulder and move to left till the chin is close to the left shoulder
Tzereh	Begin with head close to left shoulder and move to right till the chin is close to the right shoulder
Chirik	Begin straight ahead and lower head downward like a bow
Shurek	Begin head in natural upright position. Move head directly forward

slowly while vocalizing the sounds until you complete exhaling the breath. Your ending position of your head will be facing upwards and you will have exhaled all your breath. Then inhale and return your head to the normal position of looking straight ahead.

Do not breathe more than one extra breath between head movements. But between cell rows in a table you can breathe two extra breaths only, no more. After completing a table, you are permitted to breathe five breaths only, no more. It's best to breathe as little as possible between cells, rows, and tables.

A variance on the head positions, several sages state to always start with the face forward, then move to the prescribed direction. This means the head movements for the Kametz and the Tzereh would not start at one shoulder and end at the other shoulder. Instead one would start by looking straight ahead then move to the designated direction ending at the shoulder.

IMAGINATION

For tzeruf meditation to be done to the max, one needs to visualize mentally (not with the eyes) each letter of the shem hamephorish that is seeded. In the meditation of the 72 names as an example, one seeds a letter by visualizing mentally the first letter of the shem hamephorish while vocalizing it, then one gazes with his eyes at the first letter of one of the names in a cell and vocalizes it. Then one visualizes the next seeded letter of the shem hamephorish and vocalizes it, and thus repeating this process till one has done this to all the letters necessary for the completion of the seeding of the name in the cell. This visualizing method using the imagination is facilitated by the included tables that have a space between letters.

Of course the ultimate max is memorizing all of the 72 names and mentally visualizing all letters of the names and all the seeding letters while simultaneously vocalizing.

The galgal square method of meditation is typically used with visualizations of the alphabet letters from memory alone. If one is seeding a galgal square cell one visualizes the appropriate letter of the shem hamephorish letters between the two letters of a cell.

In the view of the famous Maimonides, obtaining any level of prophecy must involve an imaginative component. This facilitates the manifesting of prophecy images in the mind.

Applying Musical Tones

While doing the tzeruf vocalizations one may use tonal notes as one would use in a musical score. This helps relieve the boredom of a lengthy meditation and seems to increase it's effectiveness. This also helps tune your voice and stimulates the Daat, or bridge between mental and physical. It is a great way to disguise a meditation. People see that you are tuning your voice and not know you are doing a meditation. Your singing will also become excellent.

One example would be vocalizing the letters and their applied vowels using a vocal range from the lowest of your possible vocal tones to the your highest possible. Play a simple progression of notes up and down with one hand on the piano while vocalizing. Before transitioning to the next seeded word cell, play a major chord of the key you are leaving, move up a half step on the keyboard, then play the major chord of the key you are about to play next. Then again play the melodic progression in the new key while vocalizing the next seeded cell.

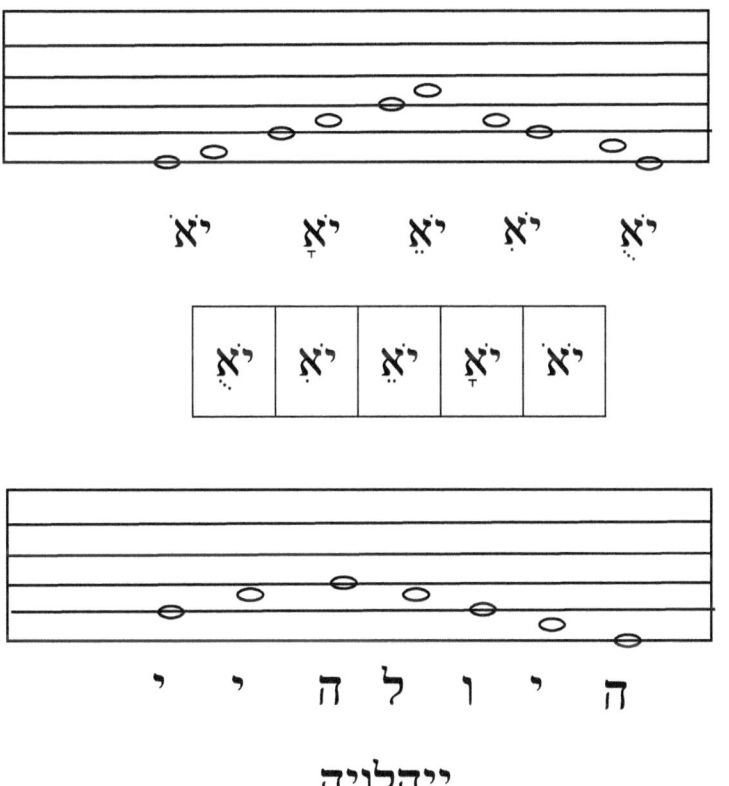

Putting in the Time

Have a minimum standard amount of different meditations that you do in a session in case you feel tired or are rushed. Try to do more than that amount every session.

At a minimum one should strive to do a session in the morning upon waking. Actually anytime is fine but you should do, at a minimum of one session during each day to produce results.

Your results are proportional to the time you spend in your meditations. It is work and requires discipline to be consistent. The more time you put in the more the results you will receive. The results come as opportunities. Be ready to recognize them. Many times you will recognize after the fact that you missed out on an opportunity. There will be times where a pure gift comes to you. Don't rest like the hare did in the hare/tortoise story. More than likely it's an opportunity that needs to be capitalized on.

Time Needed to Complete Meditations

Galgal sq - Alone

462 letter pairs (21 x 22) x 3 sec   **= 25 min**

Galgal sq - with IHVH

Forward 462 x 3 seconds each x 4 (יהוה) **= 1 ½ hr**
Reversed   **= 1 ½ hr**

Galgal Triangle

231 pairs x 3 sec = 12 min x 4 (יהוה) **= 50 min**
231 pairs Seeded x 4 sec = 15 min x 4 (יהוה) **= 1 hr**

IHVH w/ Aleph - slowly w/ head movements

50 pairs x 8 sec = 400 sec x 4 letters (יהוה), **= 25 min**

IHVH w/ Aleph - moderate speed (one breath a letter)

50 pairs x 5 sec = 250 sec x 4 letters (יהוה), **= 15 min**

IHVH w/ Aleph - lively pace

50 pairs x 2 sec = 100 sec x 4 letters (יהוה), **= 7 min**

72 names Seeded

72 x 10 sec + (tashegeviva phrase)   **= 12 min**

72 names Seeded

72 x 10 sec + (tashegeviva phrase)   **= 12 min**

72 Angels

72 names x 21 sec)   **= 25 min**

Old Kabbalists

462 pairs x 3 letters HaVaYaH יהוה **= 30 min**

Preliminary Prayers

Preliminary prayers are said to "clear the air." According to the book *Gates of Light*, *Zohar* and other Kabbalah books, there are spirits roaming in the area between the earthly dimension and the heavenly dimension. These spirits are characterized as being insecure spirits that roam like gangs that are average to very bad. When one says prayers, the spiritual essence of the prayers floats up to heaven. These initial words are blocked or partially blocked by some of these roaming spirits. By saying several prayers, it becomes too painful for these spirits to be in the area. And thus the path to heaven opens up, clearing the path for your prayers from any interference from these bad spirits. The *Gates of Light* states that King David made the Psalms for the purpose of penetrating this middle realm.

The great kabbalist Rabbi Nachman, stressed that before praying one should dedicate their prayers and hence their tzeruf meditations to a deceased *Torah* or Kabbalah sage. This deceased sage exists in another dimension. This past scholar is better able to direct and use the prayers in a way that is best needed even if it does not help the person praying at that time. Later when the person dedicating his prayers needs something, then the sage will reciprocate by helping the dedicator in an area that benefits him the most.

Dedication

The dedication in this book is written to Rabbi Abulafia who proliferated this method of meditation. One may substitute any learned sage or sages of their choosing.

Vital Prayer

Rabbi Vital wrote this as a preparation prayer to say before saying the 72 Names meditation.

Song of Sea Prayer

This is what Rabbi Vital recommends also to say before starting the 72 name tzeruf meditation. It is what the Israelites sung after they crossed the sea and saw Pharaoh's army had drowned.

Prophesy Psalm

If this Psalm is said daily, it will bring a worthy person closer to the state of prophesy.

Midnight Psalm

This is traditionally said by those who go to bed at nightfall and wake up at midnight to say prayers, then study the *Torah* or *Talmud* until they fall asleep. The *Written Torah* is aligned with the day, and the *Oral Torah* or *Talmud* is aligned with the night. Studying with an alignment strengthens the learning and brings more influx down than would otherwise happen.

Shortest Psalm

This was included for one to have a quick powerful prayer.

Shema Prayer

This is the traditional prayer said daily, in the morning and in the evening, as further elaborated on in the Talmud.

Supplication.

After you are finished praying and meditating be prepared to include a supplication. Remember to ask for what you want. In order to remember exactly what you want, you need to write down or memorize a paragraph or two. Also when doing visualizations for the future make sure that you see yourself in the picture and feel the pressures and pleasures of what your desired life will be like.

Dedication

Always dedicate your prayers and meditations. It is also a great time to set aside a Charity Donation before Praying and/or Meditating.

הֲרֵינִי   מְקַשֵׁר עַצְמִי בַּאֲמִירַת אֵלֶּה
here certainly I attach myself in words these

לְרַבֵּנוּ אַבְרָהָם אָבוּלָעְפִיָּה בֶּן שְׁמוּאֵל
to our rabbi Abraham Abulafia son Samuel

וּלְכָל הַצַּדִּיקִים שֶׁבְּדוֹרֵנוּ
to all the pious ones that in our generation

וּלְכָל הַצַּדִּיקִים כִּי אֶל־עָפָר שָׁבוּ׃
and to all the pious ones like unto - dust they returned

RABBI VITAL PRAYER

בָּרוּךְ יהוה אֲשֶׁר נָתַן חָכְמָה לִירֵאָיו הַמַּמְשִׁיל אֶת

that   the governor   to his fearing   wisdom   gives   which   ihvh   bless

הָאָדָם בְּיִרְאָתוֹ וּמַצִּיל נַפְשׁוֹת חֲסִידָיו אֲשֶׁר בְּיָדוֹ

in his hand   which   his pious   souls   who saves   in his fear   the man

נֶפֶשׁ כָּל חַי. הַמְנַחֵם בְּרֹב חֲסָדָיו הַמַּסְתִּיר וְחוֹסֶה

and who relies   the protector   his compassion   in much   the shower   life   all   soul

בְּצִלּוֹ הַמַּשְׁאִיר פְּלֵטָה לְהַחֲיוֹת, הַחוֹנֵן אֶת עֲבָדָיו

his servant   that   the pardoned   to the animals   mystical   the leaves   in shadow

חָכְמָה וּבִינָה וָדַעַת וְהַשְׂכֵּל לְדַבֵּר עִם אָדָם

Adam   with   to speak   and the intelligence   and knowing   and understanding   wise

וּבַהֲמָה וְעִם חַיָּה וְעוֹפוֹת וְדָגִים וָרֶמֶשׂ. לְהוֹדִיעַ

to honor   and insect   and fish   and birds   animals   and with   and beast

כֹּחֲךָ וְרֹב גְּבוּרָתְךָ. בָּרוּךְ וּמְבֹרָךְ שִׁמְךָ וּמְרוֹמָם

and lofty   your name   and is blessed   bless   your strength   and much   your strength

עַל כָּל בְּרָכָה וּתְהִלָּה שִׁמְךָ. כִּי שִׁמְךָ בָּךְ,

in you   your name   like   your name   and pray   who bless   all   upon

וּבְךָ מְהַדֵּר שִׁמְךָ, וּמִשִּׁמְךָ יִרְעֲשׁוּ הַכֹּל. אוֹפַנִּים

Ofanayim   the all   tremble   and from your name   your name   adorns   and in you

וּכְרוּבִים וּגְדוּדִים מְפָאֲרִים שִׁמְךָ. וְאַתָּה מַאֲזִין

from listening   and you   your name   praising   and battalions   and Cherubim

שִׁמְךָ וְשׁוֹמֵעַ שִׁירָה מִפִּי כָּל צְבָא עֶלְיוֹנִים

upper worlds   forces   all   from my mouth   song   and heeding   your name

וּמַקְשִׁיב שֶׁבַח וּתְהִלָּה מִפִּי כָּל חֲיָלֵי תַחְתּוֹנִים.

under ones   forces   all   from mouth   and prayer   praise   and listening

וְאַתָּה אֱלֹהַּ כָּל בְּרִיּוֹת וְאָדוֹן כָּל נְפָשׁוֹת בּוֹרֵא כָּל

all   creator   nafshot   all   and Adon   creatures   all   these   and you

רוּחוֹת יוֹצֵר כָּל נְשָׁמוֹת. גִּבּוֹר וְלֹא יִתַּם כֹּחוֹ,

his power   fail   and not   hero   souls   all   forming   ruchot

יָחִיד בְּעוֹלָצוֹ יוֹשֵׁב עַל כִּסְאוֹ בִּמְקוֹמוֹ שָׁרוּי בְּסִתְרֵי

in high   songs   in his place   his throne   upon   he sits   in his world   only

PRELIMINARY PRAYERS

הֵיכָל גָּבֹהַּ וּמַלְאָכִים מְשָׁרְתָיו, וְשָׂרְפֵי
לֶהָבָה וְגַלְגַּלֵּי הַמֶּרְכָּבָה וְאוֹפַנֵּי צְבָאָיו וּמַחֲנוֹת
מַלְאֲכֵי אֵשׁ סוֹבְלִים וּמִתְקַדְּשִׁים בְּנַהֲרוֹת אֵשׁ.
וּרְבָבוֹת בְּצִבְאוֹת שֶׁלֶג הַמְשׁוֹרְרִים בְּכָל כְּלֵי
שִׁיר, וְהַמַּנְעִימִים בְּכָל כְּלֵי שִׁיר, וְהַמְנַגְּנִים
בְּכִנּוֹרוֹת וּבִנְבָלִים וְחַיּוֹת עוֹמְסוֹת כִּסְאוֹ וְתִפְאֶרֶת
מְעוֹנוֹ. וְכֻלָּם בְּפֶה אֶחָד וּבְשָׂפָה אַחַת וּבְלָשׁוֹן
בָּרוּר וּבְחֵךְ עָרֵב וּבְגָרוֹן טָהוֹר וּבְלֵב נָקִי
וּבְקוֹמָה גְּחוּנָה וּבְכֹבֶד רֹאשׁ, וְנוֹתְנִים מְלוּכָה
לְמֶלֶךְ מַלְכֵי הַמְּלָכִים מַמְלִיךְ מְלָכִים וּמֵסִיר מְלָכִים
וּמַלְכוּתוֹ קַיֶּמֶת לָעַד וּמֶמְשַׁלְתּוֹ עוֹמֶדֶת לָנֶצַח.
וְהוּא חַי וְקַיָּם לְעוֹלָם וּלְעוֹלְמֵי עוֹלָמִים.
וַאֲנִי פְּלוֹנִי בֶּן פְּלוֹנִית אֲמָתֶךָ, עָפָר וָאֵפֶר, רִמָּה
וְתוֹלֵעָה, נְכֵה לֵב, וּשְׁפַל רוּחַ, צֵל עוֹבֵר וְצִיץ
נוֹבֵל. בָּטוּחַ בְּרַחֲמֶיךָ
וּבַחֲסָדֶיךָ בָּאתִי לְהַפִּיל תְּחִנָּתִי לְפָנֶיךָ
וּלְהַמְצִיא רַחֲמִים בְּשִׁמְךָ כִּי

אַתָּה קָרוֹב לְקוֹרְאֶיךָ עֲשֵׂה שְׁאֵלָתִי וּמַהֵר
   and tomorrow   my question   do   to your voice   close   you

בַּקָּשָׁתִי כִּי אַתָּה יְצַרְתַּנִי.
   it troubles me   you   like   I request

PRELIMINARY PRAYERS

Song of Sea End

Exodus Chapter 15

אָז יָשִׁיר־מֹשֶׁה וּבְנֵי יִשְׂרָאֵל אֶת־הַשִּׁירָה הַזֹּאת
the this   the song - that   Israel   and sons   Moses – he sang   then

לַיהֹוָה וַיֹּאמְרוּ לֵאמֹר
to say   and they said   to ihvh

אָשִׁירָה לַיהֹוָה כִּי־גָאֹה גָּאָה
gloriously   proud - like   to ihvh   I will sing

סוּס וְרֹכְבוֹ רָמָה בַיָּם:
in sea   leveled   and his rider   horse

1. Then sang Moses and the people of Israel this song to the Lord, and spoke, saying, I will sing to the Lord, for he has triumphed gloriously; the horse and his rider has he thrown into the sea.

עָזִּי וְזִמְרָת יָהּ וַיְהִי־לִי לִישׁוּעָה
to salvation   to me – and it is   Ya   and songs   my strength

זֶה אֵלִי וְאַנְוֵהוּ
and I will glorify him   my El   that

אֱלֹהֵי אָבִי וַאֲרֹמְמֶנְהוּ:
and I will exalt him   my father   my Elohim

2. The Lord is my strength and song, and he has become my salvation; he is my God, and I will praise him; my father's God, and I will exalt him.

יְהֹוָה אִישׁ מִלְחָמָה יְהֹוָה שְׁמוֹ:
his name   ihvh   war   man   ihvh

3. The Lord is a man of war; the Lord is his name.

מַרְכְּבֹת פַּרְעֹה וְחֵילוֹ יָרָה בַיָּם
in sea   shot   and his army   Pharaoh   from chariots

וּמִבְחַר שָׁלִשָׁיו טֻבְּעוּ בְיַם־סוּף:
end - in sea   they drowned   captains   and from chosen

4. Pharaoh's chariots and his army has he thrown into the sea; his chosen captains also are drowned in the Red Sea.

תְּהֹמֹת יְכַסְיֻמוּ
they covered them   depths

יָרְדוּ בִמְצוֹלֹת כְּמוֹ־אָבֶן:
they descended   in bottom   stone – like

5. The depths have covered them; they sank to the bottom as a stone.

יְמִינְךָ יְהֹוָה נֶאְדָּרִי בַּכֹּחַ
your right hand   ihvh   glorious   in power

יְמִינְךָ יְהֹוָה תִּרְעַץ אוֹיֵב:
your right hand   ihvh   shattered   enemy

6. Your right hand, O Lord, is glorious in power; your right hand, O Lord, has dashed in pieces the enemy.

וּבְרֹב גְּאוֹנְךָ תַּהֲרֹס קָמֶיךָ
and in much   your excellency   you destroy   your arisers

תְּשַׁלַּח חֲרֹנְךָ יֹאכְלֵמוֹ כַּקַּשׁ:
you sent forth   your fury   consumed it   like stubble

7. And in the greatness of your excellency you have overthrown those that rose up against you; you sent forth your anger, which consumed them as stubble.

וּבְרוּחַ אַפֶּיךָ נֶעֶרְמוּ מַיִם
and in wind   your nose   stacked it   water

נִצְּבוּ כְמוֹ־נֵד נֹזְלִים
stood upright   heap - like   floods

קָפְאוּ תְהֹמֹת בְּלֶב־יָם:
it frozen   depths   sea - in heart

8. And with the blast of your nostrils the waters were gathered together, the floods stood upright as a heap, and the depths were congealed in the heart of the sea.

אָמַר אוֹיֵב אֶרְדֹּף אַשִּׂיג
said   enemy   I will pursue   I will overtake

אֲחַלֵּק שָׁלָל תִּמְלָאֵמוֹ נַפְשִׁי
I will divide   plunder   will satisfy lust it   my soul

אָרִיק חַרְבִּי תּוֹרִישֵׁמוֹ יָדִי:
I will unsheathe   my sword   will destroy them   my hand

9. The enemy said, I will pursue, I will overtake, I will divide the plunder; my lust shall be satisfied upon them; I will draw my sword, my hand shall destroy them.

נָשַׁפְתָּ בְרוּחֲךָ כִּסָּמוֹ יָם
you blew   in your wind   covered them   sea

צָלֲלוּ כַּעוֹפֶרֶת בְּמַיִם אַדִּירִים:
they dived   like lead   in waters   mighty

10. You blew with your wind, the sea covered them; they sank as lead in the mighty

176

waters.

מִי־כָמֹכָה בָּאֵלִם יְהוָה
ihvh   in Elohim   like you   who

מִי כָּמֹכָה נֶאְדָּר בַּקֹּדֶשׁ
in holiness   glorious   like you   who

נוֹרָא תְהִלֹּת עֹשֵׂה פֶלֶא׃
wonders   doing   praises   awesome

11. Who is like you, O Lord, among the gods? who is like you, glorious in holiness, fearful in praises, doing wonders?

נָטִיתָ יְמִינְךָ תִּבְלָעֵמוֹ אָרֶץ׃
earth   devoured him   your right hand   you stretched

12. You stretched out your right hand, the earth swallowed them.

נָחִיתָ בְחַסְדְּךָ עַם־זוּ גָּאָלְתָּ
you redeemed   that - people   in your mercies   landing

נֵהַלְתָּ בְעָזְּךָ אֶל־נְוֵה קָדְשֶׁךָ׃
your holy   habitation - unto   in your strength   you guided

13. You in your mercy have led forth the people whom you have redeemed; you have guided them in your strength to your holy habitation.

שָׁמְעוּ עַמִּים יִרְגָּזוּן
they resented   peoples   they will hear

חִיל אָחַז יֹשְׁבֵי פְּלָשֶׁת׃
Philistia   dwellers   takes hold   sorrow

14. The people shall hear, and be afraid; sorrow shall take hold on the inhabitants of Philistia.

אָז נִבְהֲלוּ אַלּוּפֵי אֱדוֹם
Edom   chiefs   they amazed   thence

אֵילֵי מוֹאָב יֹאחֲזֵמוֹ רָעַד
trembling   it will take hold   Moab   mighty

נָמֹגוּ כֹּל יֹשְׁבֵי כְנָעַן׃
Canaan   dwellers   all   they police

15. Then the chiefs of Edom shall be amazed; the mighty men of Moab, trembling shall take hold upon them; all the inhabitants of Canaan shall melt away.

תִּפֹּל עֲלֵיהֶם אֵימָתָה וָפַחַד
and dread fear   verified   upon them   will fall

בְּגֹדֶל	זְרוֹעֲךָ	יִדְּמוּ	כָּאָבֶן
in great	your arm	they stilled	like stone

עַד־יַעֲבֹר	עַמְּךָ	יְהֹוָה
till - it pass over	your people	ihvh

עַד־יַעֲבֹר	עַם־זוּ	קָנִיתָ:
till - it pass over	people - that	you purchased

16. Fear and dread shall fall upon them; by the greatness of your arm they shall be as still as a stone; till your people pass over, O Lord, till the people pass over, whom you have purchased.

תְּבִאֵמוֹ	וְתִטָּעֵמוֹ	בְּהַר	נַחֲלָתְךָ
you will bring them	and you will plant them	in mountain	your inheritance

מָכוֹן	לְשִׁבְתְּךָ	פָּעַלְתָּ	יְהֹוָה
place	to your dwelling	you made	ihvh

מִקְּדָשׁ	אֲדֹנָי	כּוֹנְנוּ	יָדֶיךָ:
sanctuary	Adoni	established it	your hand

17. You shall bring them in, and plant them in the mountain of your inheritance, in the place, O Lord, which you have made for you to dwell in, in the Sanctuary, O Lord, which your hands have established.

יְהֹוָה	יִמְלֹךְ	לְעֹלָם	וָעֶד:
ihvh	he will reign	forever	and ever

18. The Lord shall reign forever and ever.

Prophecy Prayer - Psalm 7

שִׁגָּיוֹן לְדָוִד אֲשֶׁר־שָׁר לַיהוָה עַל־דִּבְרֵי־כוּשׁ בֶּן־יְמִינִי׃
<small>Benjamite – son   Cush - speakings – upon   to ihvh   sang - which   to David   an ecstasy</small>

1 Shiggaion of David, which he sang unto the LORD, concerning the words of Cush the Benjamite.

יְהוָה אֱלֹהַי בְּךָ חָסִיתִי הוֹשִׁיעֵנִי מִכָּל־רֹדְפַי וְהַצִּילֵנִי׃
<small>and deliver me   my persecutors - from all   save me   I take refuge   in you   my Elohim   ihvh</small>

O LORD my God, in thee do I put my trust: save me from all them that persecute me, and deliver me:

פֶּן־יִטְרֹף כְּאַרְיֵה נַפְשִׁי פֹּרֵק וְאֵין מַצִּיל׃
<small>rescuer   and isn't   rending   my soul   like lion   he prey – lest</small>

2 Lest he tear my soul like a lion, rending it in pieces, while there is none to deliver.

יְהוָה אֱלֹהַי אִם־עָשִׂיתִי זֹאת אִם־יֶשׁ־עָוֶל בְּכַפָּי׃
<small>in my palms   iniquity - there is – if   this   I have done – if   my Elohim   ihvh</small>

3 O LORD my God, if I have done this; if there be iniquity in my hands;

אִם־גָּמַלְתִּי שׁוֹלְמִי רָע וָאֲחַלְּצָה צוֹרְרִי רֵיקָם׃
<small>causeless   my foe   and I draw   bad   my at peace one   I rewarded – if</small>

4 If I have rewarded evil unto him that was at peace with me; (yea, I have delivered him that without cause is mine enemy:)

יִרַדֹּף אוֹיֵב נַפְשִׁי וְיַשֵּׂג וְיִרְמֹס לָאָרֶץ חַיָּי
<small>my life   to earth   and he trample   and he achieve   my soul   enemy   will pursue</small>

וּכְבוֹדִי לֶעָפָר יַשְׁכֵּן סֶלָה׃
<small>Selah   it dwell   to dust   and my honor</small>

5 Let the enemy persecute my soul, and take it; yea, let him tread down my life upon the earth, and lay mine honour in the dust. Selah.

קוּמָה יְהוָה בְּאַפֶּךָ הִנָּשֵׂא בְּעַבְרוֹת צוֹרְרָי
<small>my enemies   in rages   cause to lift   in your anger   ihvh   arise</small>

וְעוּרָה אֵלַי מִשְׁפָּט צִוִּיתָ׃
<small>you commanded   judgment   unto me   and awake</small>

6 Arise, O LORD, in thine anger, lift up thyself because of the rage of mine enemies: and awake for me to the judgment that thou hast commanded.

וַעֲדַת לְאֻמִּים תְּסוֹבְבֶךָּ וְעָלֶיהָ לַמָּרוֹם שׁוּבָה:
and congregation   to peoples   it surrounded you   and upon it   to high   you return

7 So shall the congregation of the people compass thee about: for their sakes therefore return thou on high.

יְהֹוָה יָדִין עַמִּים שָׁפְטֵנִי יְהֹוָה
ihvh   he will judge   peoples   judge me   ihvh

כְּצִדְקִי וּכְתֻמִּי עָלָי:
like my righteousness   and like my integrity   upon me

8 The LORD shall judge the people: judge me, O LORD, according to my righteousness, and according to mine integrity that is in me.

יִגְמָר־נָא רַע רְשָׁעִים וּתְכוֹנֵן צַדִּיק
righteous   and you establish   wicked ones   bad   now - put end

וּבֹחֵן לִבּוֹת וּכְלָיוֹת אֱלֹהִים צַדִּיק:
righteous   Elohim   and reins   hearts   and tests

9 Oh let the wickedness of the wicked come to an end; but establish the just: for the righteous God trieth the hearts and reins.

מָגִנִּי עַל־אֱלֹהִים מוֹשִׁיעַ יִשְׁרֵי־לֵב:
heart – upright   Messiah   Elohim – upon   my shield

10 My defence is of God, which saveth the upright in heart.

אֱלֹהִים שׁוֹפֵט צַדִּיק וְאֵל זֹעֵם בְּכָל־יוֹם:
day - in all   rage   and El   righteous   judger   Elohim

11 God judgeth the righteous, and God is angry with the wicked every day.

אִם־לֹא יָשׁוּב חַרְבּוֹ יִלְטוֹשׁ קַשְׁתּוֹ דָרַךְ וַיְכוֹנְנֶהָ:
and he establish it   he bent   his bow   he will sharpen   his sword   he will return   not – if

12 If he turn not, he will whet his sword; he hath bent his bow, and made it ready.

וְלוֹ הֵכִין כְּלֵי־מָוֶת חִצָּיו לְדֹלְקִים יִפְעָל:
he worked   to fueling ones   his arrows   death - instruments   prepared   and to him

13 He hath also prepared for him the instruments of death; he ordaineth his arrows against the persecutors.

הִנֵּה יְחַבֶּל־אָוֶן וְהָרָה עָמָל וְיָלַד שָׁקֶר:
lie   and begot   labor   and conceived   inequity - he travails   here

14 Behold, he travaileth with iniquity, and hath conceived mischief, and brought forth falsehood.

בּוֹר כָּרָה וַיַּחְפְּרֵהוּ וַיִּפֹּל בְּשַׁחַת יִפְעָל:
he worked   in pit   and he falls   and he dug deep it   he dug   pit

15 He made a pit, and digged it, and is fallen into the ditch which he made.

180

יָשׁוּב עֲמָלוֹ בְרֹאשׁוֹ וְעַל־קָדְקֳדוֹ חֲמָסוֹ יֵרֵד׃
it will descend   his violence   his crown - and upon   in his head   his work   he will return

16 His mischief shall return upon his own head, and his violent dealing shall come down upon his own pate.

אוֹדֶה יְהֹוָה כְּצִדְקוֹ וַאֲזַמְּרָה שֵׁם־יְהֹוָה עֶלְיוֹן׃
most high   ihvh – name   and I will sing psalms   like his righteousness   ihvh   I will praise

17 I will praise the LORD according to his righteousness: and will sing praise to the name of the LORD most high.

MIDNIGHT PSALM - PSALM 111

הַלְלוּיָהּ אוֹדֶה יְהֹוָה בְּכָל־לֵבָב בְּסוֹד יְשָׁרִים וְעֵדָה:
and congregation upright ones in assembly heart - in all ihvh I will give thanks praise Ya

1 Praise ye the LORD. I will praise the LORD with my whole heart, in the assembly of the upright, and in the congregation.

גְּדֹלִים מַעֲשֵׂי יְהֹוָה דְּרוּשִׁים לְכָל־חֶפְצֵיהֶם:
delighting them - to all sought out ones ihvh works great ones

2 The works of the LORD are great, sought out of all them that have pleasure therein.

הוֹד־וְהָדָר פָּעֳלוֹ וְצִדְקָתוֹ עֹמֶדֶת לָעַד:
to time stands and his righteousness his work and majesty – glory

3 His work is honourable and glorious: and his righteousness endureth for ever.

זֵכֶר עָשָׂה לְנִפְלְאֹתָיו חַנּוּן וְרַחוּם יְהֹוָה:
ihvh and compassionate gracious to his mystical he made memorial

4 He hath made his wonderful works to be remembered: the LORD is gracious and full of compassion.

טֶרֶף נָתַן לִירֵאָיו יִזְכֹּר לְעוֹלָם בְּרִיתוֹ:
his covenant to forever he will remember to his fearing he gave prey

5 He hath given meat unto them that fear him: he will ever be mindful of his covenant.

כֹּחַ מַעֲשָׂיו הִגִּיד לְעַמּוֹ לָתֵת לָהֶם נַחֲלַת גּוֹיִם:
nations inheritances to them to give to his people told his works strength

6 He hath shewed his people the power of his works, that he may give them the heritage of the heathen.

מַעֲשֵׂי יָדָיו אֱמֶת וּמִשְׁפָּט נֶאֱמָנִים כָּל־פִּקּוּדָיו:
his precepts – all faithful ones and judgment truth his hands works

7 The works of his hands are verity and judgment; all his commandments are sure.

סְמוּכִים לָעַד לְעוֹלָם עֲשׂוּיִם בֶּאֱמֶת וְיָשָׁר:
and uprightness in truth done ones to forever to time principled ones

8 They stand fast for ever and ever, and are done in truth and uprightness.

פְּדוּת שָׁלַח לְעַמּוֹ צִוָּה לְעוֹלָם בְּרִיתוֹ
his covenant to forever he commanded to his people he sent redemptions

Preliminary Prayers

182

קָדוֹשׁ וְנוֹרָא שְׁמוֹ:
his name and awesome holy

9 He sent redemption unto his people: he hath commanded his covenant for ever: holy and reverend is his name.

רֵאשִׁית חָכְמָה יִרְאַת יְהֹוָה
ihvh fear wisdom beginning

שֵׂכֶל טוֹב לְכָל־עֹשֵׂיהֶם תְּהִלָּתוֹ עֹמֶדֶת לָעַד:
forever stands his prayer doing them - to all good intellect

10 The fear of the LORD is the beginning of wisdom: a good understanding have all they that do his commandments: his praise endureth for ever.

Shortest Psalm - Psalm 117

הַלְלוּ אֶת־יְהוָה כָּל־גּוֹיִם
Praise　　ihvh – that　　nations – all

שַׁבְּחוּהוּ כָּל־הָאֻמִּים׃
praise him　　the peoples – all

1. O Praise the Lord, all you nations; praise him, all you peoples.

כִּי גָבַר עָלֵינוּ חַסְדּוֹ
like　　great　　upon us　　his mercy

וֶאֱמֶת־יְהוָה לְעוֹלָם הַלְלוּיָהּ׃
ihvh - and truth　　to forever　　praise Ya

2. For his loving kindness is great toward us; and the truth of the Lord endures for ever. Hallelujah!

SHEMA

DEUT 6:4-9

שְׁמַע יִשְׂרָאֵל יְהֹוָה אֱלֹהֵינוּ יְהֹוָה אֶחָד:

one   ihvh   our Elohim   ihvh   Israel   hear

4. Hear, O Israel; The Lord our God is one Lord;

[ברוך שם כבוד מלכותו לעולם ועד]

וְאָהַבְתָּ אֵת יְהֹוָה אֱלֹהֶיךָ

your Elohim   ihvh   that   and you will love

בְּכָל־לְבָבְךָ וּבְכָל־נַפְשְׁךָ וּבְכָל־מְאֹדֶךָ:

your might - and in all   your soul - and in all   your heart - in all

5. And you shall love the Lord your God with all your heart, and with all your soul, and with all your might.

וְהָיוּ הַדְּבָרִים הָאֵלֶּה אֲשֶׁר אָנֹכִי מְצַוְּךָ הַיּוֹם עַל־לְבָבֶךָ:

your heart – upon   the day   command you   I   which   the these   the speakings   and they are

6. And these words, which I command you this day, shall be in your heart;

וְשִׁנַּנְתָּם לְבָנֶיךָ וְדִבַּרְתָּ בָּם בְּשִׁבְתְּךָ בְּבֵיתֶךָ

in your house   in your sitting   in them   and you speak   to your sons   and you teach them

וּבְלֶכְתְּךָ בַדֶּרֶךְ וּבְשָׁכְבְּךָ וּבְקוּמֶךָ:

and in your rising   and in your lying down   in path   and in your going

7. And you shall teach them diligently to your children, and shall talk of them when you sit in your house, and when you walk by the way, and when you lie down, and when you rise up.

וּקְשַׁרְתָּם לְאוֹת עַל־יָדֶךָ וְהָיוּ לְטֹטָפֹת בֵּין עֵינֶיךָ:

your eyes   between   to frontlets   and they will be   your hand – upon   to sign   and you will bind them

8. And you shall bind them for a sign upon your hand, and they shall be as frontlets between your eyes.

וּכְתַבְתָּם עַל־מְזֻזוֹת בֵּיתֶךָ וּבִשְׁעָרֶיךָ:

and in your gates   your house   door mantles – upon   and you will write them

9. And you shall write them upon the posts of your house, and on your gates.

Deut 11:13-21

וְהָיָ֗ה אִם־שָׁמֹ֤עַ תִּשְׁמְעוּ֙

and it will be   hearing – with   you will hear it

אֶל־מִצְוֺתַ֔י אֲשֶׁ֧ר אָנֹכִ֛י מְצַוֶּ֥ה אֶתְכֶ֖ם הַיּ֑וֹם

unto – my commandments which   I   command   that you   the day

לְאַהֲבָ֞ה אֶת־יְהוָ֤ה אֱלֹֽהֵיכֶם֙

to love   that – ihvh   your Elohim

וּלְעָבְד֔וֹ בְּכָל־לְבַבְכֶ֖ם וּבְכָל־נַפְשְׁכֶֽם׃

and to serve him   in all – your heart   and in all – your soul

13. And it shall come to pass, if you shall give heed diligently to my commandments which I command you this day, to love the Lord your God, and to serve him with all your heart and with all your soul,

וְנָתַתִּ֧י מְטַֽר־אַרְצְכֶ֛ם בְּעִתּ֖וֹ יוֹרֶ֣ה וּמַלְק֑וֹשׁ

and I give   rain – your lands   in its season   first rain   and latter rain

וְאָסַפְתָּ֣ דְגָנֶ֔ךָ וְתִֽירֹשְׁךָ֖ וְיִצְהָרֶֽךָ׃

and you will gather   your grain   and your new wine   and your oil

14. That I will give you the rain of your land in its due season, the first rain and the latter rain, that you may gather in your grain, and your wine, and your oil.

וְנָתַתִּ֛י עֵ֥שֶׂב בְּשָׂדְךָ֖ לִבְהֶמְתֶּ֑ךָ וְאָכַלְתָּ֖ וְשָׂבָֽעְתָּ׃

and I will give   grass   in your fields   to your cattle   and you will eat   and you be full

15. And I will send grass in your fields for your cattle, that you may eat and be full.

הִשָּֽׁמְר֣וּ לָכֶ֔ם פֶּן־יִפְתֶּ֖ה לְבַבְכֶ֑ם וְסַרְתֶּ֗ם

take heed   to you   lest – it entice   your hearts   and you depart

וַעֲבַדְתֶּם֙ אֱלֹהִ֣ים אֲחֵרִ֔ים וְהִשְׁתַּחֲוִיתֶ֖ם לָהֶֽם׃

and serve them   Elohim   other ones   and you worship   to them

16. Take heed to yourselves, that your heart be not deceived, and you turn aside, and serve other gods, and worship them;

וְחָרָ֨ה אַף־יְהוָ֜ה בָּכֶ֗ם וְעָצַ֤ר אֶת־הַשָּׁמַ֙יִם֙

and kindled   anger – ihvh   in you   and stop   that – the heavens

וְלֹֽא־יִהְיֶ֣ה מָטָ֔ר וְהָ֣אֲדָמָ֔ה לֹ֥א תִתֵּ֖ן אֶת־יְבוּלָ֑הּ

and not – will be   rain   and the ground   not   it gives   that – produce

וַאֲבַדְתֶּ֣ם מְהֵרָ֗ה מֵעַל֙ הָאָ֣רֶץ הַטֹּבָ֔ה אֲשֶׁ֥ר יְהוָ֖ה נֹתֵ֥ן לָכֶֽם׃

and you lost   quickly   from upon   the earth   the good   which   ihvh   giver   to you

17. And then the Lord's anger be kindled against you, and he closed the skies, that there should be no rain, and that the land yield not her fruit; and lest you perish quickly from off the good land which the Lord gives you.

וְשַׂמְתֶּם אֶת־דְּבָרַי אֵלֶּה עַל־לְבַבְכֶם וְעַל־נַפְשְׁכֶם
your soul - and upon   your heart – upon   these   my speakings – that   and put them

וּקְשַׁרְתֶּם אֹתָם לְאוֹת עַל־יֶדְכֶם
your hand - upon   to sign   to them   and bind you

וְהָיוּ לְטוֹטָפֹת בֵּין עֵינֵיכֶם׃
your eyes   between   to frontlets   and they will be

18. Therefore shall you lay up these my words in your heart and in your soul, and bind them for a sign upon your hand, that they may be as frontlets between your eyes.

וְלִמַּדְתֶּם אֹתָם אֶת־בְּנֵיכֶם לְדַבֵּר בָּם בְּשִׁבְתְּךָ בְּבֵיתֶךָ
in your house   in your sitting   to them   to speak   your sons – that   to them   and you instruct

וּבְלֶכְתְּךָ בַדֶּרֶךְ וּבְשָׁכְבְּךָ וּבְקוּמֶךָ׃
and in your rising   and in your lying down   in way   and in your going

19. And you shall teach them to your children, speaking of them when you sit in your house, and when you walk by the way, when you lie down, and when you rise up.

וּכְתַבְתָּם עַל־מְזוּזוֹת בֵּיתֶךָ וּבִשְׁעָרֶיךָ׃
and in your gates   your house   door posts – upon   and you write them

20. And you shall write them upon the door posts of your house, and upon your gates;

לְמַעַן יִרְבּוּ יְמֵיכֶם וִימֵי בְנֵיכֶם עַל הָאֲדָמָה
the land   upon   your sons   and days   your days   they will multiply   to end

אֲשֶׁר נִשְׁבַּע יְהוָה לַאֲבֹתֵיכֶם
to your fathers   ihvh   swore   which

לָתֵת לָהֶם כִּימֵי הַשָּׁמַיִם עַל־הָאָרֶץ׃
the earth – upon   the heaven   like days   to them   to give

21. That your days may be multiplied, and the days of your children, in the land which the Lord swore to your fathers to give them, as the days of heaven upon the earth.

NUMBERS 15:37-41

וַיֹּאמֶר יְהוָה אֶל־מֹשֶׁה לֵּאמֹר׃
to say   Moses – unto   ihvh   and said

37. And the Lord spoke to Moses, saying,

דַּבֵּר אֶל־בְּנֵי יִשְׂרָאֵל וְאָמַרְתָּ אֲלֵהֶם
unto them   and you say   Israel   sons – upon   speak

וְעָשׂוּ לָהֶם צִיצִת עַל־כַּנְפֵי בִגְדֵיהֶם לְדֹרֹתָם
to their generations   their garments   wings – upon   tsitsit   to them   and you have made

187

וְנָתְנ֞וּ עַל־צִיצִ֧ת הַכָּנָ֛ף פְּתִ֥יל תְּכֵֽלֶת׃
blue   thick thread   the wing   tsitsit - upon   and you give

38. Speak to the people of Israel, and bid them that they make them fringes in the borders of their garments throughout their generations, and that they put upon the fringe of the borders a thread of blue;

וְהָיָ֣ה לָכֶם֮ לְצִיצִת֒ וּרְאִיתֶ֣ם אֹת֗וֹ
to it   and you see them   to tsitsit   to you   and it will be

וּזְכַרְתֶּם֙ אֶת־כָּל־מִצְוֺ֣ת יְהוָ֔ה וַעֲשִׂיתֶ֖ם אֹתָ֑ם
to them   and you do them   ihvh   commandments - all - that   and you remember

וְלֹֽא־תָתֻ֜רוּ אַחֲרֵ֤י לְבַבְכֶם֙ וְאַחֲרֵ֣י עֵֽינֵיכֶ֔ם
your eyes   and after   your hearts   after   you stray   and not

אֲשֶׁר־אַתֶּ֥ם זֹנִ֖ים אַחֲרֵיהֶֽם׃
after them   strainings   to you – which

39. And it shall be to you for a fringe, that you may look upon it, and remember all the commandments of the Lord, and do them; and that you seek not after your own heart and your own eyes, which incline you to go astray;

לְמַ֣עַן תִּזְכְּר֔וּ וַעֲשִׂיתֶ֖ם אֶת־כָּל־מִצְוֺתָ֑י
my commandments – all – that   and you do them   you will remember   to end

וִהְיִיתֶ֥ם קְדֹשִׁ֖ים לֵאלֹהֵיכֶֽם׃
to your Elohim   holy ones   and you be

40. That you may remember, and do all my commandments, and be holy to your God.

אֲנִ֞י יְהוָ֣ה אֱלֹֽהֵיכֶ֗ם אֲשֶׁ֨ר הוֹצֵ֤אתִי אֶתְכֶם֙ מֵאֶ֣רֶץ מִצְרַ֔יִם
Egypt   from land   to you   brought out   which   your Elohim   ihvh   I

לִהְי֥וֹת לָכֶ֖ם לֵאלֹהִ֑ים אֲנִ֖י יְהוָ֥ה אֱלֹהֵיכֶֽם׃
your Elohim   ihvh   I   to Elohim   to you   to be

41. I am the Lord your God, who brought you out of the land of Egypt, to be your God; I am the Lord your God.

Galgal Square

Galgal means cycling. In this case it is cycling through the Hebrew alphabet doing tzeruf meditation.

This is done by taking one letter of the Hebrew alphabet and pairing it with all of the Hebrew alphabet letters, one at a time. A letter is not paired with another exactly like itself. So this pairing is done with the other non-similar 21 letters of the alphabet. This makes 21 pairs. Then, the next letter in alphabetical order is again paired with the other non-similar 21 letters of the alphabet. This makes another 21 pairs. This is done with all the letters of the alphabet, making a total of 462 pairs. This method is written into a large table for vocal meditation.

It is like two wheels, one inside the other, with the Hebrew let-

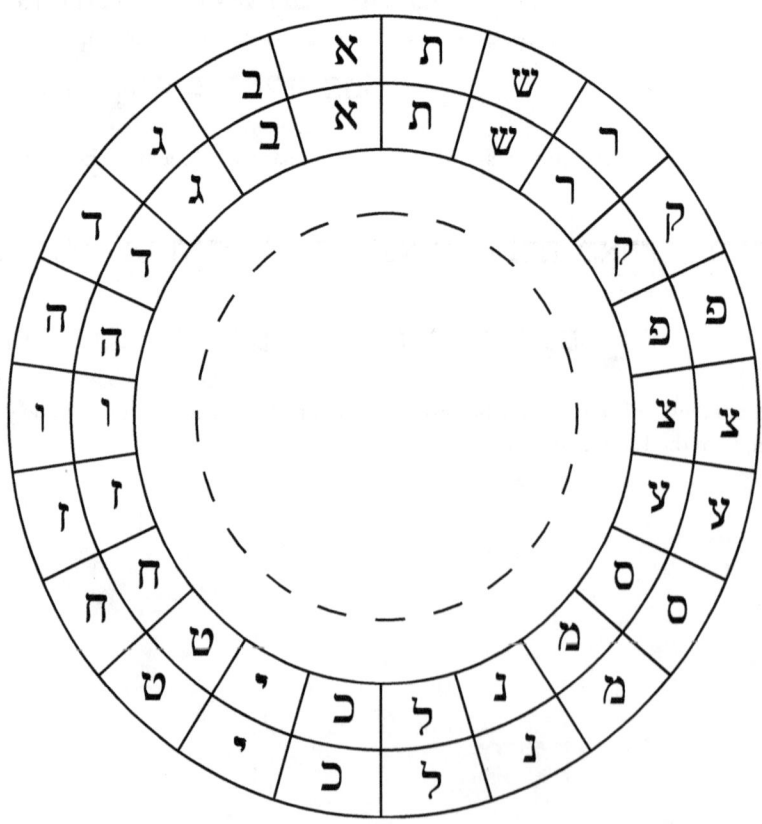

ter written on the inner and outer perimeters of the wheels. One fixes stationary the inner wheel and pairs the top outer letter with the inner letter directly below it. The first pair would be the Alef Bet.

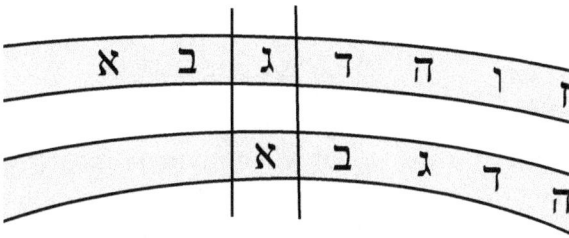

Then the outer wheel above is rotated left until the next outer circle letter appears directly below the fixed inner circle letter. This would be the next pair Alef Gimel.

This continues until all of the 21 letters of the outer wheel have been used. Then the inner wheel is turned left to the next letter, the Bet. The outer circle is repeated it's cycle of pairing all non-similar letters. This process repeats until all of the inner wheel letters have been paired with non-similar outer wheel letters.

There are two ways of doing this meditation.

METHOD 1. This method cycles one concept of creation or alphabet letter, with all the other aspects of creation (other letters in the alphabet). This is done until all 462 pairs of the alphabet letters have been paired in an ordered fashion excluding pairs with duplicated same alphabet letters.

This best performed mentally by creating a mental circle with all the Hebrew alphabet letters equally spaced around the circle. These letters are visualized as standing up facing inwardly to the middle of the circle. There is a second circle of Hebrew letters exactly the same directly on top of the first circle. One focuses on a letter on the bottom circle as a base point starting with the Alef. Then the Aleph letter on the bottom circle combines or permutes with the letter above it on the top circle. This pair is vocalized with their respective native vowel sounds. Then the top circle is rotated to the left one letter. Then with the Alef letter still in place on the bottom, it is combined with the new letter on top of the Alef at the fixed base point location. This pair is then vocalized with their native vowel sounds. After all of the 21 non-similar letters are rotated on the top circle, then the bottom circle is rotated one letter to the left and the cycle repeats. This top and bottom circles letter rotating continues in this manner producing one letter pair at a time until all letters pairs are permutated and vocalized. This process is repeated until there has been formed 462 two letter combinations.

METHOD 2. The second way is to do exactly the same that was done in method 1, but adding one more step that makes it six times longer to perform. It involves adding a seed letter of the shem hamephorash between the pair. This seed is vocalized, along with it's assigned vowel, between vocalizing the first and second letter of the pairs derived from rotating the letter circles. Thus the two letters of the pair plus the seed letter becomes a group of three letters. Since there are four letters to the shem hamephorash, this cycling of circles needs to be done four times, each with one of the shem hamephorash letters. This would make a total of 1848 three letter words. This makes for a long vocalization meditation but can be accomplished by mental focus without anything written assisting in the meditation.

Galgal Square

Part 1

Galgal Square

אה	אנ	אז	אד	אג	אב	אג	אד	אח	אז	אג
אה	בנ	בז	בד	בג	בב	בג	בד	בח	בז	בג
אז	גנ	גז	גד	גג	גב	גג	גד	גח	גז	גג
אה	דנ	דז	דד	דג	דב	דג	דד	דח	דז	דג
אה	הנ	הז	הד	הג	הב	הג	הד	הח	הז	הג
אז	ונ	וז	וד	וג	וב	וג	וד	וח	וז	וג
אה	זנ	זז	זד	זג	זב	זג	זד	זח	זז	זג
אה	טנ	טז	טד	טג	טב	טג	טד	טח	טז	טג
אה	ינ	יז	יד	יג	יב	יג	יד	יח	יז	יג
אה	כנ	כז	כד	כג	כב	כג	כד	כח	כז	כג
אה	לנ	לז	לד	לג	לב	לג	לד	לח	לז	לג
אה	מנ	מז	מד	מג	מב	מג	מד	מח	מז	מג
אה	נ	נ	נ	נ	נ	נ	נ	נ	נ	נ
אה	סנ	סז	סד	סג	סב	סג	סד	סח	סז	סג
אה	ענ	עז	עד	עג	עב	עג	עד	עח	עז	עג
אה	פנ	פז	פד	פג	פב	פג	פד	פח	פז	פג
אה	צנ	צז	צד	צג	צב	צג	צד	צח	צז	צג
אה	קנ	קז	קד	קג	קב	קג	קד	קח	קז	קג
אה	רנ	רז	רד	רג	רב	רג	רד	רח	רז	רג
אש	שנ	שז	שד	שג	שב	שג	שד	שח	שז	שג
את	תנ	תז	תד	תג	תב	תג	תד	תח	תז	תג

193

PART 2

GALGAL SQUARE

אי	אט	אח	אז	או	אה	אד	אג	אב	אא
בי	בט	בח	בז	בו	בה	בד	בג	בב	בא
גי	גט	גח	גז	גו	גה	גד	גג	גב	גא
די	דט	דח	דז	דו	דה	דד	דג	דב	דא
הי	הט	הח	הז	הו	הה	הד	הג	הב	הא
וי	וט	וח	וז	וו	וה	וד	וג	וב	וא
זי	זט	זח	זז	זו	זה	זד	זג	זב	זא
חי	חט	חח	חז	חו	חה	חד	חג	חב	חא
טי	טט	טח	טז	טו	טה	טד	טג	טב	טא
יי	יט	יח	יז	יו	יה	יד	יג	יב	יא
כי	כט	כח	כז	כו	כה	כד	כג	כב	כא
לי	לט	לח	לז	לו	לה	לד	לג	לב	לא
מי	מט	מח	מז	מו	מה	מד	מג	מב	מא
ני	נט	נח	נז	נו	נה	נד	נג	נב	נא
סי	סט	סח	סז	סו	סה	סד	סג	סב	סא
עי	עט	עח	עז	עו	עה	עד	עג	עב	עא
פי	פט	פח	פז	פו	פה	פד	פג	פב	פא
צי	צט	צח	צז	צו	צה	צד	צג	צב	צא
קי	קט	קח	קז	קו	קה	קד	קג	קב	קא
רי	רט	רח	רז	רו	רה	רד	רג	רב	רא
שי	שט	שח	שז	שו	שה	שד	שג	שב	שא
תי	תט	תח	תז	תו	תה	תד	תג	תב	תא

Part 1

Galgal Square

שא	שב	לג	קד	מה	סו	אז	עח	דט	סי	לך
רא	אב	רג	פד	שה	קו	אז	פח	רט	שי	לך
ךא	ךב	ך	ך	ך	ך	ך	ך	ך	ך	ך
וא	שב	וג	קד	מה	סו	אז	פח	דט	סי	וך
פא	פב	פג	פד	פה	פו	פז	פח	פט	פי	פך
וא	שב	וג	פד	וה	פו	פז	פח	וט	פי	פך
סא	סב	סג	סד	סה	סו	סז	סח	סט	סי	סך
הא	הב	הג	הד	הה	הו	הז	הח	הט	הי	הך
מא	שב	מג	קד	מה	סו	מז	מח	מט	סי	מך
לא	לב	לג	לד	לה	לו	לז	לח	לט	לי	לך
נא	שב	נג	נד	נה	נו	נז	נח	נט	ני	נך
יא	יב	י	י	י	י	י	י	י	י	י
פא	שב	פג	פד	פה	פו	פז	פח	פט	פי	פך
הא	הב	הג	הד	הה	הו	הז	הח	הט	הי	הך

Galgal Reversed

זא	זב	ז	ז	ז	ז	ז	ז	ז	ז	ז
וא	וב	ו	ו	ו	ו	ו	ו	ו	ו	ו
הא	הב	ה	ה	ה	ה	ה	ה	ה	ה	ה
דא	דב	ד	ד	ד	ד	ד	ד	ד	ד	ד
גא	גב	ג	ג	ג	ג	ג	ג	ג	ג	ג
בא	בב	ב	ב	ב	ב	ב	ב	ב	ב	ב
אא	אב	א	א	א	א	א	א	א	א	א

Part 2

Galgal Square

Galgal Triangle

This is the shortened version of a Galgal Square table. It entails all of the alphabet combinations with seeding all of the letters of the shem hamephorash. The difference between the Galgal Square and the Galgal Triangle is that the Galgal Square has pairs that contain the same letter combinations in some cells. The Galgal Triangle is constructed such that there are no two letter combinations that are the same in another cell. This cuts down the pairs from 462 to 231 pairs.

Under this theory when permuting only two letters, it doesn't matter the order of the letters. An Aleph Bet combination, will have the same resulting effect as if it were reversed as a Bet Aleph combination. It is one aspect of creation intermingling with another aspect of creation. It would be duplicity to also include the reverse because when two concepts mix there is no order to their mixing.

When seeding with the shem hamephorash the time to cycle through the meditation would be half that of the Galgal Square and would not involve the unnecessary duplicity of letter combinations.

The first Galgal Triangle table listed is the simple unique pairs of letters meditation. These letters can be vocalized with their native vowels with no seeding of any other letters of the shem hamephorash.

The second set of four Galgal Triangle tables are seeded with the letters of the shem hamephorash in order. The prescribed method of meditation should be as such; 1) looking at the first letter of the pair and vocalizing it's consonant sound then it's attached native vowel sound. 2) Then look at the seeded letter of the shem hamephorash between the two letters while vocalizing it and it's assigned vowel sound. 3) Then do the same with the remaining letter as was done with the first letter. Look at it while vocalizing it's consonant sound and it's native vowel sound.

The hard row to do is the row starting with Khet. When you get to it you know that you are about half done with that table. After saying the Khet row, it might be a good time to take a drink of water in order to prevent one from having a dry mouth for the rest of the vocalization.

The last Galgal Triangle table contains a space between the written pairs. This space is for you visualizing with your imagination the appropriate seeded letter of the shem hamephorash and it's assigned vowel sound. Mentally visualize the letter as if it was written between the pictured letters. The ying yang of mixing the seen earthly letters with the visualized heavenly letters of the shem hamephorash is the best way of doing this Galgal Triangle meditation.

אב	אג	אד	אה	או	אז	אח	אט	אי	אכ	אל	אמ	אנ	אס	אע	אפ	אצ	אק	אר	אש	את
בג	בד	בה	בו	בז	בח	בט	בי	בכ	בל	במ	בנ	בס	בע	בפ	בצ	בק	בר	בש	בת	
גד	גה	גו	גז	גח	גט	גי	גכ	גל	גמ	גנ	גס	גע	גפ	גצ	גק	גר	גש	גת		
דה	דו	דז	דח	דט	די	דכ	דל	דמ	דנ	דס	דע	דפ	דצ	דק	דר	דש	דת			
הו	הז	הח	הט	הי	הכ	הל	המ	הנ	הס	הע	הפ	הצ	הק	הר	הש	הת				
וז	וח	וט	וי	וכ	ול	ומ	ונ	וס	וע	ופ	וצ	וק	ור	וש	ות					
זח	זט	זי	זכ	זל	זמ	זנ	זס	זע	זפ	זצ	זק	זר	זש	זת						
חט	חי	חכ	חל	חמ	חנ	חס	חע	חפ	חצ	חק	חר	חש	חת							
טי	טכ	טל	טמ	טנ	טס	טע	טפ	טצ	טק	טר	טש	טת								
יכ	יל	ימ	ינ	יס	יע	יפ	יצ	יק	יר	יש	ית									
כל	כמ	כנ	כס	כע	כפ	כצ	כק	כר	כש	כת										
למ	לנ	לס	לע	לפ	לצ	לק	לר	לש	לת											
מנ	מס	מע	מפ	מצ	מק	מר	מש	מת												

Galgal Triangle

ט	דא	הג	וא	זר	חר	טא	יה
זא	דג	הר	וא	זר	חא	רר	
דג	דא	רא	וא	זא	חר		
זא	דא	ור	הא	זר			
רא	וא	זא	חר				
ר	הא	זר					
זא	ור						
רר							

CONTINUED

Galgal Triangle

א״ב																		
ש״א	ב״ה																	
ד״ר	ט״מ	ג״י																
פ״א	ג״ר	ש״א	ד״ז															
א״צ	ד״ק	ש״מ	ה״ז	ה״ח														
צ״א	ב״ק	צ״ר	ש״פ	ד״ת	ו״ט													
ע״א	ג״פ	ש״צ	ב״ד	ק״ר	ט״ח	ז״י												
ס״א	ס״ע	ש״ץ	י״ר	צ״ב	ס״ק	ח״ט	ח״ר											
נ״א	ד״ס	ע״צ	ש״ר	צ״ב	פ״ב	ק״ז	נ״ר	ט״ש										
מ״א	פ״ג	ס״צ	נ״ק	ע״ר	ל״ב	ד״ת	צ״ש	י״ז	נ״ד									
ל״א	מ״ר	ב״מ	ק״צ	ס״פ	ל״נ	ג״ת	פ״ש	ט״ז	י״א	צ״ה								
כ״א	נ״ב	ל״צ	מ״ק	ע״פ	ב״ת	ל״ט	ס״ש	פ״ז	י״כ	ל״ל	מ״ה							
י״א	מ״ב	כ״צ	ל״ק	נ״פ	ע״ס	מ״ט	פ״ש	ט״ז	ת״כ	ר״ל	י״ה	פ״ו						
ט״א	ל״ב	ע״ב	כ״ק	מ״פ	נ״ס	ש״ט	ע״ש	י״ז	ט״כ	ק״ל	ל״ה	צ״ו	ז״ז					
ח״א	כ״ב	נ״ב	י״ק	ל״פ	מ״ס	ד״ט	נ״ש	ע״ז	ח״כ	צ״ל	ט״ה	פ״ו	ה״ז	ר״ח				
ז״א	י״ב	מ״ב	ט״ק	כ״פ	ל״ס	ג״ט	מ״ש	ס״ז	ז״כ	פ״ל	ע״ה	נ״ו	ד״ז	ק״ח	ל״ט			
ו״א	ט״ב	ל״ב	ח״ק	י״פ	כ״ס	ב״ט	ל״ש	נ״ז	ו״כ	ע״ל	ס״ה	מ״ו	ג״ז	צ״ח	כ״ט	מ״י		
ה״א	ח״ב	כ״ב	ז״ק	ט״פ	י״ס	ט״ט	כ״ש	מ״ז	ה״כ	ס״ל	נ״ה	ל״ו	ב״ז	פ״ח	י״ט	ל״י	א״כ	
ד״א	ז״ב	י״ב	ו״ק	ח״פ	ט״ס	ח״ט	י״ש	ל״ז	ד״כ	נ״ל	מ״ה	כ״ו	א״ז	ע״ח	ט״ט	כ״י	ל״כ	ר״ב

TABLE 1 - ל'

Galgal Triangle Seeded

201

CONTINUED

אהת	אהש	אהר	אהק	אהצ	אהפ	אהע	אהס	אהנ	אהמ	אהל	אהכ	אהי	אהט	אהח	אהז	אהו	אהה	אהד	אהג	אהב
	בהת	בהש	בהר	בהק	בהצ	בהפ	בהע	בהס	בהנ	בהמ	בהל	בהכ	בהי	בהט	בהח	בהז	בהו	בהה	בהד	בהג
		גהת	גהש	גהר	גהק	גהצ	גהפ	גהע	גהס	גהנ	גהמ	גהל	גהכ	גהי	גהט	גהח	גהז	גהו	גהה	גהד
			דהת	דהש	דהר	דהק	דהצ	דהפ	דהע	דהס	דהנ	דהמ	דהל	דהכ	דהי	דהט	דהח	דהז	דהו	דהה
				ההת	ההש	ההר	ההק	ההצ	ההפ	ההע	ההס	ההנ	ההמ	ההל	ההכ	ההי	ההט	ההח	ההז	ההו
					והת	והש	והר	והק	והצ	והפ	והע	והס	והנ	והמ	והל	והכ	והי	והט	והח	והז
						זהת	זהש	זהר	זהק	זהצ	זהפ	זהע	זהס	זהנ	זהמ	זהל	זהכ	זהי	זהט	זהח
							חהת	חהש	חהר	חהק	חהצ	חהפ	חהע	חהס	חהנ	חהמ	חהל	חהכ	חהי	חהט
								טהת	טהש	טהר	טהק	טהצ	טהפ	טהע	טהס	טהנ	טהמ	טהל	טהכ	טהי
									יהת	יהש	יהר	יהק	יהצ	יהפ	יהע	יהס	יהנ	יהמ	יהל	יהכ
										כהת	כהש	כהר	כהק	כהצ	כהפ	כהע	כהס	כהנ	כהמ	כהל
											להת	להש	להר	להק	להצ	להפ	להע	להס	להנ	להמ
												מהת	מהש	מהר	מהק	מהצ	מהפ	מהע	מהס	מהנ

TABLE 2 - ה

GALGAL TRIANGLE SEEDED

Galgal Triangle (continued)

דהס	סהד	צהג	פהא	קהד	רהט	שהח	
דוס	סוד	צוג	פוצ	קוד	רוח		
דזס	סזס	צזצ	פזק	קזמ			
דחצ	סחצ	צחד	פחס				
דטק	סטד	צטמ	פטח				
דיר	סיס	צימ					
דיד	סיט	ציה					
דימ	סיח						
דיח							

GALGAL TRIANGLE

אך	את	גך	דך	הך	וך	חך	טך	יך	לך	מך	נך
אץ	הץ	גץ	דץ	הץ	וץ	טץ	יץ	כץ	מץ	נץ	סץ
אך	בך	גך	דך	הך	וך	חך	טך	לך	מך	נך	סך
אן	בן	גן	דן	הן	וּן	חן	יון	כן	לן	מן	סן
אם	בם	גם	דם	הם	חם	טם	יום	כם	לם	נם	סם
אך	בך	גך	דך	וך	חך	טך	יך	לך	מך	נך	סך
אך	בך	גך	הך	וך	חך	טך	יך	כך	לך	נך	סך
אם	גם	בם	דם	הם	טם	יום	כם	לם	נם	מש
אי	בל	גל	הל	וּל	חל	טל	יל	כל	לש	נש
אך	בך	גל	הל	ול	חל	טל	יל	כל	לש	נש
אל	גם	דם	הם	גם	חם	דם	סוף	בש	חל
אם	חל	דם	הל	טם	דל	דה	סוף	דה
אם	סם	דל	סוף	חל	דה	סוף
אם	סם	גל	דל	דה	סוף	דה
אים	סם	גל	דל	דה	וש	הה
אם	פל	דל	סוף	דל	וש	דה
אלף	סם	דל	חל	וש	דה
אינ	פל	דל	וש	דה
אף	סם	דל	דל	דה
אף	כל	דל	נוש	הה
אם	פך	כל	דל	וש
אם	אלץ	בף	סוף
אף	פב	אף	דל
אף	אלץ	פוש
אף	אלץ	פוש
אש	בת
את

TABLE 3 – ן

GALGAL TRIANGLE SEEDED

נוס	סוע	עופ	פוצ	צוק	קור	רוש	שות
נוע	סופ	עוצ	פוק	צור	קוש	רות	
נופ	סוצ	עוק	פור	צוש	קות		
נוצ	סוק	עור	פוש	צות			
נוק	סור	עוש	פות				
נור	סוש	עות					
נוש	סות						
נות							

CONTINUED

Galgal Triangle

Table 4 - יז

Galgal Triangle Seeded

נהס	סהע	עהפ	פהצ	צהק	קהר	רהש	שהת
נהע	סהפ	עהצ	פהק	צהר	קהש	רהת	
נהפ	סהצ	עהק	פהר	צהש	קהת		
נהצ	סהק	עהר	פהש	צהת			
נהק	סהר	עהש	פהת				
נהר	סהש	עהת					
נהש	סהת						
נהת							

CONTINUED

GALGAL TRIANGLE

GALGAL TRIANGLE SPACED

CONTINUED

G̲algal T̲riangle

Alef with ihvh

This involves the sounding of the first letter of the Hebrew alphabet, the Alef, with one of the letters of the shem hamephorash, יהוה. This meditation emphasizes the permutation of all of the vowel sounds in a meditation. This method is called notakeiroon. Two letter consonants are permuted, forward and reversed, not with their attached natural vowel sounds, but with each of the five vowel sounds used in the Hebrew language. This process is used with one alphabet letter (the Alef) combined with the four letters of the shem hamephorash. It also does this permuting in a reverse order.

The alphabet letter Alef symbolizes the only one God and is a shortened representation of doing a permutation with all of the letters of the Hebrew Alphabet. It is more preferable to do this with all the letters of the Hebrew alphabet but this would take a very long time to do. Many times this is not possible because of "the busy life" we live. Generally, if you are going to do this type of meditation with any one letter, it should be the Alef.

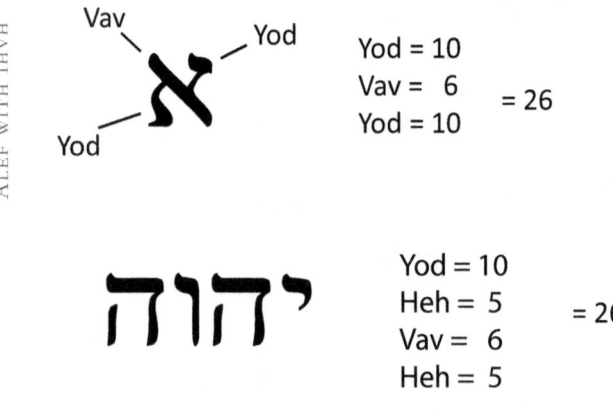

GEMATRIA OF ALEF AND IHVH

A typical more advanced meditation is using this method with the three root letters of a Hebrew word. This emphasizes a word's spiritual aspect into your life.

Methods

There are two different ways to do this meditation.

The first is to vocalize the first letter and it's attached vowel all with one exhaled breath. Inhale, then do the same for the next letter. Then inhale and go to the next cell. Thus you have two exhaled breaths per cell. This method is ideal to use in conjunction with head movements. These head movements are detailed out in the earlier chapter, Introduction to Meditation.

The second way is to vocalize both letters with their attached vowel sounds all in one exhaled breath. That would be vocalizing four sounds in one exhaled breath, or per cell. Remember to accent the consonant letter sounds, vocalizing them for a longer period than their designated vowels.

The Alef and the Yod

When the consonant Alef sound is mixed with a Kametz vowel sound, both have an "ah" sound, there needs to be a slight pause between each sound. The same is true for the consonant Yod sound when it is mixed with the Hirik "eeeh" sound.

Breaths

You are only allowed to take one full breath between each pair of letters while vocalizing. That's a breath in and an exhaled breath out without any vocalizing. And that is only if necessary. It is best to take no breaths between cell pairs. Between the tables, it is permissible to take five breaths. Pausing between the tables is a natural place to take a drink of whatever liquid you have prepared to keep your mouth moist.

ALEF א Table 1 - י

אִי	אִי	אִי	אָי	אִי
יִא	יֶא	יֵא	יָא	יֹא
יָא	יֱֶא	יַָא	יֵָא	יָָא
אָי	אֱָי	אַָי	אֵָי	אָָי
אָֻי	אֹי	אֻי	אֻי	אֻי
יֱָא	יֱא	יֱא	יֱא	יֱא
יֲא	יֲא	יֲא	יֲא	יֲא
אֲי	אֲי	אֲי	אֲי	אֲי
אֳי	אֳי	אֳי	אֳי	אֳי
יֳא	יֳא	יֳא	יֳא	יֳא

Table 2 - ה

אֹה	אָה	אֶה	אֱה	אֱה
הֹא	הָא	הֶא	הֱא	הֱא
הָא	הָא	הָא	הָא	הֹא
אָה	אֶה	אֶה	אֶה	אֹה
אֲה	אֶה	אֱה	אֹה	אֶה
הֶא	הָא	הָא	הָא	הָא
הָא	הֱא	הֹא	הָא	הֶא
אֶה	אֹה	אֹה	אָה	אֶה
אֶה	אָה	אָה	אֹה	אֱה
הֱא	הֱא	הָא	הֹא	הֱא

ALEF

Table 3 - וֹ

ALEF

אֱוֹ	אֶוֹ	אֵוֹ	אָוֹ	אֹוֹ
וֹאֱ	וֹאֶ	וֹאֵ	וֹאָ	וֹאֹ
וֹאָ	וֹאַ ‎ָ	וֹאִ ‎ָ	וֹאֶ ‎ָ	וֹאָ ‎ָ
אֹוָ	אֹוֱ ‎ָ	אֹוִ ‎ָ	אֹוֶ ‎ָ	אֹוָ ‎ָ
אָוֱ	אֹוֶ	אֶוֱ	אֶוֶ	אֱוֶ
וֹאֶ ‎ָ	וֹאֱ ‎ֶ	וֹאִ ‎ֶ	וֹאֵ ‎ֶ	וֹאֵ ‎ֶ
וֹאֶ	וֹאָ ‎ֶ	וֹאֹ	וֹאִ	וֹאֵ
אֱוֹ	אָוֹ	אֹוֹ	אֶוֹ	אֹוֹ
אֱוֹ	אֱוֹ	אָוֹ	אֹוֹ	אֱוֹ
וֹאֱ	וֹאֱ	וֹאָ	וֹאֹ	וֹאֱ

Table 4 - ה

אֵה	אֹה	אֶה	אָה	אַה
הֵא	הֹא	הֶא	הָא	הַא
הָא	הָא	הָא	הָא	הָא
אֹה	אֶה	אֵה	אֶה	אֵה
אֶה	אֹה	אֶה	אֶה	אֶה
הֵא	הֹא	הֶא	הֵא	הֵא
הֶא	הָא	הֹא	הֶא	הֶא
אֶה	אָה	אֹה	אֶה	אֶה
אֶה	אֶה	אָה	אֹה	אֶה
הֶא	הֶא	הָא	הָא	הָא

ALEF

The 72 Names

The 72 names in the following tables are derived from three verses from Exodus Chapter 14 Verses 19, 20, and 21. These are considered as one of the most powerful set of verses in the *Bible*. They refer to the parting of the Sea by Moses.

Exodus 14:19 to 21

וַיִּסַּע מַלְאַךְ הָאֱלֹהִים הַהֹלֵךְ לִפְנֵי
to before   the walker   the Elohim   angel   and it passed

מַחֲנֵה יִשְׂרָאֵל וַיֵּלֶךְ מֵאַחֲרֵיהֶם
from behind them   and it went   Israel   camp

וַיִּסַּע עַמּוּד הֶעָנָן מִפְּנֵיהֶם
from before them   the cloud   pillar   and it passed

וַיַּעֲמֹד מֵאַחֲרֵיהֶם:
from behind them   and it stood

19. And the angel of God, who went before the camp of Israel, moved and went behind them; and the pillar of the cloud went from before their face, and stood behind them;

וַיָּבֹא בֵּין מַחֲנֵה מִצְרַיִם וּבֵין מַחֲנֵה יִשְׂרָאֵל
Israel   camps   and between   Egypt   camps   between   and it came

וַיְהִי הֶעָנָן וְהַחֹשֶׁךְ
and the darkness   the cloud   and there was

וַיָּאֶר אֶת־הַלָּיְלָה
the night - that   and it lighted

וְלֹא־קָרַב זֶה אֶל־זֶה כָּל־הַלָּיְלָה:
the night - all   this- unto   this   near - and not

20. And it came between the camp of the Egyptians and the camp of Israel; and it was a cloud and darkness to them, but it gave light by night to these; so that the one came not near the other all the night.

וַיֵּט מֹשֶׁה אֶת־יָדוֹ עַל־הַיָּם
the sea - upon   his hand - that   Moses   and he stretched

וַיּוֹלֶךְ יְהוָה אֶת־הַיָּם בְּרוּחַ קָדִים עַזָּה כָּל־הַלַּיְלָה
the night - all   strong   east   in wind   the sea - that   ihvh   and he went

וַיֵּט֩ אֶת־הַיָּ֨ם לֶחָרָבָ֜ה וַיִּבָּקְע֖וּ הַמָּֽיִם׃
and he made   that - the sea   to dry   and it divided it   the sea

21. And Moses stretched out his hand over the sea; and the Lord caused the sea to go back by a strong east wind all that night, and made the sea dry land, and the waters were divided.

CONSTRUCTION OF THE NAMES.

The way the 72 names are constructed is by taking

1) the first letter of the first verse,

2) the last letter of the second verse, and

3) the first letter of the third verse,

   and making a three letter name.

   Then taking

1) the second letter in the first verse,

2) the second to the last letter in the second verse, and

3) the second letter of the third verse,

   and making the next three letter name.

This construction is continued in this manner till all of the 72 names are created. Each of the three verses have the same amount of letters.

In Hebrew, certain letters are written differently when they appear at the end of a word. These are called final letters. On the 72 name chart the Hebrew final letters are not used. The letters in the 72 name tables of this book appear as their normal depictions of the alphabet letters. No final letters are used because these names are not meant to be used as conversational Hebrew, and also this makes it easier for most to understand while meditating.

VOCALIZING

Note that in the 72 names tables the written Khet looks very similar to the written Heh when one is vocalizing during meditations. If you are not paying attention you can easily mistake a Khet for a Heh. On the 72 name seeded table a small mark has been inserted in the cell before a name containing a Khet. This is to alert one to the difference and not make a mistake pronouncing a Khet. Be sure to make the guttural sound of the Khet from the throat.

The first table "72 Names Raw" is how the names are plainly depicted in a table.

The next table "72 Names Seeded" is where these names are seeded with the four letters of the shem hamephorash in and around the three letters of each name. When vocalizing one of these cells there will be seven letter sounds plus their seven assigned vowel sounds, vocalized in order. One may use the tables that are depicted with the seeded letters to meditate, however it's best to imagine into a name the seeded letters of the shem hamephorash.

The next table "72 Names Spaced" is used for this imagining into a name. It has spaces between the letters of the names. This table is designed to facilitate the visualizations of the shem hamephorish letters with one's imagination between the written letters. The four letters of the sacred name are each to be seeded in each word mentally, by imagining the seeded letters in and around the written physical letters of one of the 72 names while vocalizing it's assigned vowel. The level of prophesy opens up by using one's imagination.

The next table "72 Names Pointed" has been found in many ancient manuscripts. Some of these texts vary slightly in the pronunciation of some of the names but still retain somewhat the same sounds. This is an example of an advanced pointing method used by the ancient sages to make the meditation more aligned with the sefirot to make the meditation more effective. However keep in mind, the major effectiveness of all meditations comes from the consonant sounds.

The last table depicts the English pronunciation of the 72 names with the attached pointing of vowels as has been depicted in many ancient texts. At the top level of performing this tzeruf meditation one should memorize all 72 names and their spellings, and mentally construct and visualize and vocalize each of the 72 names and their seedings of the shem hamephorash.

Separation Phrase

After one has seeded a name of the 72 names while vocalizing, the sages have stated that one should then say a separation phrase like "tashegeviva toveda Yah tzuruvah." This particular separator was used and depicted in the writings by the renown sage Chaim Vital. This roughly translates to "You are the most high and beneficial God (Yah) like a rock." Other phrases are used by other sages as separators. All are specially constructed to be a powerful and effective phrase. A separator phrase aids the subconscious in analyzing the three letter names as they are a part of three verses. The two sides of the brain along with your subconscious can then do the jigsaw puzzle of rearranging and processing the letters in the generation of influx.

After vocalizing the letters and their seeds in a cell, stare at the letters of the name you have just vocalized while saying the separator phrase.

Powers of the Names

Abulafia in *Or Hasekel* states that the letter names themselves have no intrinsic value. These names have attached to them spiritual powers where the meditator can bind himself to these powers through tzeruf meditation. It induces a supra state of consciousness where the meditator develops the powers himself.

In advanced tzeruf meditation from these 72 names are further enhanced and are derived 54 quadrilateral names which is the secret of drawing power from all that exists (*Gates of Light*).

הע״ב שמות של הקב״ה

והו	ילי	סיט	עלם	מהש	ללה	אכא	כהת
הזי	אלד	לאו	ההע	יזל	מבה	הרי	הקם
לאו	כלי	לוו	פהל	נלך	ייי	מלה	חהו
נתה	האא	ירת	שאה	ריי	אום	לכב	ושר
יחו	להח	כוק	מנד	אני	חעם	רהע	ייז
ההה	מיכ	וול	ילה	סאל	ערי	עשל	מיה
והו	דני	החש	עמם	ננא	נית	מבה	פוי
נמם	יילה	הרח	מצר	ומב	יהה	ענו	מחי
דמב	מנק	איע	חבו	ראה	יבמ	היי	מום

72 Names Seeded

ע"ב שמות מוטבעים ב־ע"ב אותיות

72 Names Seeded

עב שמות מרווחים / 72 Names Spaced

והו	ילי	סיט	עלם	מהש	ללה	אכא	כהת
הזי	אלד	לאו	ההע	יזל	מבה	הרי	הקם
לאו	כלי	לוו	פהל	נלך	ייי	מלה	חהו
נתה	האא	ירת	שאה	ריי	אום	לכב	ושר
יחו	להח	כוק	מנד	אני	חעם	רהע	ייז
ההה	מיכ	וול	ילה	סאל	ערי	עשל	מיה
והו	דני	החש	עמם	ננא	נית	מבה	פוי
נמם	ייל	הרח	מצר	ומב	יהה	ענו	מחי
דמב	מנק	איע	חבו	ראה	יבמ	היי	מום

72 Names Pointed

וָהוּ	יֶלִי	סִיט	עֶלֶם	מַהַשׁ	לֶלֶה	אַכָּא	כָּהַת	הֲזִי
אֶלֶד	לָאו	הַהַע	יֶזֵל	מֶבַה	הֲרִי	הַקַם	לָאו	כְּלִי
לֶוֹ	פָּהֵל	נֶלֶךְ	יִיִי	מֶלֶה	חֲהוּ	נִתָה	הָאָא	יֶרֵת
שַׁאָה	רִיִי	אוּם	לַכָּב	וַשֵׁר	יֶחֵו	לֶהַח	כְּוֵק	מֶנֵד
אֲנִי	חֲעַם	רֶהָע	יֵיֵז	הַהַה	מִיכ	וָוַל	יֶלָה	סַאֵל
עֲרִי	עֳשָׁל	מִיה	וֶהוּ	דָנִי	הֲחַשׁ	עֶמֵם	נֶנָא	נִית
מֶבָה	פּוֹי	נֶמֶם	יֵיל	הֲרַח	מַצֵר	וְמַב	יֶהַה	עֲנוּ
מֶחִי	דֶמַב	מֶנַק	אַיַע	חֲבוּ	רֶאָה	יֶבַם	הַיַי	מִוּם

Memorizing

c_hat	aca	l_lah	m_hash	alam	sit	i_li	v_hu
h_kam	h_rai	m_bah	i_zal	h_ha	l_oo	alad	hazai
kh_hu	m_lah	iiai	n_lac	p_hal	l_vu	k_li	l_oo
v_shar	l_cav	avam	r_iai	sh_ah	i_rat	haaa	n_tah
i_iaz	r_ha	khaam	ani	m_nada	r_vak	l_hakh	i_khoo
m_iah	eshal	ari	s_al	i_lah	v_vala	maiac	hahah
pavi	m_bah	n_iat	n_ni	amam	hakhesh	dani	v_hu
m_khi	aniu	i_hah	umab	m_tzar	harakh	i_ial	n_mem
mom	hiai	i_bam	r_ah	khaboo	aia	m_nak	d_mab

THE 72 ANGELS

This is an example of an advanced meditation technique of opening a bridge between the mental and the physical. The technique effectuates several aspects at the same time while seeding the revealed letter (first letter) of an angel's name, which is in this case a letter of one of the 72 names.

The first technique effected is the seeding of the shem hamephorash with the 72 names. The second technique is that each of the three individual letters of all of the 72 names are expanded to make three new words per name. These new words use as the first letter for their expanded name, a letter from one of the 72 names.

Each expanded word is composed with two parts to it. The first part of one of the expanded words is the first letter derived from the name and includes other letters that follow. This first part of the word aligns with the sefirah Binah the last sefirah of the mental level. The last part of the expanded word always ends with the letters Alef and Lamed. These two letters are one of the names of God, "El", and is aligned with the sefirah Chesed. Chesed is the first sefirah of the emotional level. Thus the last sefirah of the mental level and the first sefirah of the physical level are both stimulated. By stimulating this area it opens a bridge between the mental and physical aspects and creates a channel for the influx to easily flow down from the mental to the physical.

These names are known names of angels. The domain of the angels is at the creation level of Beriah which is aligned with sefirah Binah. We are in the domain of the physical level. Saying each angel's name is an "uhid" or uniting of the mental and physical levels. This bridging area is typically referred to as the Daat area.

METHOD

There are seven meditation steps to every seeded section in this meditation.

1) Vocalize the Hebrew letter Yod of the seeded shem hamephorash and it's natural vowel sound with one long exhaled breath. Inhale.

2) Vocalize the composed angel name drawing it out with one long exhaled breath. Inhale.

3) Vocalize the next letter of the shem hamephorash the Heh and its natural vowel with one long exhaled breath. Inhale.

Repeat this sequence for the remaining seeded letters and angel names in the first name section. Then do this process for all of the next 71 name sections of composed angels names and seeded letters of the shem hamephoriah.

    Between each 72 name column an optional separator phrase of your choice can be said (tashegeviva toveda yah tzuruvah).

    This meditation is ideal for using the head movements when vocalizing the seeded shem hamephorash that surround the various angel names.

72 Angels 1

Table 1

ל		ה		ל		ה
וֶהוּאֵל		יְלִיאֵל		סִיטאֵל		עֵלֶמִיָּה
ל		ה		ל		ה
לָאוּאֵל		אַכָאִיָּה		כַּהֲתֵאל		הֵזִיאֵל
ל		ה		ל		ה
הֲרִיאֵל		הַקָמִיָּה		לָוִיאֵל		כַּלִיאֵל
ל		ה		ל		ה
לֵוִיאֵל		פַּהֲלִיָּה		נֵלְכָאֵל		יִיאַיֵּאל
ל		ה		ל		ה
מִלָאִיאֵל		חַהֲוִיָּה		נִתַהאֵל		הָאָאִיָּה
ל		ה		ל		ה
הָרָחֵל		יִזָלאֵל		מִבַהאֵל		הֲרִיאֵל
ל		ה		ל		ה
נִיתְמֵל		הָאָאֵל		יְרַתְאֵל		שֶׁאֲהִיָּה
ל		ה		ל		ה
רֵיאִיאֵל		אוּמַבאֵל		לֶכָבאֵל		וָשָׁרִיאֵל

72 ANGELS 2

Table 2

ה		ו		ה		ו	
מִיכָאֵ״ל	ו	הַהַהאֵ״ל	ה	וְוָאלִיָ״ה	ו	יְלָיאֵ״ל	ה
וְהוּאֵ״ל	ו	יְלָיאֵ״ל	ה	סִיטְאֵ״ל	ו	עֶלֶמְיָ״ה	ה
לָאוִיָ״ה	ו	הַקֶמְיָ״ה	ה	הֲרָיאֵ״ל	ו	מְבַהאֵ״ל	ה
יֶזָלאֵ״ל	ו	מֶבָהאֵ״ל	ה	הֲרִיאֵ״ל	ו	הֲקָמְיָ״ה	ה
לָאוִיָ״ה	ו	כָלִיאֵ״ל	ה	לְוַוִיָ״ה	ו	פַהֲלִיָ״ה	ה
נֶלְכָאֵ״ל	ו	יַיָאֵ״ל	ה	מֶלָהאֵ״ל	ו	חֲהוִיָ״ה	ה
נִיתָהאֵ״ל	ו	הָאאאֵ״ל	ה	יְרָתאֵ״ל	ו	שְׂאהִיָ״ה	ה
עַםאֵ״ל	ו	מֶנָדאֵ״ל	ה	אֲנִיאֵ״ל	ו	חֲעֲמִיָ״ה	ה
רְהָעאֵ״ל	ו	יֵיזָאֵ״ל	ה	הֲהַהאֵ״ל	ו	מִיכָאֵ״ל	ה

72 Angels 3

Table 3

ז		ר		ה	
לְהַחֲיָהאֵל	ז	אָנִיאֵל	ר	לְכַבְזִיאֵל	ה
לְאַבְדִיאֵל	ז	לְהַהַעֲאֵל	ר	יְהֵרֵאֵל	ה
לְחַהֲקֻל	ז	לְמִיאֵל	ר	יַהֵוִאֵל	ה
לְאַנְפִיאֵל	ז	לְאַהֵאֵל	ר	לְאָיָאֵל	ה
לְאָזִיאֵל	ז	לְמִיסֹמֵאֵל	ר	מְסִיאֵל	ה
לְאָיעַל	ז	לְאַוְיָהִיאֵל	ר	נְצִרֵאֵל	ה
לְאַקֻמֵל	ז	לְצַאֵל	ר	חִנֻבֵאֵל	ה
הַהֵאֵל	ז	הַהֵבִיאֵל	ר	מְהַאֲמַאֵל	ה

233

Table 4

72 Angels 4

נ	הוויאל	ר	נ	מבהיאל	ר	פויאל	נ
נ	ענואל	ר	נ	יחויאל	ר	דמביאל	ר
נ	מחיאל	ר	נ	ענויאל	ר	מנקאל	ר
נ	איעאל	ר	נ	חבויאל	ר	ראהאל	ר
נ	הרחאל	ר	נ	מצראל	ר	יבמיאל	ר
נ	מומיאל	ר	נ	ההעיאל	ר	ייליאל	ר
נ	ייזאל	ר	נ	מלהאל	ר	חהויאל	ר
נ	לאויאל	ר	נ	אכאיה	ר	כהתאל	ר
נ	נתהיה	ר	נ	הזיאל	ר	אלדיאל	ר

72 Angels 5

Table 5

ל		ה		ו		ה	
לפֿהֿיִאֵל		והֿוּיָאֵל		לעֿוּיָאֵל		
לסֿלִיָאֵל		הַהֿהֿיָאֵל		בִּיתֿיָאֵל		
לאֿוּיָאֵל		והֿוּיָאֵל		היֿהֿיָאֵל		
קלִיָאֵל		ודֿוּיָאֵל		הפֿוּיָאֵל		
אלִיָאֵל		ורֿיָאֵל		לאֿוּ		
נפֿוּיָאֵל		ערֿיָאֵל		ניָאֵל		
ננֿוּיָאֵל		בהֿהֿיָאֵל		גדֿיָאֵל		
לאֿנֿיִ		יוֿנָיָאֵל		זכֿוּיָאֵל		

72 ANGELS 6

Table 6

ני	הרחאלאל	ני	נמאמיהאל	ני	ענואלאל	ני	מחיאל
ני	דמביהאל	ני	ייליאל	ני	ננאאלאל	ני	עריאל
ני	מנקאל	ני	ייהוהיאל	ני	ייהוהאל	ני	מבהיאל
ני	הוהיאל	ני	ללביהאל	ני	יאהאל	ני	אהיאל
ני	יבמיאל	ני	אמביאל	ני	סהסאל	ני	בבסיאל
ני	יוביראל	ני	הוהבאל	ני	הירבאל	ני	יובראל
ני	יאל	ני	מהסהאל	ני	יאהליאל	ני	יאהליאל
ני	האויאל	ני	ייקהבאל	ני	הומלאל	ני	הוהלאל

72 Angels 7

Table 7

ו		ה		ו		ה	
ו	ונדניאל	ה	ננהיאל	ו	ירתאל	ה	ןו
ו	נודריאל	ה	נוסמיאל	ו	יסמסיאל	ה	ןו
ו	נוכורבאל	ה	ננאריאל	ו	מאנתאאל	ה	ןו
ו	ועפציאל	ה	נחתריאל	ו	וחריאל	ה	ןו
ו	נונפסאל	ה	נוסיאל	ו	אכריאל	ה	ןו
ו	נוברוא	ה	יאריאל	ו	ננוריאל	ה	ןו
ו	נחכיאל	ה	נואל	ו	נוריאל	ה	ןו
ו	סראל	ה	נורריאל	ו	ונסמריאל	ה	ןו

72 Angels 8

Table 8

ני	המומיה.אל	ני	דמבה.אל	ני	מנקאל.אל	ני	יהה.אל	ע
ני	ענואאל	ני	מהיאל.אל	ני	ההעשיה.אל	ני	דניאל	ע
ני	ננאאל	ני	נידה.אל	ני	מבהיה.אל	ני	פויאל	ע
ני	מיכאל	ני	ויהאל	ני	ייליאל	ני	נממיה	ע
ני	איעאל	ני	חבויה	ני	רואאל	ני	יחואל	ע
ני	הרחאל	ני	מצראל	ני	ההאל	ני	לכבאל	ע
ני	מצראל	ני	ומבאל	ני	יהויאל	ני	מהיאל	ע
ני	מומאל	ני	מנקאל	ני	יבמיה	ני	היאאל	ע

72 Angels 9

Table 9

ויהויה	ו	ילהיה	ו	סיטאל	ו	עלמיה	ו
מהשיה	ו	ללהאל	ו	אכאיה	ו	כהתאל	ו
הזיאל	ו	אלדיה	ו	לאויה	ו	ההעיה	ו
יזלאל	ו	מבהאל	ו	הריאל	ו	הקמיה	ו
לאויה	ו	כליאל	ו	לוויה	ו	פהליה	ו
נלכאל	ו	יייאל	ו	מלהאל	ו	חהויה	ו
נתהיה	ו	האאיה	ו	ירתאל	ו	שאהיה	ו
ריייאל	ו	אומאל	ו	לכבאל	ו	ושריה	ו

Later Kabbalists

This is an example of an advanced meditation. Generally a Hebrew root word consists of three root letters. The first letter of a word depicts it's revealed character. The other two letters that follow reveal aspects of it's concealed character. However each letter of the shem hamephorash shows revealed character. Spelling out the letter names of each letter of the shem hamephorash will then yield each letter's revealed aspect and each letter's two concealed aspects. Thus by spelling out the four letters of the shem hamephorash, there now is a total of twelve letters with 4 revealed aspects and 8 concealed aspects. This is called milui, meaning in English, pregnant.

Milui

In milui, a word that has it's letter's nominative names spelled out is considered complete. Each letter of any word is considered pregnant with a word. For example the word Chen has two letters which are the Chet and the Nun. The name of Chet is spelled; Chet, Yod, Tav, and has a gematria value of 418. The name of Nun is spelled; Nun, Vav, Nun, and has a gematria value of 106. Thus, the pregnant value of the word Chen by milui computation is 524.

The shem hamephorash can be spelled in milui different ways. The letter Heh can be spelled out 1) Hei, Yod 2) Hei Hei 3) Hei, Alef. Also the letter Vav can be spelled out 1) Vav, Yod, Vav 2) Vav, Alef, Vav 3) Vav, Vav. These different spellings affect the numerical values of the milui.

Three letters of the shem hamephorash, Hei, Vav, and again Hei, have three variants of spelling. This is 27 different possible spellings of the sacred name. There are 13 possible numerical values of the shem hamephorash ranging from 44 to 72.

The following chart shows the four generally accepted and most essential spellings of the shem hamephorash. This is because the numerical values are harmonious with Chochmah (72), Binah (63), Chesed to Yesod (45), and Malchut (52). These values are referred to by their Hebrew numerical values sounds as if it were a word;

AV – עב 72, SaG – סג 63, MaH – מה 45, BeN – בן 52.

	Havayah of 72		Havayah of 63		Havayah of 45		Havayah of 52	
Yod	י ו ד	20	י ו ד	20	י ו ד	20	י ו ד	20
Heih	ה י	15	ה י	15	ה א	6	ה ה	10
Vav	ו י ו	22	ו א ו	13	ו א ו	13	ו ו	12
Heh	ה י	15	ה י	15	ה א	6	ה ה	20
	Total	72	Total	63	Total	45	Total	52

Latter Kabbalist's Method

On the far left side of the "Later Kabbalist" tables there is a vertical column. The spelled out or pregnant names of the shem hamephorash are listed vertically down the column. These individual letters are to be seeded mentally between the letters appearing in the eleven cells to the right.

One is to vocalize the first letter of the cell, then vocalize a seeded letter, then vocalize the last letter in the cell. The letter to be seeded for the row appears in the outlined box to the far left of that individual row. In each row the seeded letter will change.

This is example of how advanced tzeruf meditations can get more complicated.

Later Kabbalists

Later Kabbalists - Table 1

Chokma / עב

חש	קל	מג	אך	מה	לל	אכא	הזי	אלד	לאו	הוה
עה	לב	סע	צא	הה	לא	הקם	הרי	לאו	זלי	מבה
אך	מה	לל	אכא	הזי	אלד	לאו	הוה	יה	לט	סט
צא	הה	לא	הקם	הרי	לאו	זלי	מבה	סט	עלם	מהש
אכא	הזי	אלד	לאו	הוה	יה	לט	סט	עלם	מהש	ללה
הקם	הרי	לאו	זלי	מבה	סט	עלם	מהש	ללה	אכא	כהת
לאו	הוה	יה	לט	סט	עלם	מהש	ללה	אכא	כהת	הזי
זלי	מבה	סט	עלם	מהש	ללה	אכא	כהת	הזי	אלד	לאו
			ה	י				ה	י	וה

Table 1 Continued

אָז ... בִּינָה

Later Kabbalists - Table 2

The Six — מה

אל	אכ	אי	אט	אח	אז	או	אה	אד	אג	אב
בך	בי	בט	בח	בז	בו	בה	בד	בג	בב	בא
גי	גט	גח	גז	גו	גה	גד	גג	גב	גא	סמ
דט	דח	דז	דו	דה	דד	דג	דב	דא	סמ	עב
הח	הז	הו	הה	הד	הג	הב	הא	סמ	עב	מב
וז	וו	וה	וד	וג	וב	וא	סמ	עב	מב	ל״ב
זו	זה	זד	זג	זב	זא	סמ	עב	מב	ל״ב	אטב
חה	חד	חג	חב	חא	סמ	עב	מב	ל״ב	אטב	תב
טד	טג	טב	טא	סמ	עב	מב	ל״ב	אטב	תב	בר
כג	כב	כא	סמ	עב	מב	ל״ב	אטב	תב	בר	בר
לב	לא	סמ	עב	מב	ל״ב	אטב	תב	בר	בר	מה
שם	בר	אב	יד	בר	יד	אב	בד	פב	פא	יה
י	י	ו	הי	א	ו	א	ו	הי	א	יה

אמ	נס	עפ	קצ	רש	תב	גד	הו	זח	טי	כל	י
אנ	סע	פצ	קר	שת	בג	דה	וז	חט	יכ	למ	ו
אס	עפ	צק	רש	תב	גד	הו	זח	טי	כל	מנ	ד
אע	פצ	קר	שת	בג	דה	וז	חט	יכ	למ	נס	ה
אפ	צק	רש	תב	גד	הו	זח	טי	כל	מנ	סע	ה
אצ	קר	שת	בג	דה	וז	חט	יכ	למ	נס	עפ	ו
אק	רש	תב	גד	הו	חז	טי	כל	מנ	סע	פצ	ו
אר	שת	בג	דה	וז	חט	יכ	למ	נס	עפ	צק	ה
אש	תב	גד	הו	זח	טי	כל	מנ	סע	פצ	קר	ה
את	בג	דה	וז	חט	יכ	למ	נס	עפ	צק	רש	יהו

בן   **TABLE 2 CONTINUED**   **MALKUT**

About Psalm 119

Baal Shem Tov prayed this Psalm every day. He continually recommended to his followers that this Psalm should be said daily. He said if said on a continuous daily bases, it will put one into a meditative state where one will receive mental impressions of a person while they are talking to them. This will happen even when one is engaged in conversation with a total stranger. Sometimes this can make the practitioner feel very self-conscious while listening to another person talking.

One doesn't start noticing the results until saying it daily for three or four weeks. When starting, it's best to say this psalm twice a day, once in the morning, and once in the evening. Don't feel surprised if you want to stop this meditation after you have experienced the effects. Eventually you will control your feelings from the impressions. When the sages of old write about "the light" you know the awe they are referring to.

This is the longest Psalm. In this Psalm there are twenty-two sections with each letter of the Hebrew alphabet representing a section. The first word of each the verses in a section starts with the representative Hebrew alphabet letter for that section. In this psalm there are an abnormally high occurrence of words that refer to meditation.

There are eight verses per alphabet letter section. The number eight in the *Bible* has spiritual significance. Seven is the biblical number associated with perfection in the physical world. Eight is the level above this level and thus signifies the spiritual world beyond. Circumcision was commanded to be done on the eighth day. In the festival of Succot there are seven days that are celebrated regarding the nations of the world. The eighth day of celebration is set aside for those that transcend the physical world to the spiritual realm. There are many other examples in the *Bible* related to the number eight.

Advanced Meditation

One of the advanced meditations is to meditate on a chosen Hebrew word and effectuate a meditation by taking each of the letters of that word and saying their corresponding letter sections found in Psalm 119. Thus generally only three sections are read assuming there were only three letters in the word being meditated on.

Psalm 119

א

אַשְׁרֵי תְמִימֵי דָרֶךְ הַהֹלְכִים בְּתוֹרַת יְהֹוָה׃
ihvh   in Torah   the walking ones   way   perfect   happy

1. Happy are those whose way is blameless, who walk in the Torah of the Lord.

אַשְׁרֵי נֹצְרֵי עֵדֹתָיו בְּכָל־לֵב יִדְרְשׁוּהוּ׃
they seek him   heart - in all   his testimonies   preservers   happy

2. Happy are those who keep his testimonies, and who seek him with the whole heart.

אַף לֹא פָעֲלוּ עַוְלָה בִּדְרָכָיו הָלָכוּ׃
they walk   in his way   inequity   they act   not   then

3. They also do no iniquity; they walk in his ways.

אַתָּה צִוִּיתָה פִקֻּדֶיךָ לִשְׁמֹר מְאֹד׃
greatly   to heed   your precepts   commanded   you

4. You have commanded us to keep your precepts diligently.

אַחֲלַי יִכֹּנוּ דְרָכָי לִשְׁמֹר חֻקֶּיךָ׃
your statutes   to heed   my way   you established   my tent

5. O that my ways were directed to keep your statutes!

אָז לֹא אֵבוֹשׁ בְּהַבִּיטִי אֶל כָּל מִצְוֹתֶיךָ׃
your commandments   all   unto   in my observing   I will be ashamed   not   then

6. Then I shall not be ashamed, when I observe to all your commandments.

אוֹדְךָ בְּיֹשֶׁר לֵבָב בְּלָמְדִי מִשְׁפְּטֵי צִדְקֶךָ׃
your righteous   judgments   in my learning   heart   in upright   I thank you

7. I shall give thanks with uprightness of heart, when I learn your righteous judgments.

אֶת חֻקֶּיךָ אֶשְׁמֹר אַל תַּעַזְבֵנִי עַד מְאֹד׃
greatly   till   you forsake me   don't   I will heed   your statutes   that

8. I will keep your statutes; O do not forsake me utterly

בּ

בַּמֶּה יְזַכֶּה־נַּעַר אֶת־אָרְחוֹ לִשְׁמֹר כִּדְבָרֶךָ׃
like your sayings   to heeding   road   that   youth   he clean   in what

9. How can a young man keep his way pure? By guarding it according to your word.

בְּכָל־לִבִּי דְרַשְׁתִּיךָ אַל־תַּשְׁגֵּנִי מִמִּצְוֺתֶיךָ׃
from your commandments   you stray me   don't   I sought you   my heart   in all

10. With my whole heart I have sought you; O do not let wander from your commandments!

בְּלִבִּי צָפַנְתִּי אִמְרָתֶךָ לְמַעַן לֹא אֶחֱטָא־לָךְ׃
to you   I will sin   not   to end   your word   I have hid   in my heart

11. I have hidden your word in my heart, that I might not sin against you.

בָּרוּךְ אַתָּה יְהוָה לַמְּדֵנִי חֻקֶּיךָ׃
your statutes   teach me   ihvh   you   blessed

12. Blessed are you, O Lord; teach me your statutes.

בִּשְׂפָתַי סִפַּרְתִּי כֹּל מִשְׁפְּטֵי־פִיךָ׃
your mouth   judgments   all   I declared   in my lips

13. With my lips I have declared all the judgments of your mouth.

בְּדֶרֶךְ עֵדְוֺתֶיךָ שַׂשְׂתִּי כְּעַל כָּל־הוֹן׃
fulfillment   all   like upon   I rejoiced   your testimonies   in way

14. I have rejoiced in the way of your testimonies, as much as in all riches.

בְּפִקֻּדֶיךָ אָשִׂיחָה וְאַבִּיטָה אֹרְחֹתֶיךָ׃
your road   light   and I observe   I will meditate   in your precepts

15. I will meditate in your precepts, and observe your ways.

בְּחֻקֹּתֶיךָ אֶשְׁתַּעֲשָׁע לֹא אֶשְׁכַּח דְּבָרֶךָ׃
your sayings   I will forget   not   I will delight   in your statutes

16. I will delight myself in your statutes; I will not forget your word.

ג

גְּמֹל עַל עַבְדְּךָ אֶחְיֶה וְאֶשְׁמְרָה דְבָרֶךָ׃
_{your sayings   and I will heed   I will live   your servant   upon   treat}

17. Deal bountifully with your servant, that I may live, and keep your word.

גַּל עֵינַי וְאַבִּיטָה נִפְלָאוֹת מִתּוֹרָתֶךָ׃
_{from your Torah   mysticals   and I will behold   my eye   wave}

18. Open my eyes, that I may behold wondrous things in your Torah.

גֵּר אָנֹכִי בָאָרֶץ אַל תַּסְתֵּר מִמֶּנִּי מִצְוֺתֶיךָ׃
_{your commandments   from me   you secret   don't   in earth   I am   stranger}

19. I am a stranger on earth; do not hide your commandments from me.

גָּרְסָה נַפְשִׁי לְתַאֲבָה אֶל מִשְׁפָּטֶיךָ בְכָל עֵת׃
_{times   in all   your judgments   unto   to longing   my soul   version}

20. My soul is consumed with longing for your judgments at all times.

גָּעַרְתָּ זֵדִים אֲרוּרִים הַשֹּׁגִים מִמִּצְוֺתֶיךָ׃
_{from your commandments   erring ones   cursed ones   arrogant ones   you rebuked}

21. You have rebuked the arrogant who are cursed, who wander from your commandments.

גַּל מֵעָלַי חֶרְפָּה וָבוּז כִּי עֵדֹתֶיךָ נָצָרְתִּי׃
_{I kept   your testimonies   like   and contempt   insult   from upon me   wave}

22. Remove from me insult and contempt; for I have kept your testimonies.

גַּם יָשְׁבוּ שָׂרִים בִּי נִדְבָּרוּ עַבְדְּךָ יָשִׂיחַ בְּחֻקֶּיךָ׃
_{in your statutes   meditated   your servant   they spoke   in me   princes   they sat   also}

23. Princes also sat and spoke against me; but your servant meditated in your statutes.

גַּם עֵדֹתֶיךָ שַׁעֲשֻׁעָי אַנְשֵׁי עֲצָתִי׃
_{my advisors   my counselors   my delights   your testimonies   also}

24. Your testimonies also are my delight and my counselors.

ד

דָּבְקָה לֶעָפָר נַפְשִׁי חַיֵּנִי כִּדְבָרֶךָ:
like your sayings　give me life　my soul　to dust　clings

25. My soul cleaves to the dust; revive me according to your word.

דְּרָכַי סִפַּרְתִּי וַתַּעֲנֵנִי לַמְּדֵנִי חֻקֶּיךָ:
your statutes　teach me　and you answered　I declared　my path

26. I have declared my ways, and you heard me; teach me your statutes.

דֶּרֶךְ פִּקּוּדֶיךָ הֲבִינֵנִי וְאָשִׂיחָה בְּנִפְלְאוֹתֶיךָ:
in your wonders　and I will meditate　the my understand　your precepts　path

27. Make me understand the way of your precepts; so I shall talk of your wondrous works.

דָּלְפָה נַפְשִׁי מִתּוּגָה קַיְּמֵנִי כִּדְבָרֶךָ:
like your sayings　strengthen me　from sorrow　my soul　melts

28. My soul melts away for sorrow; strengthen me according to your word.

דֶּרֶךְ שֶׁקֶר הָסֵר מִמֶּנִּי וְתוֹרָתְךָ חָנֵּנִי:
grant me　and your torah　from me　remove　lie　the path

29. Put the ways of falsehood away from me; and grant me your Torah graciously.

דֶּרֶךְ אֱמוּנָה בָחָרְתִּי מִשְׁפָּטֶיךָ שִׁוִּיתִי:
laid before me　your judgments　I chose　truth　path

30. I have chosen the way of truth; your judgments have I laid before me.

דָּבַקְתִּי בְעֵדְוֺתֶיךָ יְהֹוָה אַל תְּבִישֵׁנִי:
you shame me　don't　ihvh　in your testimonies　I cleaved

31. I cleave to your testimonies; O Lord, put me not to shame.

דֶּרֶךְ מִצְוֺתֶיךָ אָרוּץ כִּי תַרְחִיב לִבִּי:
my heart　it will enlarge　like　I run　your commandments　the path

32. I will run the way of your commandments, when you shall enlarge my heart.

ה

הוֹרֵ֣נִי יְ֭הוָה דֶּ֥רֶךְ חֻקֶּ֗יךָ וְאֶצְּרֶ֥נָּה עֵֽקֶב׃
<small>end　and I will keep　your statutes　path　ihvh　teach me</small>

33. Teach me, O Lord, the way of your statutes; and I shall keep it to the end.

הֲ֭בִינֵנִי וְאֶצְּרָ֥ה תוֹרָתֶ֗ךָ וְאֶשְׁמְרֶ֥נָּה בְכָל־לֵֽב׃
<small>heart　in all　and I will heed it　your Torah　and I will keep　the my understanding</small>

34. Give me understanding, and I shall keep your Torah; I shall observe it with my whole heart.

הַ֭דְרִיכֵנִי בִּנְתִ֣יב מִצְוֺתֶ֑יךָ כִּי־ב֥וֹ חָפָֽצְתִּי׃
<small>I delight　in it　like　your commandments　in lead　the path of me</small>

35. Lead me in the path of your commandments; for I delight in it.

הַט־לִ֭בִּי אֶל־עֵדְוֺתֶ֗יךָ וְאַ֣ל אֶל־בָּֽצַע׃
<small>unjust gain　unto　and don't　your testimonies　unto　my heart　incline</small>

36. Incline my heart to your testimonies, and not to unjust gain.

הַעֲבֵ֣ר עֵ֭ינַי מֵרְא֣וֹת שָׁ֑וְא בִּדְרָכֶ֥ךָ חַיֵּֽנִי׃
<small>give me life　in your way　vanity　from seeing　my eyes　the pass</small>

37. Turn away my eyes from beholding vanity; and give me life in your way.

הָקֵ֣ם לְ֭עַבְדְּךָ אִמְרָתֶ֑ךָ אֲ֝שֶׁ֗ר לְיִרְאָתֶֽךָ׃
<small>to fearing you　which　your word　to your servant　confirm</small>

38. Confirm to your servant your word. which is for those who fear you.

הַעֲבֵ֣ר חֶ֭רְפָּתִי אֲשֶׁ֣ר יָגֹ֑רְתִּי כִּ֖י מִשְׁפָּטֶ֣יךָ טוֹבִֽים׃
<small>good ones　your judgments　like　it my routine　which　my insult　the pass</small>

39. Turn away my insult which I fear; for your judgments are good.

הִ֭נֵּה תָּאַ֣בְתִּי לְפִקֻּדֶ֑יךָ בְּצִדְקָתְךָ֥ חַיֵּֽנִי׃
<small>give me life　in your righteousness　to your precepts　I longed　here is</small>

40. Behold, I have longed after your precepts; give me life in your righteousness.

ו

וִיבֹאֻנִי חֲסָדֶךָ יְהוָה תְּשׁוּעָתְךָ כְּאִמְרָתֶךָ:
   and come to me your mercies ihvh your salvation like your word

41. Let your loving kindness come also to me, O Lord, your salvation, according to your word.

וְאֶעֱנֶה חֹרְפִי דָבָר כִּי בָטַחְתִּי בִּדְבָרֶךָ:
   and I will answer my insulter speech like my trust in your sayings

42. So shall I have an answer for him who insults me; for I trust in your word.

וְאַל תַּצֵּל מִפִּי דְבַר אֱמֶת עַד מְאֹד
   and don't take away from my mouth speech truth till again

כִּי לְמִשְׁפָּטֶךָ יִחָלְתִּי:
   like to your judgments I hoped

43. And do not take the word of truth utterly from my mouth; for I have hoped in your judgments.

וְאֶשְׁמְרָה תוֹרָתְךָ תָמִיד לְעוֹלָם וָעֶד:
   and I will heed your Torah always to forever and time

44. So shall I keep your Torah continually for ever and ever.

וְאֶתְהַלְּכָה בָרְחָבָה כִּי פִקֻּדֶיךָ דָרָשְׁתִּי:
   and I will walk in liberty like your precepts I seek

45. And I will walk at liberty; for I seek your precepts.

וַאֲדַבְּרָה בְעֵדֹתֶיךָ נֶגֶד מְלָכִים וְלֹא אֵבוֹשׁ:
   and I will speak in testimonies before kings and not I will be ashamed

46. I will also speak of your testimonies before kings, and will not be ashamed.

וְאֶשְׁתַּעֲשַׁע בְּמִצְוֹתֶיךָ אֲשֶׁר אָהָבְתִּי:
   and I will delight in your commandments which I loved

47. And I will delight myself in your commandments, which I have loved.

וְאֶשָּׂא כַפַּי אֶל מִצְוֹתֶיךָ אֲשֶׁר אָהָבְתִּי
   and I will lift my palms onto your commandments which I loved

וְאָשִׂיחָה בְחֻקֶּיךָ:
   and I will meditate in your statutes

48. My hands also I will lift up to your commandments, which I have loved; and I will meditate in your statutes.

256

ז

זְכָר־דָּבָר לְעַבְדֶּךָ עַל אֲשֶׁר יִחַלְתָּנִי:
it [gives] hope to me   which   upon   to your servant   speak   remember

49. Remember the word to your servant, whereby you have given me hope.

זֹאת נֶחָמָתִי בְעָנְיִי כִּי אִמְרָתְךָ חִיָּתְנִי:
life [to] me   your word   like   in my affliction   I comforted   this is

50. This is my comfort in my affliction; for your word has revived me.

זֵדִים הֱלִיצֻנִי עַד־מְאֹד מִתּוֹרָתְךָ לֹא נָטִיתִי:
I turned away   not   from your torah   greatly   till   cause me derision   the proud ones

51. The arrogant have had me greatly in derision; but I have not turned away from your Torah.

זָכַרְתִּי מִשְׁפָּטֶיךָ מֵעוֹלָם יְהוָה וָאֶתְנֶחָם:
and I am comforted   ihvh   from forever   your judgments   I remembered

52. I remembered your judgments of old, O Lord; and have comforted myself.

זַלְעָפָה אֲחָזַתְנִי מֵרְשָׁעִים עֹזְבֵי תּוֹרָתֶךָ:
your Torah   forsakers   from wicked ones   took hold of me   horror

53. Horror has taken hold of me because of the wicked who forsake your Torah.

זְמִרוֹת הָיוּ־לִי חֻקֶּיךָ בְּבֵית מְגוּרָי:
my pilgrimage   in house   your statutes   to me   have been   songs

54. Your statutes have been my songs in the house of my pilgrimage.

זָכַרְתִּי בַלַּיְלָה שִׁמְךָ יְהוָה וָאֶשְׁמְרָה תּוֹרָתֶךָ:
your Torah   and I heeded   ihvh   your name   in night   I remembered

55. I have remembered your name, O Lord, in the night, and have kept your Torah.

זֹאת הָיְתָה־לִּי כִּי פִקֻּדֶיךָ נָצָרְתִּי:
I kept   your precepts   like   to me   I had   this

56. This I had, because I kept your precepts.

ח

חֶלְקִי יְהוָה אָמַרְתִּי לִשְׁמֹר דְּבָרֶיךָ׃

your sayings to heed I said ihvh my portion

57. You are my portion, O Lord; I have said that I would keep your words.

חִלִּיתִי פָנֶיךָ בְכָל־לֵב חָנֵּנִי כְּאִמְרָתֶךָ׃

like your word grant me heart - in all your face I entreated

58. I entreated your favor with my whole heart; be merciful to me according to your word.

חִשַּׁבְתִּי דְרָכָי וָאָשִׁיבָה רַגְלַי אֶל עֵדֹתֶיךָ׃

your testimonies unto my feet and returned toward my ways I thought

59. I thought on my ways, and turned my feet to your testimonies.

חַשְׁתִּי וְלֹא הִתְמַהְמָהְתִּי לִשְׁמֹר מִצְוֹתֶיךָ׃

your commandments to heed I delayed and not I hastened

60. I made haste, and did not delay to keep your commandments.

חֶבְלֵי רְשָׁעִים עִוְּדֻנִי תּוֹרָתְךָ לֹא שָׁכָחְתִּי׃

I forgot not your Torah still me wicked ones bands

61. Bands of wicked men have robbed me; but I have not forgotten your Torah.

חֲצוֹת־לַיְלָה אָקוּם לְהוֹדוֹת לָךְ עַל מִשְׁפְּטֵי צִדְקֶךָ׃

your righteous judgments upon to you to thankings I will rise night - mid

62. At midnight I will rise to give thanks to you because of your righteous judgments.

חָבֵר אָנִי לְכָל־אֲשֶׁר יְרֵאוּךָ וּלְשֹׁמְרֵי פִּקּוּדֶיךָ׃

your precepts and to heeders they fear you which - to all I friend

63. I am a companion of all those who fear you, and of those who keep your precepts.

חַסְדְּךָ יְהוָה מָלְאָה הָאָרֶץ חֻקֶּיךָ לַמְּדֵנִי׃

teach me your statutes the earth full ihvh your mercy

64. The earth, O Lord, is full of your loving kindness; teach me your statutes.

ט

טוֹב עָשִׂיתָ עִם־עַבְדְּךָ יְהֹוָה כִּדְבָרֶךָ׃

like your sayings   ihvh   your servant - with   you did   good

65. You have dealt well with your servant, O Lord, according to your word.

טוּב טַעַם וָדַעַת לַמְּדֵנִי כִּי בְמִצְוֹתֶיךָ הֶאֱמָנְתִּי׃

the I believed   in your commandments   like   teach me   and knowledge   taste   good

66. Teach me good judgment and knowledge; for I have believed your commandments.

טֶרֶם אֶעֱנֶה אֲנִי שֹׁגֵג וְעַתָּה אִמְרָתְךָ שָׁמָרְתִּי׃

I heed   your word   and now   [on] roof   I   I afflicted   before

67. Before I was afflicted I went astray; but now I observe your word.

טוֹב־אַתָּה וּמֵטִיב לַמְּדֵנִי חֻקֶּיךָ׃

your statutes   teach me   and beneficial   you - good

68. You are good, and you do good; teach me your statutes.

טָפְלוּ עָלַי שֶׁקֶר זֵדִים אֲנִי בְּכָל־לֵב אֶצֹּר פִּקּוּדֶיךָ׃

your precepts   I will keep   heart - in all   I   arrogant ones   lies   upon me   they smear

69. The arrogant smear me with lies; but I will keep your precepts with my whole heart.

טָפַשׁ כַּחֵלֶב לִבָּם אֲנִי תּוֹרָתְךָ שִׁעֲשָׁעְתִּי׃

my delight   your torah   I   their heart   like fat   gross

70. Their heart is gross like fat; but I delight in your Torah.

טוֹב־לִי כִי־עֻנֵּיתִי לְמַעַן אֶלְמַד חֻקֶּיךָ׃

your statutes   I will learn   to end   I afflicted - like   to me - Good

71. It is good for me that I have been afflicted; that I might learn your statutes.

טוֹב־לִי תוֹרַת־פִּיךָ מֵאַלְפֵי זָהָב וָכָסֶף׃

and silver   gold   from thousand   your mouth   Torah   to me - good

72. The Torah of your mouth is better to me than thousands of gold and silver.

ר

יָדֶיךָ עָשׂוּנִי וַיְכוֹנְנוּנִי הֲבִינֵנִי
your hands   made me   and they established me   the my understanding

וְאֶלְמְדָה מִצְוֺתֶיךָ:
and I will learn   your commandments

73. Your hands have made me and fashioned me; give me understanding, that I may learn your commandments.

יְרֵאֶיךָ יִרְאוּנִי וְיִשְׂמָחוּ כִּי לִדְבָרְךָ יִחָלְתִּי:
your fearing   they will see me   and they will be happy   like   to your saying   I hoped

74. Those who fear you will be glad when they see me; because I have hoped in your word.

יָדַעְתִּי יְהוָה כִּי־צֶדֶק מִשְׁפָּטֶיךָ וֶאֱמוּנָה עִנִּיתָנִי:
I know   ihvh   like - righteous   your judgments   and faithfulness   afflicted me

75. I know, O Lord, that your judgments are right, and that you in faithfulness have afflicted me.

יְהִי־נָא חַסְדְּךָ לְנַחֲמֵנִי כְּאִמְרָתְךָ לְעַבְדֶּךָ:
it be - now   your mercy   to comfort me   like your word   to your servant

76. Let, I pray you, your loving kindness be for my comfort, according to your word to your servant.

יְבֹאוּנִי רַחֲמֶיךָ וְאֶחְיֶה כִּי תוֹרָתְךָ שַׁעֲשֻׁעָי:
they come to me   your mercies   and I will live   like   your Torah   my delight

77. Let your mercies come to me, that I may live; for your Torah is my delight.

יֵבֹשׁוּ זֵדִים כִּי־שֶׁקֶר עִוְּתוּנִי אֲנִי אָשִׂיחַ בְּפִקּוּדֶיךָ:
they ashamed   arrogant ones   like – lies   dealt perversely me   I   will meditate   in your precepts

78. Let the arrogant be ashamed; for they dealt perversely with me without a cause; but I will meditate on your precepts.

יָשׁוּבוּ־לִי יְרֵאֶיךָ וְיֹדְעֵי עֵדֹתֶיךָ:
they return - to me   your fearing ones   and his knowing   your testimonies

79. (K) Let those who fear you turn to me, and those who have known your testimonies.

יְהִי־לִבִּי תָמִים בְּחֻקֶּיךָ לְמַעַן לֹא אֵבוֹשׁ:
it be - my heart   perfect   in your statutes   to end   not   I ashamed

80. Let my heart be sound in your statutes; that I be not ashamed.

כ

כָּלְתָה לִתְשׁוּעָתְךָ נַפְשִׁי לִדְבָרְךָ יִחָלְתִּי:
I hope   to your saying   my soul   to your salvation   languishes

81. My soul languishes for your salvation; I hope in your word.

כָּלוּ עֵינַי לְאִמְרָתֶךָ לֵאמֹר מָתַי תְּנַחֲמֵנִי:
you will comfort me   when   to say   to your word   my eyes   spent

82. My eyes fail longing for your word, saying, When will you comfort me?

כִּי־הָיִיתִי כְּנֹאד בְּקִיטוֹר חֻקֶּיךָ לֹא שָׁכָחְתִּי:
I forgot   not   your statutes   in smoke   like wineskin   I was - like

83. For I have become like a wineskin in the smoke; yet I do not forget your statutes.

כַּמָּה יְמֵי־עַבְדֶּךָ מָתַי תַּעֲשֶׂה בְרֹדְפַי מִשְׁפָּט:
judgment   in my persecutors   will you do   how long   your servant   days   how many

84. How many are the days of your servant? When will you execute judgment on those who persecute me?

כָּרוּ־לִי זֵדִים שִׁיחוֹת אֲשֶׁר לֹא כְתוֹרָתֶךָ:
like to your torah   not   which   pits   proud ones   to me - they dug

85. The arrogant dug pits for me, which are not according to your Torah.

כָּל־מִצְוֹתֶיךָ אֱמוּנָה שֶׁקֶר רְדָפוּנִי עָזְרֵנִי:
help me   they persecute me   lies   faithful   your commandments - all

86. All your commandments are faithful; they persecute me wrongfully; help me.

כִּמְעַט כִּלּוּנִי בָאָרֶץ וַאֲנִי לֹא־עָזַבְתִּי פִקּוּדֶיךָ:
your precepts   have forsaken   not   and I   in earth   consumed me   like a little

87. They had almost consumed me on earth; but I have not forsaken your precepts.

כְּחַסְדְּךָ חַיֵּנִי וְאֶשְׁמְרָה עֵדוּת פִּיךָ:
your mouth   testimonies   and I will heed   give me life   like your kindness

88. In your loving kindness spare my life; so I shall keep the testimony of your mouth.

ל

לְעוֹלָם יְהוָה דְּבָרְךָ נִצָּב בַּשָּׁמָיִם:
in heavens   fixed   your sayings   ihvh   to forever

89. For ever, O Lord, your word is fixed in heaven.

לְדֹר וָדֹר אֱמוּנָתֶךָ כּוֹנַנְתָּ אֶרֶץ וַתַּעֲמֹד:
and it stands   earth   you established   your faithfulness   and generation   to generation

90. Your faithfulness endures to all generations; you have established the earth, and it stands firm.

לְמִשְׁפָּטֶיךָ עָמְדוּ הַיּוֹם כִּי הַכֹּל עֲבָדֶיךָ:
your servants   the all   like   the day   they stand   to your judgements

91. They continue this day according to your ordinances; for all are your servants.

לוּלֵי תוֹרָתְךָ שַׁעֲשֻׁעָי אָז אָבַדְתִּי בְעָנְיִי:
in my affliction   I perished   then   my delight   your torah   had it not been

92. If your Torah had not been my delight, I should have perished in my affliction.

לְעוֹלָם לֹא אֶשְׁכַּח פִּקּוּדֶיךָ כִּי בָם חִיִּיתָנִי:
life to me   in them   like   your precepts   I will forget   not   to forever

93. I will never forget your precepts; for with them you have given me life.

לְךָ אֲנִי הוֹשִׁיעֵנִי כִּי פִקּוּדֶיךָ דָרָשְׁתִּי:
I sought   your precepts   like   save me   I   to you

94. I am yours, save me; for I have sought your precepts.

לִי קִוּוּ רְשָׁעִים לְאַבְּדֵנִי עֵדֹתֶיךָ אֶתְבּוֹנָן:
I will consider   your testimonies   to destroy me   the wicked   they waited   to me

95. The wicked have waited for me to destroy me; but I will consider your testimonies.

לְכָל תִּכְלָה רָאִיתִי קֵץ רְחָבָה מִצְוָתְךָ מְאֹד:
greatly   your commandment   broad   limits   I saw   perfection   to all

96. I have seen a limit to all perfection; but your commandment is exceedingly broad.

מ

מָה אָהַבְתִּי תוֹרָתֶךָ כָּל הַיּוֹם הִיא שִׂיחָתִי:
my meditation | it | the day | all | your torah | I loved | how

97. O how I love your Torah! It is my meditation all the day.

מֵאֹיְבַי תְּחַכְּמֵנִי מִצְוֹתֶךָ כִּי לְעוֹלָם הִיא לִי:
to me | it | to forever | - like | your commandments | it made me wise | from my enemies

98. Your commandments have made me wiser than my enemies; for they are always with me.

מִכָּל מְלַמְּדַי הִשְׂכַּלְתִּי כִּי עֵדְוֹתֶיךָ שִׂיחָה לִי:
to me | meditation | your testimonies | like | I comprehended | my teachers | from all

99. I have more understanding than all my teachers; for your testimonies are my meditation.

מִזְּקֵנִים אֶתְבּוֹנָן כִּי פִקּוּדֶיךָ נָצָרְתִּי:
I keep | your precepts | like | I understand | from elder ones

100. I understand more than the elders, because I keep your precepts.

מִכָּל אֹרַח רָע כָּלִאתִי רַגְלָי לְמַעַן אֶשְׁמֹר דְּבָרֶךָ:
your sayings | I will heed | to end | my feet | I refrained | bad | way | from all

101. I have refrained my feet from every evil way, that I might keep your word.

מִמִּשְׁפָּטֶיךָ לֹא סָרְתִּי כִּי אַתָּה הוֹרֵתָנִי:
taught me | you | like | I departed | not | from your judgments

102. I have not departed from your judgments; for you have taught me.

מַה נִּמְלְצוּ לְחִכִּי אִמְרָתֶךָ מִדְּבַשׁ לְפִי:
to my mouth | from honey | your words | to my taste | they sweet | how

103. How sweet are your words to my taste! Sweeter than honey to my mouth!

מִפִּקּוּדֶיךָ אֶתְבּוֹנָן עַל כֵּן שָׂנֵאתִי כָּל אֹרַח שָׁקֶר:
lies | roads | all | I hate | thus | upon | I understand | from your precepts

104. Through your precepts I get understanding; therefore I hate every false way.

נ

נֵר לְרַגְלִי דְבָרֶךָ וְאוֹר לִנְתִיבָתִי׃
                to my path   and light   your sayings   to my feet   lamp
105. Your word is a lamp to my feet, and a light to my path.

נִשְׁבַּעְתִּי וָאֲקַיֵּמָה לִשְׁמֹר מִשְׁפְּטֵי צִדְקֶךָ׃
              your righteous   judgments   to heed   and I will execute   I swore
106. I have sworn, and I will perform it, that I will keep your righteous judgments.

נַעֲנֵיתִי עַד מְאֹד יְהוָה חַיֵּנִי כִדְבָרֶךָ׃
              like your word   give me life   ihvh   greatly   till   I'm afflicted
107. I am very much afflicted; revive me, O Lord, according to your word.

נִדְבוֹת פִּי רְצֵה נָא יְהוָה וּמִשְׁפָּטֶיךָ לַמְּדֵנִי׃
              teach me   and your judgements   ihvh   now   accept   my mouth   handouts
108. Accept, I beseech you, the freewill offerings of my mouth, O Lord, and teach me your ordinances.

נַפְשִׁי בְכַפִּי תָמִיד וְתוֹרָתְךָ לֹא שָׁכָחְתִּי׃
              I forget   not   and your torah   always   in my palm   my soul
109. My soul is continually in my hand; yet I do not forget your Torah.

נָתְנוּ רְשָׁעִים פַּח לִי וּמִפִּקּוּדֶיךָ לֹא תָעִיתִי׃
              I strayed   not   and from your precepts   to me   snare   the wicked   they gave
110. The wicked have laid a snare for me; yet I have not strayed from your precepts.

נָחַלְתִּי עֵדְוֹתֶיךָ לְעוֹלָם כִּי שְׂשׂוֹן לִבִּי הֵמָּה׃
              they are   my heart   rejoicing   like   to forever   your testimonies   my heritage
111. Your testimonies I have taken as a heritage for ever; for they are the rejoicing of my heart.

נָטִיתִי לִבִּי לַעֲשׂוֹת חֻקֶּיךָ לְעוֹלָם עֵקֶב׃
              very end   to forever   your statutes   to doing   my heart   I inclined
112. I have inclined my heart to perform your statutes always, to the end.

ס

סֵעֲפִים שָׂנֵאתִי וְתוֹרָתְךָ אָהָבְתִּי:
113. I hate vain thoughts; but I love your Torah.

סִתְרִי וּמָגִנִּי אָתָּה לִדְבָרְךָ יִחָלְתִּי:
114. You are my hiding place and my shield; I hope in your word.

סוּרוּ מִמֶּנִּי מְרֵעִים וְאֶצְּרָה מִצְוֺת אֱלֹהָי:
115. Depart from me, you evil doers; for I will keep the commandments of my God.

סָמְכֵנִי כְאִמְרָתְךָ וְאֶחְיֶה וְאַל תְּבִישֵׁנִי מִשִּׂבְרִי:
116. Uphold me according to your word, that I may live; and do not let me be ashamed of my hope.

סְעָדֵנִי וְאִוָּשֵׁעָה וְאֶשְׁעָה בְחֻקֶּיךָ תָמִיד:
117. Hold me up, and I shall be safe; and I will observe your statutes continually.

סָלִיתָ כָּל שׁוֹגִים מֵחֻקֶּיךָ כִּי שֶׁקֶר תַּרְמִיתָם:
118. You have trampled down all those who stray from your statutes; for their deceit is vain.

סִגִים הִשְׁבַּתָּ כָל רִשְׁעֵי אָרֶץ לָכֵן אָהַבְתִּי עֵדֹתֶיךָ:
119. You put away all the wicked of the earth like dross; therefore I love your testimonies.

סָמַר מִפַּחְדְּךָ בְשָׂרִי וּמִמִּשְׁפָּטֶיךָ יָרֵאתִי:
120. My flesh trembles for fear of you; and I am afraid of your judgments.

ע

עָשִׂיתִי מִשְׁפָּט וָצֶדֶק בַּל תַּנִּיחֵנִי לְעֹשְׁקָי׃

121. I have done what is just and right; do not leave me to my oppressors.

עֲרֹב עַבְדְּךָ לְטוֹב אַל יַעַשְׁקֻנִי זֵדִים׃

122. Be surety for your servant for good; do not let the arrogant oppress me.

עֵינַי כָּלוּ לִישׁוּעָתֶךָ וּלְאִמְרַת צִדְקֶךָ׃

123. My eyes fail with watching for your salvation, and for the word of your righteousness.

עֲשֵׂה עִם עַבְדְּךָ כְחַסְדֶּךָ וְחֻקֶּיךָ לַמְּדֵנִי׃

124. Deal with your servant according to your loving kindness, and teach me your statutes.

עַבְדְּךָ אָנִי הֲבִינֵנִי וְאֵדְעָה עֵדֹתֶיךָ׃

125. I am your servant; give me understanding, that I may know your testimonies.

עֵת לַעֲשׂוֹת לַיהוָה הֵפֵרוּ תּוֹרָתֶךָ׃

126. It is time for you, Lord, to act; for they have made void your Torah.

עַל כֵּן אָהַבְתִּי מִצְוֹתֶיךָ מִזָּהָב וּמִפָּז׃

127. Therefore I love your commandments above gold; above fine gold.

עַל כֵּן כָּל פִּקּוּדֵי כֹל יִשָּׁרְתִּי כָּל אֹרַח שֶׁקֶר שָׂנֵאתִי׃

128. Therefore I esteem all your precepts to be entirely right; and I hate every false way.

פ

פְּלָאוֹת עֵדְוֺתֶיךָ עַל כֵּן נְצָרָתַם נַפְשִׁי:
my soul   kept them   thus   upon   your testimonies   mystical

129. Your testimonies are wonderful; therefore my soul keeps them.

פֵּתַח דְּבָרֶיךָ יָאִיר מֵבִין פְּתָיִים:
simple ones   from understanding   it shines   your sayings   opening

130. The unfolding of your words gives light; it gives understanding to the simple.

פִּי פָעַרְתִּי וָאֶשְׁאָפָה כִּי לְמִצְוֺתֶיךָ יָאָבְתִּי:
it my love   to your commandment   like   and I will strive   I open   mouth

131. I open my mouth and pant; because I long for your commandments.

פְּנֵה אֵלַי וְחָנֵּנִי כְּמִשְׁפָּט לְאֹהֲבֵי שְׁמֶךָ:
your name   to lovers   like judgment   and be merciful to me   unto me   face

132. Look upon me, and be merciful to me, as you are to those who love your name.

פְּעָמַי הָכֵן בְּאִמְרָתֶךָ וְאַל תַּשְׁלֶט בִּי כָל אָוֶן:
inequity   all   in me   it dominated   and don't   in your word   the thus   my steps

133. Order my steps in your word; and do not let any iniquity have dominion over me.

פְּדֵנִי מֵעֹשֶׁק אָדָם וְאֶשְׁמְרָה פִּקּוּדֶיךָ:
your precepts   and I will heed   Adam   from oppression   deliver me

134. Save me from the oppression of man; and I will keep your precepts.

פָּנֶיךָ הָאֵר בְּעַבְדֶּךָ וְלַמְּדֵנִי אֶת חֻקֶּיךָ:
your statutes   that   and teach me   in your servant   the shine   your face

135. Let your face shine upon your servant; and teach me your statutes.

פַּלְגֵי מַיִם יָרְדוּ עֵינָי עַל לֹא שָׁמְרוּ תוֹרָתֶךָ:
your Torah   they heeded   not   upon   my eyes   they descend   water   rivers

136. Rivers of water run down my eyes, because they do not keep your Torah.

צ

צַדִּיק אַתָּה יְהֹוָה וְיָשָׁר מִשְׁפָּטֶיךָ׃
your judgments   and upright   ihvh   you   righteous

137. You are righteous, O Lord, and upright are your judgments.

צִוִּיתָ צֶדֶק עֵדֹתֶיךָ וֶאֱמוּנָה מְאֹד׃
greatly   and faithful   your testimonies   righteous   you commanded

138. You have commanded your testimonies in righteousness and in all faithfulness.

צִמְּתַתְנִי קִנְאָתִי כִּי שָׁכְחוּ דְבָרֶיךָ צָרָי׃
my enemies   your sayings   they forgot   like   my zeal   consumes me

139. My zeal consumes me, because my enemies have forgotten your words.

צְרוּפָה אִמְרָתְךָ מְאֹד וְעַבְדְּךָ אֲהֵבָהּ׃
loves it   and your servant   greatly   your word   very pure

140. Your word is very pure; therefore your servant loves it.

צָעִיר אָנֹכִי וְנִבְזֶה פִּקֻּדֶיךָ לֹא שָׁכָחְתִּי׃
I forget   not   your precepts   and despised   I am   young

141. I am small and despised; yet I do not forget your precepts.

צִדְקָתְךָ צֶדֶק לְעוֹלָם וְתוֹרָתְךָ אֱמֶת׃
truth   and your Torah   to forever   right   your righteousness

142. Your righteousness is an everlasting righteousness, and your Torah is the truth.

צַר־וּמָצוֹק מְצָאוּנִי מִצְוֹתֶיךָ שַׁעֲשֻׁעָי׃
my delights   your commandments   took hold of me   and anguish - trouble

143. Trouble and anguish have taken hold of me; yet your commandments are my delights.

צֶדֶק עֵדְוֹתֶיךָ לְעוֹלָם הֲבִינֵנִי וְאֶחְיֶה׃
and I will live   the give me understanding   to forever   your testimonies   righteous

144. The righteousness of your testimonies is everlasting; give me understanding, and I shall live.

ק

קָרָ֣אתִי בְכָל־לֵ֭ב עֲנֵ֥נִי יְהוָ֗ה חֻקֶּ֥יךָ אֶצֹּֽרָה׃
 I will keep　your statutes　ihvh　answer me　heart - in all　I cry

145. I cry with my whole heart; answer me, O Lord; I will keep your statutes.

קְרָאתִ֥יךָ הוֹשִׁיעֵ֑נִי וְ֝אֶשְׁמְרָ֗ה עֵדֹתֶֽיךָ׃
your testimonies　I will heed　save me　I cried to you

146. I cry to you: save me, and I shall keep your testimonies.

קִדַּ֣מְתִּי בַ֭נֶּשֶׁף וָאֲשַׁוֵּ֑עָה לִדְבָרְךָ֥ יִחָֽלְתִּי׃
I hope　to your sayings　and I cry out　in before dawn　I proceed

147. (K) I rise before dawn, and I cry out; my hope is in your word.

קִדְּמ֣וּ עֵ֭ינַי אַשְׁמֻר֑וֹת לָ֝שִׂ֗יחַ בְּאִמְרָתֶֽךָ׃
in your word　to meditate　watches of night　my eyes　they proceed

148. My eyes open before the watches of the night, that I may meditate on your saying.

קוֹלִ֣י שִׁמְעָ֣ה כְחַסְדֶּ֑ךָ יְ֝הוָ֗ה כְּֽמִשְׁפָּטֶ֥ךָ חַיֵּֽנִי׃
give me life　like your judgment　ihvh　like your mercy　hear　my voice

149. Hear my voice according to your loving kindness; O Lord, revive me according to your judgment.

קָ֭רְבוּ רֹדְפֵ֣י זִמָּ֑ה מִתּוֹרָתְךָ֥ רָחָֽקוּ׃
they far　from the torah　mischief　persuers　they near

150. Those who follow after mischief draw near; they are far from your Torah.

קָר֣וֹב אַתָּ֣ה יְהוָ֑ה וְֽכָל־מִצְוֺתֶ֥יךָ אֱמֶֽת׃
truth　your commandments - and all　ihvh　you　near

151. You are near, O Lord; and all your commandments are truth.

קֶ֣דֶם יָ֭דַעְתִּי מֵעֵדֹתֶ֑יךָ כִּ֖י לְעוֹלָ֣ם יְסַדְתָּֽם׃
you founded them　to forever　like　from your testimonies　I knew　of ancient time

152. Concerning your testimonies, I have known of old that you have founded them for ever.

ר

רְאֵה־עָנְיִי וְחַלְּצֵנִי כִּי־תוֹרָתְךָ לֹא שָׁכָחְתִּי:
I forget   not   your Torah – like   and rescue me   my affliction – see

153. Consider my affliction, and save me; for I do not forget your Torah.

רִיבָה רִיבִי וּגְאָלֵנִי לְאִמְרָתְךָ חַיֵּנִי:
give me life   to your word   and save me   my cause   plead

154. Plead my cause, and save me; give me life according to your word.

רָחוֹק מֵרְשָׁעִים יְשׁוּעָה כִּי־חֻקֶּיךָ לֹא דָרָשׁוּ:
they seek   not   statutes - like   salvation   from wicked ones   far

155. Salvation is far from the wicked; for they do not seek your statutes.

רַחֲמֶיךָ רַבִּים יְהוָה כְּמִשְׁפָּטֶיךָ חַיֵּנִי:
give me life   like your judgments   ihvh   many ones   your compassion

156. Great is your compassion, O Lord; give me life according to your justice.

רַבִּים רֹדְפַי וְצָרָי מֵעֵדְוֺתֶיךָ לֹא נָטִיתִי:
I turned   not   from your testimonies   my enemies   my persecutors   many

157. Many are my persecutors and my enemies; yet I do not swerve from your testimonies.

רָאִיתִי בֹגְדִים וָאֶתְקוֹטָטָה אֲשֶׁר אִמְרָתְךָ לֹא שָׁמָרוּ:
they heeded   not   your word   which   and I am grieved   transgressor ones   I see

158. I look at the transgressors, and I am grieved; because they do not keep your saying.

רְאֵה כִּי־פִקּוּדֶיךָ אָהָבְתִּי יְהוָה כְּחַסְדְּךָ חַיֵּנִי:
give me life   like your kindness   ihvh   I loved   your precepts - like   you see

159. Consider how I love your precepts; revive me, O Lord, according to your loving kindness.

רֹאשׁ־דְּבָרְךָ אֱמֶת וּלְעוֹלָם כָּל־מִשְׁפַּט צִדְקֶךָ:
your righteous   judgment - all   and to forever   truth   your sayings - beginning

160. The sum of your word is truth; and every one of your righteous judgments endures for ever.

ש

שָׂרִים רְדָפוּנִי חִנָּם וּמִדְּבָרְיךָ פָּחַד לִבִּי:

161. (K) Princes have persecuted me without cause; but my heart in awe of your word.

שָׂשׂ אָנֹכִי עַל־אִמְרָתֶךָ כְּמוֹצֵא שָׁלָל רָב:

162. I rejoice at your word, like one who finds great booty.

שֶׁקֶר שָׂנֵאתִי וַאֲתַעֵבָה תּוֹרָתְךָ אָהָבְתִּי:

163. I hate and loathe lying; but I love your Torah.

שֶׁבַע בַּיּוֹם הִלַּלְתִּיךָ עַל מִשְׁפְּטֵי צִדְקֶךָ:

164. Seven times a day I praise you because of your righteous judgments.

שָׁלוֹם רָב לְאֹהֲבֵי תוֹרָתֶךָ וְאֵין לָמוֹ מִכְשׁוֹל:

165. Great peace have those who love your Torah; and nothing can make them stumble.

שִׂבַּרְתִּי לִישׁוּעָתְךָ יְהוָה וּמִצְוֹתֶיךָ עָשִׂיתִי:

166. Lord, I have hoped for your salvation, and done your commandments.

שָׁמְרָה נַפְשִׁי עֵדֹתֶיךָ וָאֹהֲבֵם מְאֹד:

167. My soul has kept your testimonies; and I love them exceedingly.

שָׁמַרְתִּי פִקּוּדֶיךָ וְעֵדֹתֶיךָ כִּי כָל־דְּרָכַי נֶגְדֶּךָ:

168. I have kept your precepts and your testimonies; for all my ways are before you.

ת

תִּקְרַב רִנָּתִי לְפָנֶיךָ יְהוָה כִּדְבָרְךָ הֲבִינֵנִי׃
the give understanding to me   like your sayings   ihvh   to your presence   my joy cry   will near

169. Let my cry come before you, O Lord; give me understanding according to your word.

תָּבוֹא תְחִנָּתִי לְפָנֶיךָ כְּאִמְרָתְךָ הַצִּילֵנִי׃
rescue me   like your word   to your face   my supplication   will come

170. Let my supplication come before you; save me according to your word.

תַּבַּעְנָה שְׂפָתַי תְּהִלָּה כִּי תְלַמְּדֵנִי חֻקֶּיךָ׃
your statutes   you taught me   like   praise   my lips   will utter

171. My lips shall utter praise, when you have taught me your statutes.

תַּעַן לְשׁוֹנִי אִמְרָתֶךָ כִּי כָל־מִצְוֺתֶיךָ צֶּדֶק׃
just   commandments - all   like   your word   my tongue   will answer

172. My tongue shall speak of your word; for all your commandments are just.

תְּהִי־יָדְךָ לְעָזְרֵנִי כִּי פִקּוּדֶיךָ בָחָרְתִּי׃
I've chosen   your precepts   like   to help me   your hand - let be

173. Let your hand help me; for I have chosen your precepts.

תָּאַבְתִּי לִישׁוּעָתְךָ יְהוָה וְתוֹרָתְךָ שַׁעֲשֻׁעָי׃
my delight   and your Torah   ihvh   your salvation   I long

174. I long for your salvation, O Lord; and your Torah is my delight.

תְּחִי־נַפְשִׁי וּתְהַלְלֶךָּ וּמִשְׁפָּטֶךָ יַעְזְרֻנִי׃
they help me   and your judgments   and will praise you   my soul - you let live

175. Let my soul live, and it shall praise you; and let your judgments help me.

תָּעִיתִי כְּשֶׂה אֹבֵד בַּקֵּשׁ עַבְדֶּךָ
your servant   seek   lost   like a sheep   I went astray

כִּי מִצְוֺתֶיךָ לֹא שָׁכָחְתִּי׃
I forget   not   your commandments   like

176. I have gone astray like a lost sheep; seek your servant; for I do not forget your commandments.

SUPPLICATION

It is very important that after you do your praying and meditations, you take the time to ask ... for what you want. The Baal Shem Tov, Rabbi Nachman, and many other great kabbalah teachers have stated that this as a very important stage. After saying prayers and after doing the meditations, be sure to ask, with clarity, WHAT YOU WANT.

When doing this you should go to a visualization board with pictures and prepared paragraphs of your visions of the future. Spend quality time looking at the pictures and reciting prepared paragraphs. This is the time to feel with your emotions how you will be reacting as you visualize your future.

Rabbi Nachman has stated those who study *Torah* have their requests answered more readily and thoroughly.

Advanced Meditations

This book only covers the basics. There is a level above this involving the hand writing of permutations in various ways. After the fundamental levels, there are many advanced methods involving high spiritual theory.

Examples of writing analysis techniques are combinations and permutations, engraving or hewing (kakika), carving (chatziva), weighing (shikul), substitution (hamira), subdivision & separation, composi-

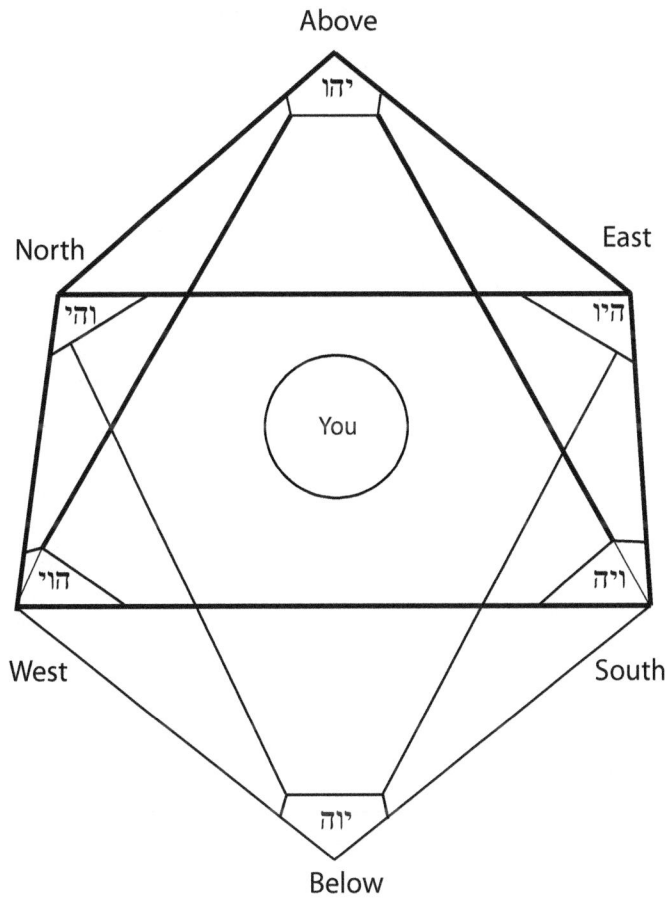

As depicted in Sefer Yitzerah

tion, pronunciation (nikud), dilug, quantity, gematria, and skipping & leaping, and many more.

By doing long advanced meditations over a period of time one's dreams become extremely vivid, pronounced and easily remembered. Eventually this leads one to the advanced dream states where one consciously directs their dreams. This eventually leads to the breaking through the rakia. The renown Kabbalish Baal Shem Tov stated numerous times that when he slept at night he would go to the Supernal Torah Academy in the heavens to learn Torah.

In advanced meditations one can also direct their energy to a more specific target. Advanced methods also involve using the high tech physical world to help align the mental and physical levels.

Appendix

Abraham Abulafia, ben Samuel

Founder

The type of meditations described in this book are attributed to Abulafia who openly taught and published these techniques. He is considered the founder of the school of "Prophetic Kabbalah." He called it the Kabbalah of Letters. He was born in Saragossa, Spain. He lived from 1240 to 1291. He died when he was 51 years old.

Prophetic Kabbalah School

He lead a life of ceaseless wandering. However he had noted followers who later wrote kabbalah books which today are considered classics. His most important disciple was R. Joseph Gikatilla who took over Abulafia's established school after he passed on. R. Cordovero was also one of his renown students who also wrote kabbalah books that are classics. Chaim Vital was another of his student who is renown for his classics on Abulafia's teachings. At the height of Abulafia's teachings he experienced an excess of rebuke from the other rabbis of that time eventually leading him to live a self exile towards the end of his life.

Famous Journey to Rome

In obedience to an inner voice, he went in 1280 to Rome, in order to effect the conversion of Pope Nicholas III on the day before the Jewish New Year, 5041. The Pope, then in nearby Suriano, heard of it, and issued orders to "burn the fanatic" as soon as he reached the city. Close to the inner gate a stake was erected in preparation. But not in the least disturbed, Abulafia set out for Suriano and reached there August 22. While passing through the outer gate, he heard that the Pope had died from an apoplectic stroke during the preceding night. Returning to Rome, he was thrown into prison by the Minorites, but was liberated after four weeks of detention. He was next heard of in Sicily, where he appeared as he describes his end result, a prophet.

His most influential books teach one how to achieve prophetic meditation: *Chayei ha-Olam ha-Ba* (1280), *Or ha-Sekhel, Sefer ha-Cheshek,* and *Imrei Shefer* (1291). In all Abulafia has written 25 books.

It is believed he is buried somewhere on the little island of Comino, Maltese archipelago, where the last traces of him were found.

JOSEPH GIKATILLA, BEN ABRAHAM

Gikatilla was one of the noted students of Abulafia who considered Gikatilla the continuation of his school. Gikatilla was said to be able to work miracles. Because of this others called him Joseph the master prophet (Ba'al ha-Nissim). He lived from 1248 to sometime after 1305. He died somewhere around the age of 57.

The books he is most known for are;

Ginnat Egoz. He wrote when he was 26. The first word of the title is an acrostic for Gematria, Notarkon, and Temurah. The second word means Nut, the emblem of mysticism i.e. a hard shell with great fruit inside.

Sha're Orah. Has ten chapters that detail out the names of God.

Sefer ha-Orah, Sha'are Zedek. Both on the ten sefirot.

Sefer ha-Nikkud. A book on vowel points and what they represent.

MOSES CORDOVERO, BEN JACOB

He was born in Saragossa, Spain. (1522 to 1570) His acronym is "the Ramak." He was one of the top student of Abulafia, and furthered his teachings. He established the school of Cordoveran Kabbalah. The academy was located in Safed, Israel, where he taught for approximately 20 years. He died at the age of 48.

He is noted for his two classics works. *Pardes Rimonim* (Orchard of Pomegranates) is his most known book written in 1548. It consists of three very large volumes. His other classic is *Ohr Yakar* (Precious Light). This work is considered his magnum opus of his life. It was a commentary on mainly the *Zohar* and the *Sefer Yetzirah*. It was originally 16 volumes but today consists of more writings and is 22 volumes.

One of his best students was Chaim Vital who later became the official recorder of the teachings of the Ari, Rabbi Isaac Luria.

CHAIM VITAL, BEN YOSEF

Also known as Rabbi Chaim Vital Calabrese. His family was from Calabria, Italy). He studied under Moses Cordovero (Ramak). He is renown as the official note keeper of the famous kabbalist the Ari. He was born 1543, and passed away 1620 at age of 77.

His first teacher Cordovero, appeared to him in a dream a few months after his passing. Chaim adjured him to tell him the truth; whether they should study Kabbala according to the Ramak's system or according to the Arizal's system. "In the Heavenly Academy," his former teacher replied, "Both approaches are true. However, my approach is the simple one, suitable for beginners in the wisdom of Kabbala. Whereas the teachings of your current teacher [the Arizal] are deeper and his teachings are the primary approach. I, too, in the Heavenly Academy, study only according to the approach of your current master."

When the Arizal started teaching he prohibited others from taking notes, but gave only this privilege only to Rabbi Chaim Vital to record his teachings. Today these writings are known as Kitvei Arizal.

Chaim studied under the Arizal for only two years. Then the Arizal passed away. Chaim was universally regarded as his successor and was regarded as a great Kabbalist.

Chaim Vital gained a reputation as a miracle worker, a healer and a master of practical kabbala. He was able to discern the nature and history of the souls of men.

Isaac Luria (the "Arizal") Ben Solomon

The Arizal lived from 1534 to July 25, 1572. He died when he was 38.

The Arizal arrived in Safed on the exact day of the funeral of Moshe Cordovero (the Ramak) in 1570 after arriving from Egypt. When he joined in the funeral procession, he realized that only he saw a pillar of fire following the Ramak's procession. When the procession was going straight but the pillar of fire turned down another way, the Ari called out to the others and told them to turn and follow the pillar of fire. Where the pillar stopped was where they buried the Ramak. The students had been told previously by the Ari before he died that the person who sees this pillar of fire leading the procession was meant to succeed him in leadership. And so the Ari took over leadership after six months when he found his chosen disciple, Chaim Vital. The Ari radically changed the system of meditation in just the two years he taught.

After the passing of the Ari, two schools developed, the Cordoveran and the Lurianic. The Lurianic teachings were comprised of completely new doctrines of Kabbalah. The Lurianic teachings superseded the Cordoveran in the Hasidic communities of which eighty per cent are Ashkenazim Jews. The Sephardim Jews continued to embrace Cordoveran along with the Lurianic.

Baal Shem Tov, Rabbi Yisroel ben Elieze

The Baal Shem Tov was the founder of today's Hasidic movement. He was born on the 18th of Elul 5458 (August 27, 1698) to Rabbi Eliezer and his wife Sarah. He was an orphaned at a young age. He was born in what is known today as the Ukraine.

According to Hasidic tradition, he learned how to work miracles with the name of the shem hamephorash. The Baal Shem Tov passed away on Shavuos, 5520 (May 23, 1760) at age 62, having founded the Hasidic movement that lives on today.

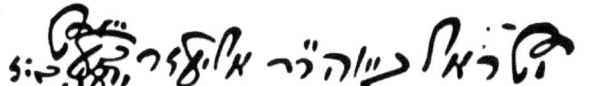 Baal Shem Tov's signature

About the Author

Daniel A. Elias, J.D., is an author, lecturer, who is renown as a world authority on tzeruf meditation. Throughout his life he has been interested in what effects sounds have on the mind. He became interested in sounds in grade school when he bought a silent dog whistle (inaudible sound to humans) to call the family dog.

At eighteen he began to widen his study of religions by studying in person with Maharish Mehesh Yogi, the Beatle's guru. He studied under a college professor who had practiced zen meditation all his life. He has tried the many different world meditations and has experienced many wellness programs such as Gestalt therapy, primal scream therapy, hug therapy, subliminal/sound therapy, rational fasting, alkaline detox, acupuncture, Tai Chi etc., etc. He is a subliminal sound mixing expert who has successfully helped others with sound therapy.

He became fascinated after reading that the shem hamephorash was not to be pronounced out loud and also about its true pronunciation only being known to the high priest of Jerusalem who would only pronounce it once a year on the holiest day of the year. This led him to discover tzeruf meditation which vocalizes the shem hamephorash while combined or seeded with Hebrew letters to affect a person's mind and surrounding circumstances. He was lured also because of the dream states resulting from the advanced vocalization meditations, leading one into penetrating the Rakia of higher dream dimensions.

For many years the author has daily practiced tzeruf meditation. His daily practice also involves reading and studying Torah. The rest of his time he spends reading ancient texts about advanced tzeruf meditations and writing about them.

INDEX

Abraham	vi, xiv, 1-3, 29, 38, 42, 81-84, 89, 91, 175, 281-282
Abulafia	vi, vii, 3, 6-8, 113, 162, 165-166, 173, 175, 224, 281-282
acidic	108
Adonai	79-80, 84-85
Aliens	156
alkaline	108-110, 285
alkalinity	108
Amulets	118
Anakim	156
Angels	x, 34, 36, 97, 171, 177, 233-243
Appendix	281
Arizal	3, 283-284
Ashkenazi	165, 284
Ashlag, Rabbi	90
Asiyah	89, 100
Atzilut	90, 100, 151
Baalai	79
Babylon	36, 92
barakah	89, 146, 149, 159
Beriah	233
Beriya	90, 100, 151
Bernays	105
Buddha	119, 126
Byblos	13
Calling in name	ix, xiii, 1
Chaiya	100, 282
chemicals	104-105, 110
Cherubim	176
Chesed	61, 63, 102, 124, 139, 141-142, 233, 245
Chinese writing	2, 12
Chiyah	150
Chlorella	108
Christian	125, 126, 154

Clinton, President 110
Table of Contents ix
Conversion xix, 13 281
Copyright v
Cordovero 3, 56, 281-284
Council, Nicaea 125
Counting the Omer 136
dagesh xviii, 57, 73
danger 3, 6-7, 110
Dedication ix, 173, 175
Derush 89
destiny 2, 145, 150
disease 110, 105
distill 105
dreams 5-6, 35, 102, 112, 121, 155, 158, 279
Elohai Elohaynu 82
Elohim xvi, xvii, 39, 65-72, 75, 80-85, 106, 125, 128, 137, 146-149, 179, 181, 183-184, 189-190, 192, 221, 269
emotional ix, 4, 42, 76, 100, 102, 111, 132-136, 139, 141-143, 233, 277
Farben Co, I. G. 105
Flavius 9, 78
fluoride, FLUoxetene 104-105
Frontlet 114-118, 189, 191
fructose 110
Gehinnom 35, 153-154
Gematria 19, 31, 33, 39, 42-43, 54-56, 82, 89, 121, 245, 279, 282
Gevurah 61, 63, 102, 124, 139, 141-142
Gikatilla 3, 281-282
Gilgal 207, 209, 211, 213
Gilgul 154
Goliath 156
HaKodesh 18, 97, 126
hamburger 109
HaShem 19
Hasidic 159, 284
hatred 124
haughty 124
Haunebu 3

Havaya	1 80, 171
herbivores	107
idolatry	40, 92, 124, 127
influx	4, 7, 79, 100, 102, 104, 110-111, 120-121, 128-129, 132, 135, 139, 141-142, 146, 164, 174, 224, 233
insane	7
insect	9, 176
Israel	xvi, xvii, xix, 13, 35-36, 74, 79-81, 86, 91-93, 95, 116-118, 123, 154, 179, 189, 191-192, 221, 282
Israelites	2, 33, 39, 80, 91-92, 107, 109, 153, 156, 173
jealous	5, 83
Josephus	78
jubilee	26, 34, 39
Lashon HaKodesh	18
Lashone	7
Longhorn	109
Lurianic	284
Luzzatto	79
Maimonides	167
Masora	86
Masoretes masoretic, massoreh	48, 86
Matthew	125
Messiah	25-26, 27 32, 34, 79, 94 125-126, 184
Mezuzah	111
mikvah	113
Minorites	281
Moharan, Likutey	124
mosquito	9
Moses	33
Nachman	78, 122, 124, 158, 173, 277
Nephilim	156
Neshama	100, 149-150, 154
Nicaea	125
Notarkon	282
Ofanayim	56, 176-177
ordinal	55
palate	45-46
papyrus	13
Pardes	3, 56, 89, 282

Passover	26-27, 91, 136
patriarchs	1, 84
Phoenician	13
planets	73, 88
Poverty	124
Preface	ix, xviii
prefix	xviii, 24, 76, 78
pregnant	33, 39, 76, 82, 89 245-246
Propaganda	105
Prophecy	x, 6, 35, 93, 121, 150, 94 167, 174, 154 183 223
prophet	1 82, 83 90-92, 97, 125 281-282
prosperity	94, 124
Proverbs	26, 87, 94
Provoking God	9
PROZAC	105
Publisher	v
Purgatory	153
quails	107
rectifying	150-151
Rephaim	156
sabbath	26, 127-128, 136-137, 145, 158
Saturday	125, 129
seeded	x, 75, 162, 167-168, 170-171, 201-202, 205, 207, 209, 211, 222-223, 227, 233-234, 246-247, 285
sefirah	19, 32, 61, 65, 77, 79-80, 84, 100, 102-104, 120-121, 124, 126, 129, 131, 136, 139, 141, 144, 146, 151, 153-154, 164, 233
sefirot	xviii, 26, 29, 42, 53, 61, 64-65, 75 76, 82-83, 100, 102-103, 121, 128, 131-132, 134-136, 139, 141-142, 144, 146, 151, 223, 282
selfish	78, 112
Sephardi	165, 284
Shaarey Orah	3
Shabbat	26, 35-36
Shadai, El	83-84
slander	124
spinach	108
stealing	122
steroids	110
Succot	26-27, 36, 39, 253

suffixes	76, 78
Sumerian	2
Sunday	125, 127, 145
Talmud	xix, 26, 33, 40, 82-84, 89, 129, 159, 174
Tanach	76, 82, 83 84, 90-91
Thailand	119
Tiberias	48
Tiferet	63, 79, 84, 139, 141-142
Tikunei HaKlali	90
Traimit	119
Triangle	x, 170, 201-203, 205, 207, 209, 211, 213
tsitsit	117, 191-192
Tzavaot	83
Tzereh	167
tzitzit	117
vamana	3
Vespasian	9
vessel	ix, 28, 76, 104, 108-111, 120
vowels	ix, 1, 48-49, 53, 78, 125, 159, 162, 164, 168, 201, 216, 223
wealth	124, 130, 148-149
woolen	113, 114
Yechidah	100, 150
Yetzirah	89, 100, 151, 283
Yio-Zeus	125

Index

www.ingramcontent.com/pod-product-compliance
Lightning Source LLC
Chambersburg PA
CBHW061424040426
42450CB00007B/893